The Bitter Fruits

The Civil War Comes to a Small Town in Pennsylvania

The Bitter Fruits

The Civil War Comes to a Small Town in Pennsylvania

by David G. Colwell

Cumberland County Historical Society

The Society is grateful to the
Wells Foundation for their financial
assistance with this project.

Published by
Cumberland County Historical Society
Carlisle, Pennsylvania

Book Design by Keevin Graham

Printed by Reprographics

CONTENTS

The Bitter Fruits

The Civil War Comes to a Small Town in Pennsylvania

Photo captions include the title or description of the photo, the date if known, the photographer if known, and the source (donor, collection or repository). Photos from the Cumberland County Historical Society's collection are noted with the abbreviation CCHS.

Civil War era illustrations were selected from books in the CCHS Collection. These captions include a description of the image, the book's title, the author or publisher, the date of publication, and the abbreviation CCHS.

Acknowledgments

The evolution of this story from a master's thesis manuscript to a fully edited and illustrated book was the result of many people's efforts. We are indebted to them all for their expertise and assistance.

The telling of this previously little known story became the passion of one man, David Colwell, great grandson of the Civil War soldier, James S. Colwell. His enthusiasm and willingness to share this story with others is the raison d'être for this book. The Society sincerely thanks him for allowing us to publish the results of his years of study and research. Mr. Colwell was especially helpful by supplying and entrusting us with a wealth of supplementary materials, including many original letters, documents and photographs.

The editing and adaptation of Mr. Colwell's text involved the incorporation of many endnotes into the main text or as sidebars. The editorial committee, composed of myself, Dr. Paul Gill, Dr. Steven Hattleberg, and Wayne Wachsmuth, closely reviewed the text for accuracy and content and made necessary revisions and additions. Mary Rosenbaum provided her professional services to proofread the text. We thank all these individuals for their work and contributions to this publication.

The photographs and illustrations in this book came primarily from the Colwell Family Collection and the Photo and Library Archives of the Cumberland County Historical Society. Additional important illustrations were located with the aid of Randy Hackenburg and Michael Winey at the U.S. Military History Institute, and Barbara Bartos at the Shippensburg Historical Society. Jim Bradley of Mother Cumberland Publications and Wayne Wachsmuth produced the quality contemporary photographs that were needed. James and Miriam Steinmetz were helpful as always by producing quality prints. We sincerely thank all these people whose help added greatly to the visual quality of this publication.

We are especially grateful to Keevin Graham for his professional services to lay out and design this work. His meticulous attention to detail and tireless dedication to this publication are reflected in the beautiful presentation of the text.

The Society's staff was helpful in innumerable ways. I personally thank them all for their patience and assistance as I was preoccupied so long with this project. A special thank you goes to our curator, Mike Strong, for sharing his Civil War knowledge and answering my numerous questions.

In conclusion, I would like to express my gratitude to the Society and to David Colwell for entrusting me with this project. Having met twice with Mr. Colwell and exchanged letters for a number of years, his passion for this project soon became my own. It was my goal to present this story in a manner that would be worthy of the people who lived it. Their personal experiences during this turbulent period of our history are representative of the experiences of thousands of others, the effects of which are still present in our lives today. My sincere hope is that all who read these words will be moved by this story and will appreciate the extreme sacrifice that so many made for a noble cause.

Richard L. Tritt

Photo Curator

Preface

David G. Colwell

In 1992, two years after the death of my father, when his New Jersey house had been sold and its attic emptied, I received in California three trunks full of family papers which had come originally from the family home in Carlisle, Pennsylvania. They came to New Jersey in 1948 after the death of my great-aunt, Mary Hall Colwell, the last of our family to live in Carlisle. Those papers had never been examined; they were in great disorder. The Carlisle Colwells were pack-rats: they never saw a piece of paper they didn't want to save. There were, I suppose, between two and three thousand letters, documents, bills, school papers and report cards, wills, and old newspapers and clippings in those trunks, a few from the 1700s, most from the 1800s, some from the early 1900s.

At the time I received those papers, I had recently returned to school on a part-time basis to obtain a master's degree in history. As I read through those papers one by one, I came upon 179 letters exchanged between James Smith Colwell and his wife, Ann Hall Colwell, my great-grandparents, during the period from June 1861, when he went on active duty with the Union Army, until his death in September 1862. I decided to base my master's thesis on those letters and the story of Carlisle itself during the first seventeen months of the Civil War. This book is the result.

The story told here is not only the personal history of my great-grandparents for that period. It is also the story of how attitudes and opinions in the town of Carlisle changed from lighthearted, flag-waving patriotism at the war's onset to grim determination as the months passed and casualties mounted - until it finally came to be recognized that there would be no negotiated peace, and that the war would end only with victory by one side or the other, and that victory itself could be achieved only through battles, more casualties, and sacrifice.

It is an honor that the Cumberland County Historical Society has chosen to publish this story. I want to thank all those involved with this undertaking at the Society, Mr. Richard Tritt in particular, for their work in preparing this book for publication. I must also thank the staff of the History Department at California State University, Los Angeles, especially Professor Lamont Yeakey, for advice and counsel on this project.

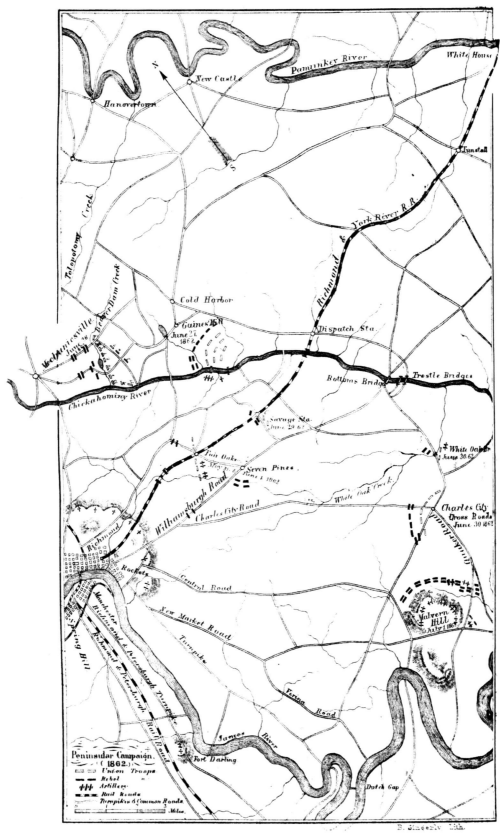

Map of Peninsula Campaign, 1862. (*History of Pennsylvania Volunteers, 1860-5*, Samuel P. Bates, 1869, CCHS.)

Time Line: *The Bitter Fruits*

by Dr. Paul Gill

April 1813	James Colwell is born near Shippensburg, Pa.
Feb. 18, 1833	Ann Barbara Hall is born in Baltimore, Md.
1839	James Colwell graduates from the College of New Jersey (later Princeton University).
1840-41	James Colwell attends Harvard Law School.
Jan. 9, 1843	James Colwell is admitted to the Pennsylvania Bar and begins to practice law in Carlisle.
Dec. 13, 1853	James Colwell marries Ann Barbara Hall.
1855-60	Two boys and two girls are born to James and "Annie" Colwell.
March 1857	Dred Scott Decision by the U.S. Supreme Court – Slavery is constitutionally protected in the U.S. Territories.
October 1859	John Brown seizes the United States Arsenal at Harper's Ferry, Virginia.
December 1859	John Brown is tried and executed for treason against the U.S.
November 1860	Abraham Lincoln is elected President of the United States.
Dec. 20, 1860	South Carolina is the first Southern state to secede from the Union.
Apr. 12, 1861	Confederate artillery bombards Fort Sumter.
Apr. 15, 1861	President Lincoln calls for 75,000 militia to suppress the rebellion.
April 1861	James Colwell is appointed First Lieutenant in the Carlisle Fencibles.
June 1861	The Carlisle Fencibles are called to active Federal Service as Company A, 7th Regiment, Pennsylvania Reserve Volunteer Corps.
July 27, 1861	James Colwell's regiment is sworn into Federal Service as the 36th Regiment, Pennsylvania Volunteers, better known as the 7th Pennsylvania Reserves.
October 1861	James Colwell's regiment is moved to Camp Pierpont, near Langley, Virginia, where it spends the winter.
May 31 & June 1, 1862	Battle of Seven Pines or Fair Oaks, Virginia.
June 25 - July 1, 1862	James Colwell's regiment participates in the Seven Days' Battles in Virginia.
July 4, 1862	James Colwell is promoted to Captain and given command of Company A.
Aug. 29 & 30, 1862	Second Battle of Manassas or Bull Run, Virginia
Sept. 4, 1862	Lee's army crosses the Potomac and enters Maryland.
Sept. 6, 1862	Stonewall Jackson's men occupy Frederick. Md.
Sept. 7, 1862	The Federal Army of the Potomac under Gen. McClellan begins slow movements northward from Washington searching for Lee's Army.
Sept. 11, 1862	Confederate forces enter Hagerstown, Md. Gov. Andrew G. Curtin of Pennsylvania calls for fifty thousand men.
Sept. 12, 1862	Union forces enter Frederick, Md.
Sept. 14, 1862	Battle of South Mountain, Stonewall Jackson besieges Harper's Ferry.
Sept. 15, 1862	Confederates capture Harper's Ferry.
Sept. 16, 1862	Lee concentrates his forces along the Antietam Creek near Sharpsburg, Md.
Sept. 17, 1862	Battle of Antietam – James Colwell is killed as his Company moves to attack the Cornfield.
Sept. 22, 1862	The Preliminary Emancipation Proclamation is announced. The Federals reoccupy Harper's Ferry.
Sept. 26, 1862	James Colwell is buried in the Old Carlisle Graveyard.
1871	The Soldiers Monument is erected in Carlisle, memorializing the 344 men from Cumberland County who died in the Civil War, including James Colwell.
1881	The Grand Army of the Republic Post #201 is established in Carlisle, named after Captain James S. Colwell.
May 29, 1907	James Colwell's widow, Annie, dies in Carlisle.

CHAPTER 1

Prelude to War: Carlisle, Pennsylvania

By the mid-nineteenth century most of the European world had abolished slavery. Britain outlawed the Atlantic slave trade in 1807 and freed the slaves in her colonies in 1833. France did likewise in 1848. Following independence from Spain, the Latin American republics one by one abolished slavery after 1820, although it was frequently replaced by debt peonage. By the time of the Civil War, slavery in the Americas persisted only in the Spanish and Dutch Caribbean islands, Brazil, and the United States.[1] And in the American North, despite near-universal agreement that blacks were an inferior race, slavery was by 1860 generally considered to be a violation of both Christian and democratic principles.[2]

As the world turned against the institution, however, the economy of the South became more dependent on it. With the invention of the cotton gin in 1793 and the subsequent breaking of fertile virgin land for cotton in Alabama, Mississippi, Louisiana, and, after the Mexican War, in east Texas, fortunes were made in the production of cotton and its export to Europe, chiefly to Britain. Cotton, and to a lesser extent other labor-intensive commodity crops such as rice, sugar, and tobacco, depended on relatively cheap slave labor. Slave states further north found that trading in slaves was itself extremely profitable. Breeding slaves on land poorly suited for agriculture, then selling them "down the river" to newer cotton states in the deep South, was lucrative for plantation owners in Virginia and Maryland.

The economy, the political strength, and the social structure of the South came under increasing pressure, however, as the decades passed. The census returns showed that the population of Northern free states was growing far faster than that of the South; the number of territories which would enter the Union as free states surpassed the number of possible future slave states; and the economy of the North was stronger and growing more rapidly than the economy of the South. Bitterly fought compromises in 1820, when Missouri and Maine entered the Union, and in 1850, when California was granted statehood, were portents of the deep-rooted animosity which caused the Civil War.

For Sale,
THE TIME OF A
Mulatto Girl,
WHO HAS NINE YEARS TO SERVE—
She is remarkable strong and healthy, about Nine Years of age.
For Terms apply to the Printer.
Dec. 13.

WILL BE-SOLD,
THE TIME OF A LIKELY YOUNG
Negro wench,
Who has Six-Years to serve—Enquire of the Printer.

TO BE SOLD,
THE TIME OF A STOUT, HEALTHY,
Negro Boy,
between 19 and 20 years of age, recorded agreeably to Law, he has been accustomed to take care of horses and work on a farm. For terms enquire of the Printer.
February 28th, 1804.

For Sale
A NEGRO WENCH,
A SLAVE for life, about 38 years of age, capable of doing any kind of house work.— Also a NEGRO BOY about 7 years of age, who has to serve until 28—for terms apply to
JAMES DAVIS.
Silver Springs, February 27th, 1806.

Sale ads for slaves in Cumberland County from issues of the Carlisle *Herald* 18 Jan. 1805, 4 Aug. 1802, 29 Feb. 1804, 28 Feb. 1806.

After 1850 there were no more compromises. The divisive issue of slavery tore the country apart in the decade that followed. The 1851 publication of *Uncle Tom's Cabin* and the increasing activity of Northern abolitionists provoked Southern anger. The near civil war in Kansas which followed passage of the Kansas-Nebraska Act in 1854 intensified Free Soil sentiment and led to the formation of the Republican Party at Ripon, Wisconsin, in 1854. The 1857 Dred Scott decision of the Supreme Court, declaring that slavery followed the flag throughout the continent, and overturning seventy years of precedents, aroused the North.

Sectional rancor was fueled by the biting, abusive language of such Southern "fire-eaters" as Robert Barnwell Rhett and Lawrence Keitt of South Carolina, Louis Wigfall of Texas, and William L. Yancey of Alabama. Their opponents in the North were such staunch abolitionists as Wendell Phillips and William Lloyd Garrison. Asserting that slavery was a monstrous evil which must be eradicated root and branch, some advocated immediate action, by force if necessary, to bring the institution to an end. Others favored severing all ties with the slave states and permitting them to secede. Although the abolitionists found only limited support in the North, their speeches and writings inflamed Southern opinion. At Harper's Ferry, in October of 1859, John Brown led a doomed attempt to establish a home for fugitive slaves, an act which the South saw as proof that the North sought to end slavery by force.

The attitudes and opinions of small towns in the North, such as Carlisle, the county seat of Cumberland County, Pennsylvania, reflected the simmering national dispute, which had roiled the nation almost continuously since the end of the Mexican War. Cumberland County, the sixth county of colonial Pennsylvania, was settled originally by immigrants from Ulster. Lowland Scots, transplanted to Northern Ireland during the seventeenth century, were drawn to Pennsylvania by economic opportunity and the freedom of religion that Penn's colony offered.

View of the Carlisle Public Square, c.1860. Left to right—the corner of the Courthouse, the Washington Hotel which burned in April of 1861, N. Courthouse Ave. with the spire of the First Reformed Church on W. Louther Street in the background, and the First Presbyterian Church. In the foreground is part of the roof of the open-air Market House. (Attributed to Charles L. Lochman, CCHS.)

Settling initially in Lancaster County to the east of the Susquehanna River in central Pennsylvania, these immigrants, who came to be called Scotch-Irish,[3] spilled across the Susquehanna by the mid-1730s. Cumberland County, sometimes called the "Mother County" for the Scotch-Irish in America, was formed a few years later in 1750.

In 1751 the town of Carlisle was laid out as the county seat. Initially the residents of Carlisle and Cumberland County were overwhelmingly Scotch-Irish immigrants. The Scotch-Irish were footloose, however; the grass forever looked greener somewhere else. By 1800 large numbers of German newcomers had moved into the county, replacing many of the original settlers. The two groups generally got along well, but the Germans still spoke an English often incomprehensible to Scotch-Irish descendants who dominated political life in the county and always referred to the Germans as "Dutch," a corruption of "Deutsche."

The population of Carlisle in 1860 was 5,700, that of Shippensburg, the second largest town, about 2,000, and that of the county 40,100. The county's prosperous farms attested to the rich soil of the Cumberland Valley. Numerous grist and flour mills, breweries, distilleries, and tanneries bespoke the county's agricultural base. The county's forests supported saw mills and a paper mill. Significant deposits of iron ore occurred throughout the valley and an important ironworks and forge had operated since Revolutionary times at Boiling Springs, five miles from Carlisle.[4] A railroad was completed from the Susquehanna River to Carlisle in 1837. A bridge was built across the river in 1839 and service extended to Harrisburg; by 1860 the line had advanced as far south as Hagerstown, Maryland, thirty miles from Harper's Ferry on the Potomac.

A scar from the Confederate shelling of 1 July 1863, on one of the pillars of the County Courthouse, 1997. (Jim Bradley, Mother Cumberland Collection.)

A storied town, Carlisle was the site of a major Indian conference in 1753; the base for Braddock's inglorious march to the west in 1755; a defensive stronghold from Indian attacks during the French and Indian War; the organization site for the Forbes and Bouquet western expeditions during that conflict; the onetime home of three signers of the Declaration of Independence, James Wilson, James Smith, and George Ross; a military supply point for Washington's forces during the Revolution; and the site of Carlisle Barracks, founded in 1777, now the second-oldest active army base in the country. Dickinson Grammar School, founded in Carlisle in 1773, became Dickinson College in 1783. Washington made Carlisle his headquarters during the Whiskey Rebellion in 1794. Carlisle was occupied by Confederate troops in 1863. Scars left by two Confederate cannonballs are still clearly visible on the front of the County Courthouse and an historical plaque three miles north of town today indicates the exact spot the Confederate cavalry reached immediately prior to the Battle of Gettysburg. After the Civil War the Indian School was located at Carlisle Barracks; a monument to Jim Thorpe now stands in the town square. The Barracks is today the site of the National War College.[5]

Images Representative of Cumberland County

The Burkholder thatched
roof barn, c.1910.
(A. A. Line, CCHS.)

Early whiskey distillery,
located on E. South St.,
Carlisle, that operated until
about 1838. (CCHS.)

"The Pioneer," a light passenger locomotive built in 1851 for the Cumberland Valley Railroad, 1901. (A. A. Line, CCHS.)

Iron forge and mill at the "Carlisle Iron Works" in Boiling Springs, c.1876. (J. N. Choate, Eddy Collection, CCHS.)

Irwin's Mill on the Big
Spring, c.1905. (CCHS.)

Given Brothers Paper Mill at
Papertown, now Mt. Holly
Springs, burned in 1864.
(Charles L. Lochman, Robin
Stanford Collection, CCHS.)

Civil War Era Views of Carlisle

South Hanover Street from the square, c.1876.
(A. A. Line, CCHS.)

North Hanover Street from the square, c.1876.
(A. A. Line, CCHS.)

West High Street from the square, c.1886.
(J. C. Bailey, CCHS.)

East High Street from the square, c.1872.
(Charles L. Lochman, CCHS.)

Courthouse seen over the market sheds on a winter day, c.1865. (Charles L. Lochman, CCHS.)

Open air Market House in 1878 on the south-east corner of the Public Square. (A. A. Line, CCHS.)

Two views of market day in Carlisle, c.1862, taken from a window
overlooking South Hanover Street and the Public Square.
(Charles L. Lochman, CCHS.)

South College, part of Dickinson College, located on the south side of W. High Street facing Old West, c.1864. (Charles L. Lochman, Robin Stanford Collection, CCHS.)

Dickinson College buildings seen from N. College Street, c.1864. Old West on the left, East College on the right. (Charles L. Lochman, CCHS.)

Carlisle was the leading market town in the county, the site of Dickinson College, and the seat of county government, the courts, and the social and political life of the county. In the mid-nineteenth century four weekly newspapers were published in Carlisle and one in Shippensburg. The *Carlisle American*, originally a supporter of the American Party, was edited by George Zinn. The Carlisle *Herald*, established in 1799 to support the Federalists, was edited until 1857 by Ekuries Beatty, by William Porter until mid-1862, and thereafter by A. K. Rheem. These two papers and the *Shippensburg News*, edited by E. E. Curriden, opposed the national Democratic Party and the extension of slavery into the territories. The Democrats were championed by the Carlisle *American Democrat*, edited by E. Cornman, which, supportive of the national Democratic Party, was also a pro-Union organ.

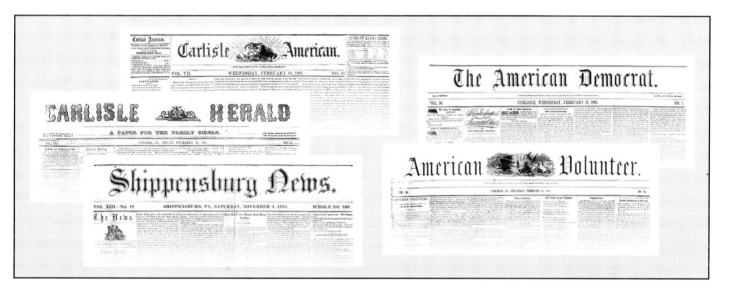

Carlisle and Shippensburg newspaper banners from the 1860s. (CCHS and the Shippensburg Historical Society.)

Volunteer building on Liberty Avenue. Wagon scales and south-east corner of the old market sheds in foreground. John Bratton, standing in the first door on right, and William Kennedy on the pavement without a hat, were editors of the *Volunteer*, c.1870. (A. A. Line, CCHS.)

Carlisle's *American Volunteer*, the leading Democratic paper in the county, was always sympathetic to the grievances of the South. The Democratic papers customarily referred to their opposition as "black Republicans;" in turn the anti-administration papers consistently alluded to the Democratic Party as the "sham democracy" or the "shamocracy." John Bratton, the combative, acid-tongued editor of the *American Volunteer*, a strong supporter of President Franklin Pierce (who had appointed him postmaster of Carlisle) and of 1856 Democratic nominee James Buchanan, engaged in frequent biting polemics with his competitors.

More often than not, the majority of the people of Carlisle voted Democratic. Dickinson College enrolled many students from the South and their presence may have had an influence. A more important factor may have been the Carlisle Barracks, an army post since the Revolution. Hundreds of Southern army officers had served tours of duty there and socialized with the town's residents over the decades. Perhaps their marriages to Carlisle girls lessened anti-Southern feelings in the town.

Portico of the Officers' Quarters at Carlisle Barracks, c.1861. (Charles L. Lochman, Robin Stanford Collection, CCHS.)

Sarah (Sallie) Gibson, daughter of John Bannister Gibson, and a cousin of Ann Hall Colwell, married Richard H. Anderson, a regular army officer, in 1850. Ann wrote about the marriage in a letter to her brother George in California on 3 October 1850. "On Tuesday our cousin Sallie Gibson is to be metamorphosed into Mrs. Lieutenant Anderson 2nd Dragoon U.. S.. A.. He is very respectable though not rich & does not know whether he'll be ordered to Santa Fe or yet remaining here. It is to be in the morning & a church affair so that is all I know about it."[6]

Richard H. Anderson, a native of Charleston, S.C., resigned his commission in 1861 to accept one in the Confederate army. By the end of the war R. H. Anderson was a Confederate Lieutenant General and Corps Commander.[7]

Richard H. Anderson. (*Battles and Leaders of the Civil War,* Grant-Lee Edition, CCHS.)

A group of Civil War era officers and wives posed before the Officers' Quarters at the Carlisle Barracks, c.1861. (Charles L. Lochman, CCHS.)

The consequences of the growing crisis on the lives of families in small towns across the North are exemplified by its effect on the lives of James Smith Colwell, his wife, Ann Hall Colwell, and their four small children in the years before the Civil War. Their ancestors were among the earliest residents of the county. Robert Caldwell, as the name was originally spelled, came to Cumberland County in the early 1730s. His son James, born in Ulster in 1730, emigrated to America with his father and was five when his father died. James Colwell bought land north of Shippensburg in Cumberland County in 1768, where he built a stone house and a grist mill on a small stream that ran through his property. After serving in the Revolution,[8] he built a larger house on the property. Both houses still stand. James left the smaller house and grist mill to a younger son, John,[9] the father of James Smith Colwell.[10] John Colwell died in 1831, leaving a widow, one married daughter, three unmarried daughters, and his eighteen-year-old son, James, to whom he left the grist mill and part of his land.[11]

James entered Princeton (then the College of New Jersey) in 1837 as a sophomore at the age of twenty-four.[12] He graduated in 1839, ranking tenth in his final examinations among his college class of sixty.[13]

Following graduation from Princeton, James attended Harvard Law School for a year in 1840-1841, but did not graduate. When he returned to Cumberland County, he established his residence at Carlisle, read law in a Carlisle law office, and was admitted to the bar January 9, 1843. He opened a law office in Carlisle; a year later he established a partnership with Robert P. McClure, a Princeton classmate and resident of Shippensburg. McClure, five years his junior, handled legal business originating in that town; James dealt with business and court appearances in Carlisle.[14]

James Smith Colwell, c.1860.
(J. N. Choate cabinet card, Colwell Family Collection.)

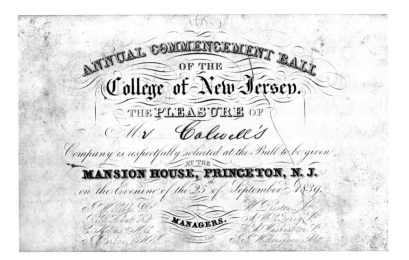

James Colwell's invitation to the Annual Commencement Ball at Princeton, 25 September 1839. (Colwell Family Collection.)

James Colwell's admission to the bar, dated 9 January 1843. The authorities perhaps decided to use the spelling "Caldwell" as shown on his baptismal record. (Colwell Family Collection.)

Colwell & McClure partnership agreement, 1 April 1844. (Colwell Family Collection.)

Colwell & McClure ad from the Carlisle *Herald*, 24 April 1844.

James Colwell began his law practice in 1844 in a building "one door west of the Jail," c.1875. (A. A. Line, CCHS.)

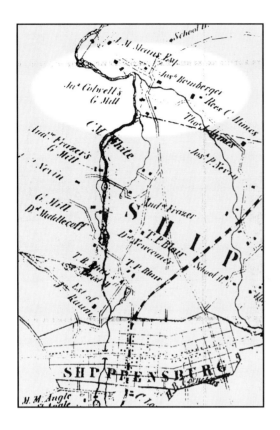

Detail of the 1858 Map of Cumberland County by H. F. Bridgens. The Colwell properties were the grist mill, the house on the opposite side of the road, and the nearby house owned by Joseph Bomberger, which he purchased from the Colwells in 1837.

The Colwell Grist Mill was built in 1788 on the road from Shippensburg to Middle Spring (Route 696). James Colwell inherited this mill in 1831 and owned it when he died in 1862. The mill was demolished when the road was straightened in the 1960s. Photo dated 1936. (J. Huston McCullogh, Shippensburg Historical Society.)

All that remains of the Colwell Grist Mill is a mill stone, located in front of a brick house opposite the mill site, 1997. (Jim Bradley, Mother Cumberland Collection.)

The James Colwell house was built in colonial days on land purchased in 1768. James deeded it to his son John in 1797. John's son, James, was born and raised here and inherited the property when his father died. Photo taken 1997. (Jim Bradley, Mother Cumberland Collection.)

Around 1776 James Colwell built a second larger stone house along Burd Run near his first house. He left this house to his son Samuel Colwell who sold it to Joseph Bomberger in 1837 (see the 1858 map detail). Photo taken 1997. (Jim Bradley, Mother Cumberland Collection.)

Colwell family graves in the Middle Spring Presbyterian Church Cemetery. John Colwell and his three wives are buried under the four flat stones in the foreground, 1997. (Jim Bradley, Mother Cumberland Collection.)

Details of the tombstones of John and Nancy Colwell, parents of James Colwell. James's middle name was Smith, his mother's maiden name, 1997. (Jim Bradley, Mother Cumberland Collection.)

In
Memory of
JOHN COLWELL
who departed this life
January 28th, 1831
in the 63rd Year of his Age

IN
MEMORY OF
NANCY
wife of
John Colwell &
daughter of Hugh &
Elizabeth Smith
died July 4th 1818
in the 33rd year of her age

The great-grandfather of Ann Barbara Hall Colwell,
James Galbraith, arrived in Pennsylvania with his father in
1718, served in the Pennsylvania Assembly and was
sheriff and justice of the peace in Lancaster County. He
moved across the Susquehanna in 1761 and built a house
which still stands. His youngest son, Andrew, Ann
Colwell's grandfather, who also served in the Revolution,
left seven surviving daughters.[15] The youngest, only four
years old on her father's death, was Ann Galbraith, who
married in 1825 and settled in Baltimore with her husband, Charles Hall, a recent immigrant from Ulster.
There Ann Barbara Hall, born in 1833, her three brothers, and one sister lived until 1845 when Charles Hall
died. In time Ann Galbraith Hall, the widow, moved to
Carlisle. Since four of her mother's six sisters had
married Carlisle residents, Ann Barbara Hall was surrounded by numerous relatives as she grew to adulthood.
The families were always close; aunts and cousins were
important figures in Annie's life.

At some point after the return of the widow, Ann
Galbraith Hall, and her family to Carlisle, James met the Hall
family and was attracted to Ann Barbara.[16] In December 1853
they were married; at forty he was twice her age. While James
pursued his law career, Annie produced four children in rapid suc-
cession: Anna ("Nan") in 1855, John Charles in 1856, Mary ("Daisy")
in 1858, and James Hall in 1860.

Ann Barbara Hall Colwell, tintype from a
carte de visite photo album, c.1858-60.
(Colwell Family Collection.)

Annie's older brother, George, succumbed to gold fever in 1849 and left for
California to seek his fortune. In a letter dated 22 June 1849 Ann Galbraith Hall
wrote her son, George, in California, "I can scarcely trust myself to trace on the
map the tremendous distance you are removed from us," and referred in the letter
to "your old kind friend...Mr. Caldwell," who had visited the Hall household.

James was a serious, patient, and persistent man; a later letter makes clear
that his visits to the Hall home had more to do with his as yet unspoken interest
in Ann, at age sixteen, twenty years younger than he, than in his friendship with
her brother, George. In a letter written by young Ann to her brother George on
19 October 1849, she noted that "quite a change has been wrought on our friend
Mr. Colwell since you were here. He has been really transformed into a galant."

Ann and James were engaged in 1850. Ann's mother, Ann Galbraith Hall,
confided to her son George in a letter dated 8 October 1851 that "As it respects
Annie's marriage, I cannot say when it will be. She and Mr. C. have been
engaged nearly a year. I am quite satisfied for he is truly a worthy honourable
man. He is very respectable in his connections and also stands high in his
profession and for integrity of character not surpassed by any of our acquaintances. This is confidential. When you write do not say anything of what I
have told you."

A cased daguerreotype of Ann Hall (Colwell) and her mother Ann Galbraith Hall, c.1850. (Colwell Family Collection.)

The Galbraith family graves in the Silver Spring Presbyterian Church Cemetery. Ann Galbraith Hall's stone is directly in front of the upright monument on the left, 1997. (Jim Bradley, Mother Cumberland Collection.)

Detail of the Ann Galbraith Hall gravestone. She was the mother of Ann Hall Colwell, 1997. (Jim Bradley, Mother Cumberland Collection.)

While James pursued his law career in the 1840s and 1850s, the face of American politics was changing. As the Whig Party fragmented in those years, its successors included the Liberty Party, the nativist American Party whose more extreme adherents became known as "Know-Nothings," and the Free Soil Party, interested chiefly in preventing the spread of slavery into the territories. Also opposed to the extension of slavery was the Republican Party, formed in 1854, which ultimately incorporated most of the supporters of the Liberty, American, and Free Soil parties.[17] These political strands would appear in Pennsylvania under various names in the 1850s; such designations as the American Party, the American Republican Party, the Republican Party, the Peoples Party, and the Union Party appeared on Pennsylvania ballots into the 1860s.

The 1856 election was the first in which the Republican Party appeared on the national scene. Editor Beatty of the *Herald* described clearly what was at stake in the 1856 election, as seen from the viewpoint of those across the North who opposed the extension of slavery:

> The question is between FREEDOM and SLAVERY. It is not to decide whether slavery is to be abolished in the states where it now exists. No one advocates that. But it is to decide whether Slavery shall be confined to its present limits, or extended farther into territory now free.... Whether this country, professing to be a free Republic, shall become the propagandist of Slavery.... Whether Cuba shall be forcibly seized and annexed, and whether Nicaragua shall be made a Slave State, and annexed. Whether Kansas shall be free, or whether Slavery shall be imposed upon a territory by force and fraud against the wishes of the people.... Whether intimidation, violence and idle threats of Disunion on the part of the South shall be stronger than Northern principle and courage.[18]

In the three-way 1856 race with Republican John Fremont and the American Party candidate, Millard Fillmore, James Buchanan gained 174 electoral votes, Fremont 114, and Fillmore only 8; but Buchanan was a minority president, winning 44 percent of the vote while Fremont won 35 percent and Fillmore 21 percent. Buchanan swept Pennsylvania, but his support for the extension of slavery to the territories cost the Pennsylvania Democratic Party dearly. After the election the Pennsylvania State Senate numbered only fifteen Democrats against eighteen Republicans and Americans combined. The state House of Representatives had fifty-three Democrats and forty-seven in opposition. Although the Democrats had a combined majority of sixty-eight to sixty-five in the two houses, at a joint meeting in January 1857 the state's legislators elected Simon Cameron, a Republican, to the U.S. Senate by a single vote over John Forney, publisher of the *Philadelphia Press*, Democratic State Chairman, and the man most responsible for Buchanan's election as president. The Carlisle *Herald* headlined Cameron's election, "Great Republican Triumph," and so it was.[19] Buchanan lost political control of his own state party before he even took office.

Simon Cameron, U.S. Senator and Lincoln's Secretary of War. (Massachusetts Commandery Military Order of the Loyal Legion and the U.S. Army Military History Institute.)

Sectional animosity was further aroused throughout the North by the Dred Scott decision of March 1857. Issuing nine separate opinions, a Supreme Court majority decided that slavery was constitutionally protected throughout the country and the territories, thereby overturning precedents established by the 1787 Northwest Ordinance, the 1820 Missouri Compromise, and the many laws under which free states had entered the Union since 1789. Further, declared Chief Justice Roger Taney, himself a graduate of Carlisle's Dickinson College, blacks, whether slave or free, were beings "of an inferior order" not entitled to full United States citizenship, overturning additional precedents established in many states where free blacks had long been accorded rights to vote and sue in federal courts.

The South exulted at the decision. The North considered it tainted and invalid, the result of collusion between Buchanan, also a graduate of Dickinson College, and a sectionally packed court. Rather than removing the issue of slavery from the political arena, the decision divided the Democratic Party and inflamed Northern opinion. An editorial in the Carlisle *Herald* spoke for many in the North when it commented: "[A]s might have been expected from the Southern affinities and sympathies of the majority of the Court the great principles of Freedom are virtually repudiated."[20]

James Buchanan, 1865. (*Battles and Leaders of the Civil War,* Grant-Lee Edition, CCHS.)

Four years of bitter rhetoric followed, as the sectional breach widened. Buchanan's attempts to have Kansas admitted as a state under a pro-slavery constitution, an effort overwhelmingly opposed by the anti-slavery majority in the territory, infuriated the North. In May 1858, only eighteen months after Buchanan's election, former Pennsylvania Democratic State Chairman John Forney broke with Buchanan and publicly suggested the formation of a new anti-slavery coalition to include "good Democrats...opposed to the admission of Kansas under the [pro-slavery] Lecompton Constitution."[21] In a speech four months later he accused Buchanan of betraying his trust and trying to subvert the will of the majority in Kansas. "I find myself turned out of the Democratic Party," said Forney.[22]

The 1858 elections demonstrated the deep and permanent split in both the country and the Democratic Party, as anti-slavery Americans and Republicans combined to elect a majority in the House of Representatives.[23] John Brown's attack on Harper's Ferry in October 1859, which he hoped would lead to a general uprising of slaves in Maryland and western Virginia and to the establishment of a free home for fugitive slaves, further inflamed Southern opinion. Although all Northern political leaders and newspapers condemned the raid as the work of a fanatic, Southern opinion was nearly unanimous in attributing the event to constant Northern criticism of slavery.

John Brown. (*Battles and Leaders of the Civil War,* Grant-Lee Edition, CCHS.)

The 1860 political conventions brought the crisis to a head. The Democratic convention met at Charleston on April 23. Unhappy with the treatment of slavery in the platform, delegates from nine Southern states walked out and Stephen Douglas never gained the two-thirds majority required for nomination. After ten days the convention adjourned to meet again in Baltimore on June 18. Seeking compromise, delegates from twenty-four border and Northern states met at the Constitutional Union Party convention in Baltimore on May 9, 1860. There moderates interested chiefly in maintaining the Union nominated John Bell, a conservative pro-slavery Southerner who supported the right of Congress to limit the extension of slavery into the territories. Republicans, scenting victory in the air at what was only their second national convention, met in Chicago on May 16. Trailing New York Senator William H. Seward on the first two ballots, Lincoln clinched the nomination mid-way through the third ballot to wild acclaim.

The Democratic Convention reconvened in Baltimore on June 18. When it declared that delegates who had walked out of the Charleston convention should be replaced by new pro-Douglas men, delegates from Virginia, North Carolina, and Tennessee promptly walked out. Douglas was then nominated as the presidential candidate of the National Democratic Party. Simultaneously in Baltimore, a rump convention of those who had walked out of the regular Democratic meetings in Charleston and Baltimore chose U.S. Vice President John C. Breckinridge as the nominee of the Constitutional Democratic Party.

The root of all the bitterness in the 1860 campaign was, of course, the matter of slavery. As opinions in the world and the country toward slavery slowly changed, the problem of the races in America grew. While few Northerners regarded blacks as their equals, most in the North, Abolitionists or not, considered slavery a moral wrong.[24] The country did not know how to solve the problem of slavery. The sectional vote in the 1860 election only made clear that the country could not tolerate the institution much longer.

Nationally, Lincoln won the North and West, Bell the border states, and Breckinridge the deep South. Only Douglas campaigned both North and South, and he came in fourth in the Electoral College with just twelve votes, although he was second only to Lincoln in the popular vote. Lincoln's victory brought to a boil the long-simmering dispute over slavery and its extension to the territories.

Abraham Lincoln in 1857 at 48 years of age. This was the first photograph of Lincoln circulated throughout the country for campaign purposes. (A. A. Line copy, CCHS.)

Upon Lincoln's nomination "The audience stood up, the cheers and the confusion became deafening.... The intelligence of the nomination, when conveyed to the people outside, caused a scene of the wildest excitement, beggaring description." (Carlisle *Herald*, 23 May 1860.)

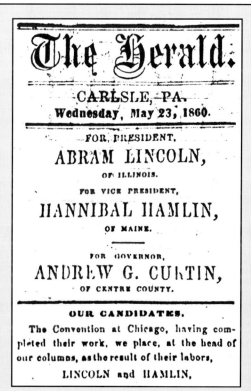

The Herald.

CARLSLE, PA.
Wednesday, May 23, 1860.

FOR PRESIDENT,
ABRAM LINCOLN,
OF ILLINOIS.

FOR VICE PRESIDENT,
HANNIBAL HAMLIN,
OF MAINE.

FOR GOVERNOR,
ANDREW G. CURTIN,
OF CENTRE COUNTY.

OUR CANDIDATES.

The Convention at Chicago, having completed their work, we place, at the head of our columns, as the result of their labors,
LINCOLN and HAMLIN,

Endnotes

[1] For a wide-ranging discussion of slavery in the European world see David Brion Davis, *The Problem of Slavery in Western Culture* (Ithaca: Cornell University Press, 1966), and *Slavery and Human Progress* (New York: Oxford University Press, 1984). For a general history of slavery in the United States see Peter Kolchin, *American Slavery: 1619-1877* (New York: Hill and Wang, 1993).

[2] George Winston Smith and Charles Judah, *Life in the North during the Civil War* (Albuquerque: University of New Mexico Press, 1966) xv. Davis, *Slavery and Human Progress*, 109-111, 259-279.

[3] "Scots" and "Scottish" are the more correct forms, but "Scotch" survives, among other usages, in "Scotch-Irish." For a history of the Scotch-Irish see Charles Knowles Bolton, *Scotch-Irish Pioneers in Ulster and America* (Baltimore: Genealogical Publishing Company, 1967); Wayland F. Dunaway, *The Scotch-Irish of Colonial Pennsylvania* (London: Archon Books, 1962); Charles A. Hanna, *The Scotch-Irish, or the Scot in North Britain, North Ireland, and North America* (Baltimore: Genealogical Publishing Company, 1968); Joseph E. Illick, *Colonial Pennsylvania: A History* (New York: Charles Scribners Sons, 1976); William C. Lehman, *Scottish and Scotch-Irish Contributions to Early American Life and Culture* (London, Kennekat Press, 1978).

[4] The Carlisle Iron Works was owned by members of the Ege family, cousins of Ann Colwell, whose aunt had married Michael Ege in 1810. A history of the Iron Works may be found in Wing, *Cumberland County*, 216-217.

[5] *History of Cumberland and Adams Counties* (Chicago: Warner Beers & Co., 1886); I. Rupp, *The History and Topography of Dauphin, Cumberland, Franklin, Bedford, Adams, and Perry Counties* (Lancaster, Pa.: Gilbert Hills, 1846); Conway P. Wing, *History of Cumberland County, Pennsylvania* (Philadelphia: James D. Scott, 1879).

[6] Letter of Ann Hall to George Hall, 3 October 1850. The Colwell Family Papers.

[7] C. Irvine Walker, *The Life of Lieutenant General Richard Heron Anderson* (Charleston, S.C.: Art Publishing Company, 1917).

[8] Information regarding James's service during the Revolution is from copies of records supplied by the Pennsylvania Historical and Museum Commission, Harrisburg, Pa. William Caldwell, a nephew who came from Ulster to visit James in the mid-1770s, chose the other side and went to Detroit where he became a well-known military figure among the British forces on the Revolution's western frontier. Lyman Copeland Draper Manuscript Collection, 1980 Microfilm Edition, Wisconsin State Historical Society, Madison, Wisconsin, Mss 17 S 213-214.

[9] Will of James Colwell, dated 20 December 1798. The spelling, "Colwell," is used in James's will. The Colwell Family Papers.

[10] The baptismal record, dated 13 April 1813, gives the name as James Smith Caldwell. Wilbur J. McElwain, *Genealogical Data Abstracted from History of Middle Spring Church, Middle Spring, Pennsylvania 1738-1900* (Bowie, MD.: Heritage Books, Inc., 1992), 21.

[11] Will of John Colwell, dated 4 January 1831. Both spellings, "Caldwell" and "Colwell," occur in the will. The Colwell Family Papers.

[12] With its heritage of Scottish Presbyterianism, many Scotch-Irish descendants matriculated at Princeton when family finances permitted. Although James had inherited the small grist mill and some land from his father, the money arising from the sale of the remaining property had gone to his sisters and stepmother. It was probably a shortage of cash that delayed his college education.

[13] Records from the Office of the Registrar, Princeton University, Princeton, NJ.

[14] Partnership Agreement dated 1 April 1844 "between James S. Colwell of the one part and Robert P. McClure of the other." They were each to pay the expenses of their own offices. James was the senior partner: "of every sum of five dollars of such profits the said Colwell shall be entitled to three dollars & the said McClure to two dollars." The Colwell Family Papers.

[15] A fragment of Andrew's diary survives, written during the period when, as a prisoner of war, he was confined to a British prison ship in New York harbor. The Colwell Family Papers.

[16] See James Smith Colwell's (hereafter noted as JSC) letter to Ann Hall Colwell (hereafter noted as AHC) dated 21 August 1862 on page 150. All letters between them referenced hereafter in this book are from the Colwell Family Papers.

[17] The best description of the philosophical and ideological foundations of the Republican Party is Eric Foner, *Free Men, Free Soil, Free Men: The Ideology of the Republican Party before the Civil War* (New York: Oxford University Press, 1970).

[18] Carlisle *Herald*, 29 October 1856.

[19] Carlisle *Herald*, 14 January 1857. In an unusual move, three anti-slavery Democrats broke party ranks to vote for Republican Cameron, presaging the 1860 split in the Democratic Party.

[20] Carlisle *Herald*, 11 March 1857.

[21] Carlisle *Herald*, 5 May 1858.

[22] Carlisle *Herald*, 15 September 1858.

[23] In Illinois, where the Lincoln-Douglas debates had drawn national attention, the Republican state ticket out-polled the Democrats by 5,000. Had the Senate seat been filled by popular vote, Lincoln would have won. Due to the manner of the state's legislative districting, however, Douglas Democrats were in a majority when the two houses of the state legislature met in joint session and Stephen Douglas was returned to his seat in the Senate. Carlisle *Herald*, 10 November 1858.

When asked about his loss, Lincoln answered, "I suppose I am too big to cry about it, but it hurts too awful bad to laugh," a story which another Illinois politician, Adlai Stevenson, repeated nearly a century later. *Shippensburg News*, 29 January 1859.

[24] Foner, *Free Soil, Free Labor, Free Men*; Davis, *Slavery and Human Progress*; and Smith and Judah, *Life in the North* discuss the status of slavery as a moral issue in the North, prior to the Civil War.

CHAPTER 2

"None But the Brave Deserve the Fair"

As North-South animosity over slavery and its extension to the territories divided the nation, the same concerns affected Carlisle. Forefathers of many of the town's residents had fought in the Revolution to create a new nation; the state had abolished slavery in 1780 in the midst of that conflict. The town's citizens realized, as did the country, that the South had dominated the country's political life for eighty years. Now the North, together with its new ally, the West, had grown stronger and was no longer willing to permit Southern domination of the national government. In addition, most Carlisle residents would not willingly countenance the expansion of slavery into the territories, although few, if any, supported abolition in the states where slavery already existed.

Annie's wealthy cousin, Galbraith Ege, inherited the Carlisle Iron Works from his father, Michael, who married Annie's aunt, Mary Galbraith, in 1810. Galbraith Ege sold the iron works to another member of the Ege family in 1847 and a few years later moved to Kansas where he became one of the larger landowners in the territory. In 1857 when pro-slavery and anti-slavery forces were contesting the future of the territory, Galbraith Ege visited Carlisle, "gave a glowing account of the new territory, which in the richness of the soil...cannot be surpassed," and made arrangements "to take 25 or 30 of the young men of our town" back to Kansas. "We hope they will do all in their power to save that fair territory from the blighting effects of slavery." Thus did both sides seek to increase the population of Kansas. (Carlisle *Herald*, 11 March 1857.)

James Powell, known as "Pompey Jim," a former slave who lived in Carlisle, c.1860. (CCHS.)

The "Act of Abolition" was passed by the Pennsylvania legislature on March 1, 1780. The law did not actually free any slaves but made provision for a gradual abolition. Only black and mulatto children born after March 1, 1780, were to be freed and then only after they served their mothers' master for twenty-eight years. Those whose masters failed to register them would be freed. In 1840, there were still twenty-four slaves listed in the tax lists of Cumberland County.

Buchanan, a native of nearby Lancaster, carried Carlisle in 1856, gaining 406 votes to 215 for Fremont and 186 for Fillmore. John Bratton, editor of Carlisle's *American Volunteer*, whose appointment as postmaster was renewed by Buchanan, was the leading pro-administration Democratic voice in the community. He refused to acknowledge the growing crisis in his party and the country, termed the slaves "three millions of degraded negroes,"[1] and predicted in December 1857:

> Our opponents—we cannot call them by name, for they have none—this nondescript party, without name, head, tail, or principles—is jubilant over what they term "a split in the Democratic party".... [O]ur zebra opponents...have shouted too soon.... There is no "split in the Democratic party," nor is there likely to be.[2]

Two months later in February 1858 he forecast that Kansas would be admitted under its pro-slavery constitution within a month and opined in his usual caustic manner, "We may look for a perfect calm in the 'nigger market' in thirty days.... Peace dawns and strife is banished."[3]

The 1858 elections in Cumberland County reflected hardening Northern sentiment. When a Republican defeated a pro-Buchanan candidate in the three-county congressional district that included Carlisle, the results were celebrated in Carlisle with victory bonfires, a brass band, and a torchlight procession through the town.[4] Kansas had nothing to do with the 1858 Democratic losses, the *American Volunteer* editorialized: the cause was the 1857 economic crisis and unrelated to the Administration's pro-slavery policies.[5] A month later Bratton admitted that the Democrats "have met a disastrous defeat in the Northern and Western States," while finding solace in the fact that Cumberland was the only county in Pennsylvania "that proved true to the Democratic party."[6]

As attention focused increasingly on the coming 1860 presidential election, and the split in the Democratic Party widened, the *Volunteer* predicted that

> [I]n 1860...the old national flag of Democracy...will infuse the ancient Democratic fire into the bosoms of the masses.... [E]verything like opposition, Abolition, nigger worshiping, nigger marrying, spiritual rapping and kindred isms will be totally overthrown and forgotten.[7]

Bratton fulminated that anti-slavery Democrats who refused to follow the national party were only "disappointed office-seekers, defeated candidates...grumblers...'sore-heads'...spavined politicians...corrupt disorganizers and demagogues...hypocrits."[8]

While controversy over slavery boiled at the national level, the issue was brought home more immediately and with great excitement to Cumberland County in June 1859, when the Butlers, a black

MISCELLANEOUS ITEMS.

Daring Abduction of Negroes.

One of the most outrageous cases of kidnapping ever done in this county, occurred on Friday night last, in Dickinson township. A colored man named Butler, his wife and two children, residing near Weakley's Saw mill, were captured between the hours of 9 and 10 o'clock, P. M., by parties unknown, and forcibly carried off. A carriage track was found leading to the house and from thence to Papertown, where it was lost. Late in the evening, a carriage, supposed to be the same, forced its way through the Holly toll-gate. The secrecy with which the affair was conducted, leaves little room to doubt but that the parties were well acquainted with both the neighborhood and their nefarious business. Although the cabin from which the abduction took place is in a thickly settled spot, some four or five families of whites being within a stone's throw, not the slightest alarm was raised, and the fact was not discovered till the next day, when the house was found entirely deserted; the articles of clothing strewn about, the half rumpled bed of the little girl, and bread left to rise on the hearth, showing that this outrage had been perpetrated in the most sudden and precipitate manner. The Butler family came into this county from Adams about a year ago, and are highly esteemed by their neighbors for sobriety, industry and general good conduct.

Article about the Butler affair from the *Carlisle American*, 15 June 1859.

family composed of husband, wife, and daughter, were kidnapped at night from their home eight miles from Carlisle by one Emanuel Myers, a Maryland man who specialized in the recovery of fugitive slaves. The family, freed by a Maryland widow several years previously, had fled to Pennsylvania in 1858 when the legality of the manumission was disputed in Maryland. Myers's Maryland home was only a few feet from the Pennsylvania state line. The Cumberland County sheriff traveled to the state line, enticed Myers to the Pennsylvania side through a ruse, and there arrested him after a violent struggle. The *Carlisle American* called it "one of the most outrageous cases of kidnapping ever done in the county," while the normally pro-Southern *Volunteer* expressed the hope that "the vile scoundrels who have been guilty of this meanest of crimes may all be arrested and severely punished." At his trial in August, Myers was found guilty of kidnapping but was allowed to go free upon his promise to return the Butler family to their Cumberland County home, which in due course he did.[9]

The Harper's Ferry raid in October 1859 also touched Carlisle when Albert Hazlett, one of John Brown's associates, was arrested and jailed there on suspicion that he had been a member of Brown's party. When the State of Virginia sought extradition, three leading members of the Carlisle bar defended him, attempting to establish it as a case of mistaken identity, The defense failed; Hazlett was returned to Harper's Ferry, tried, convicted, and hanged.[10]

In February 1860, John Forney, only four years earlier Pennsylvania Democratic State Chairman, was elected clerk of the Republican-controlled House of Representatives in Washington, illustrating the split among Northern Democrats over slavery. Raged Bratton, "Another apostate has been rewarded for his treachery—another traitor purchased at a price." Forney's election "by the Black Republicans," the editorial continued, "is an evidence of the degradation of that detestable and shameless party."[11]

As the 1860 political conventions approached, local newspapers chose their favorite candidates. The *Carlisle American* proclaimed its support of Edward Bates of Missouri for president. The *Herald* and *Shippensburg News* supported native son Simon Cameron for president. Reflecting the profound division in the national Democratic Party, the *American Volunteer* ignored the contest for the Democratic presidential nomination. But when delegates from nine Southern states walked out of the Charleston Democratic convention, the stridently Democratic *Volunteer* for once spoke out against those Southerners. Optimistically predicting that the reconvening of the delegates at Baltimore would be "the means of reconciling all difficulties," *Volunteer* editorials characterized the seceding delegates as men "determined to rule or ruin"[12] and urged Democrats to "speak out in terms of thunder, against the disunionists of the North and South.... [T]his Union of ours 'must and shall be preserved.'"[13]

The Conviction of Hazlett.

CHARLESTOWN, VA., Feb. 11.—The trial of Hazlett was concluded on Friday evening. Mr. Green, the counsel for the prisoner, making an able defence. The case was then submitted to the jury, and the court adjourned. On the re-opening of the Court this morning, the jury rendered a verdict of guilty of murder in the first degree. The prisoner received the announcement with the same degree of indifference that has characterized his conduct throughout the trial.

It will be remembered that HAZLETT is the man who was arrested in Carlisle, by officer HOUSER, of Chambersburg, on the 22d of October last. At the time of his arrest he was supposed to be Capt. COOK, for whose arrest a large reward was offered by the authorities of Virginia. HAZLETT was confined in our jail for a couple of weeks, and was finally delivered up to the officers of Virginia, in compliance with the requisition of the Governor of that State. HAZLETT is quite a young man—say 25—and when arrested here, he made no resistance, notwithstanding he was armed with three revolvers and two Bowie knives. He gave his name as WILLIAM HARRISON, and denied having any knowledge of the raid of JOHN BROWN at Harper's Ferry. Witnesses from Virginia, however, who were here at his trial before Judge GRAHAM, on the writ of *habeas corpus*, testified positively that the prisoner at the bar was one of the persons who invaded Harper's Ferry; that they had conversed with him there, and that they recognized him. One of the witnesses, Mr. COPELAND, said that he had seen the flash of his rifle when in the act of shooting at a citizen. No one of the witnesses knew the name of the man, nor did they ever see him before they saw him in the streets of Harper's Ferry. The same witnesses testified against him at Charlestown, during his trial.

Poor fellow!—we really feel a sympathy for this young man, for he was evidently led into wickedness and crime by the advice of older heads. His appearance is that of a mild man, but yet appearance is often deceptive. The fact that he took deliberate aim at and fired upon citizens of Harper's Ferry—citizens who had never harmed him—was evidence that he was willing to obey to the letter the orders of his desperate and blood-thirsty chief, old BROWN. Of course, HAZLETT will suffer death upon the gallows. We repeat, we are sorry for this young man, but at the same time we must confess that his punishment is just.

Article about Albert Hazlett from the *American Volunteer*, 16 Feb. 1860.

When Republicans nominated Lincoln as their candidate, the reactions of Cumberland County papers were predictable. The *Carlisle American* termed Lincoln "clean handed and pure...indebted to the people—not to the politicians—for the nomination";[14] and the *Shippensburg News* declared that he "comes up from the ranks of the people.... [H]is humble birth and his poverty fresh upon him...[with] a reputation for honesty and integrity."[15] As might have been expected, the *Volunteer* thought otherwise: "The mongrel opposition," wrote Bratton, "have selected a bigoted Abolitionist...extremist and agitator." Bratton supported Douglas, a man of "giant strength...the idol of millions, who admire him for his great intellect, his patriotism, and love of country."[16] Exhorted the *Volunteer*, "*The regular candidates of the party must be sustained* at all costs.... Democrats of Cumberland, stand by your regular nominees."[17]

Animosity over the issue of slavery reached the local level. At the July graduation exercises of Dickinson College, President Buchanan, an alumnus, "was sneered at by more than one of the young men who took part in the Commencement exercises." Complained the *Volunteer*, "nearly half the speeches delivered during Commencement week, were devoted to the praise of '*Sam*,'" as the paper contemptuously referred to blacks.[18]

An October 3 meeting at the courthouse to hear speakers supporting John Bell for president drew a large audience:

> [A] large number of Republicans attended from curiosity, and a larger number of Democrats...were drawn there probably from sympathy.... It was frankly admitted that Douglas and Breckinridge were both "dead cocks in the pit."[19]

Two weeks later the *Volunteer* accurately predicted:

> As sure as there is a God in Heaven, we will have fearful times in our country should the North elect Lincoln.... Where now reigns peace and quiet, we will hear the clash of arms and the shrieks of the vanquished.[20]

The *Herald*, headlining an editorial "SINK THE 'NIGGER QUESTION,'" declared,

> Slavery agitation comes from the democratic side of the house.... It is only the struggle of the Democracy to carry slavery where it does not exist, that produces this "agitation of the nigger question."[21]

Pennsylvania's 1860 elections for state offices, held in October four weeks before the presidential vote, produced an overwhelming victory for the People's Party, as the combined opposition to the Democrats styled itself that year. Andrew Curtin, the party's nominee for governor, swept the state with a majority of more than 30,000 votes; both houses of the state legislature returned large majorities of People's Party candidates. "Let the Eagle Scream" proclaimed the *Carlisle American.*[22]

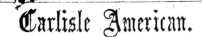

Carlisle American.

The Largest Circulation in the County.

CARLISLE, PA.

Wednesday, May, 30, 1860.

FOR PRESIDENT,

ABRAHAM LINCOLN,

OF ILLINOIS.

FOR VICE PRESIDENT,

HANNIBAL HAMLIN,

OF MAINE.

FOR GOVERNOR,

ANDREW G. CURTIN,

OF CENTRE COUNTY.

LINCOLN CLUB.

The citizens of the Borough of Carlisle without distinction of party, favorable to protection to American industry, the perpetuation of our glorious Union, the maintainance of all rights guarantied by the National Constitution, and by our local and general laws, and of internal peace, union and liberty, are requested to assemble at the Public House of Henry Glass, on Saturday evening the 2d June next, at 7½ o'clock, for the purpose of forming a "LINCOLN CLUB" and organizing generally for the Campaign. Able Speakers will be present to address the meeting.

MANY.

Headline and "Lincoln Club" announcement from the *Carlisle American*, 30 May 1860.

Andrew G. Curtin, 1860. (*Lincoln and Men of War Times*, A. K. McClure, 1892, CCHS.)

The way Pennsylvania has United the "National Democracy!

A cartoon printed during the 1860 election campaign in the *Shippensburg News*. It depicts Lincoln hoisting two rat-like figures representing Douglas and Breckinridge with a split rail. It appeared after Republican victories in Pennsylvania's October state-wide elections and before the presidential election in November.

VICTORY!!

FREEMEN
RENEW YOUR SHOUTS!!

LINCOLN AND HAMLIN
ELECTED!!!
Pennsylvania O. K.

THE NEW YORK PANIC MAKERS
SUBMERGED.

The Disunion Fortress Razed
From Turret to Foundation Stone!!
AND THE

OLD FLAG
OUR FATHERS STAR'D
AND DEDICATED TO
GOD, OUR COUNTRY AND LIBERTY,
FLOATS IN TRIUMPH!!

The battle is over, the victory won, Free Speech, Free Homes, Free Soil, and Free Labor vindicated in the election of ABRAHAM LINCOLN and HANNIBAL HAMLIN.— Hang out your banners, Light your torches and chant your songs of triumph—
"Freemen rejoice, the port to which we've passed, O'er destiny's dark wave, beams out at last. Victory is our own———"

THE RESULT.
PENNSYLVANIA.

The Keystone of the Arch has proved true as steel. The majority for Curtin has been largely increased. It is not necessary to give reported majorities. Suffice it to say that the State has gone Republican by not less than

75.000!

Headlines proclaiming Lincoln's election from the *Carlisle American*, 7 Nov. 1860.

With bands, torchlight parades, and marches by Wide-Awake clubs (the name given to local Republican campaign groups), the contest continued into November, when Lincoln carried Pennsylvania by over 70,000 votes. "VICTORY! VICTORY!! GRAND TRIUMPH OF THE PEOPLE! LINCOLN ELECTED PRESIDENT! DISUNION REBUKED," headlined the *Herald*.[23] Equally dramatic were the headlines in the *Carlisle American*, "THE DISUNION FORTRESS RAZED FROM TURRET TO FOUNDATION STONE AND THE OLD FLAG OUR FATHERS STAR'D AND DEDICATED TO GOD, OUR COUNTRY, AND LIBERTY FLOATS IN TRIUMPH."[24]

The Carlisle and Cumberland county vote showed the deep split in local sentiment and the strength of the Democrats:

Carlisle
Lincoln – Republican 425
Bell – Constitutional Union 53
Douglas-Breckinridge – Fusion Democratic ticket ..... 406 [25]
Douglas – Straight Democratic ticket .... 13 [26]

Cumberland County
Lincoln 3593
Bell 147
Douglas-Breckinridge – Fusion ticket 3207
Douglas 26

Lincoln's majority over the two Democratic tickets was only 6 votes in Carlisle and 360 votes in the county. As historic Democratic strongholds, Carlisle gave Lincoln only 47 percent of its vote and Cumberland County 51.5 percent.

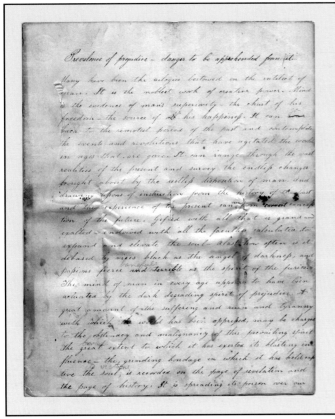

An undated school paper (probably written when James Colwell was about sixteen) is headed, "Prevalence of prejudice—danger to be apprehended from it," and refers to the "dark, degrading spirit of prejudice." He states that "It is spreading its poison over our own country, undermining the fair frame of her noble institutions and the independence of her free born citizens." He continues that "the peace and good order of society [is] disturbed and even the dissolution of the union threatened by agitators on the subject of slavery." He concludes "But let us lay aside these dark apprehensions. Let us hope that the diffusion of intelligence will correct false opinions, and that the people will burst the bonds of prejudice and resolve to be free." (Colwell Family Papers.)

James Colwell was an intelligent and thoughtful man. With respect to slavery, in a letter written when he was twenty, he supported the colonization of Africa by American slaves, a vain proposal popular among many anti-slavery adherents:

> And why then not send them [the slaves] back to their own land where they can enjoy liberty, be governed by their own laws, choose their own rulers, and enjoy all the privileges in their own country, which we as a free nation enjoy here.[27]

By 1856 James had become a Free Soil man. Although not an abolitionist, he strongly opposed the extension of slavery to the territories. When his wife Annie gave birth to their first son on August 10, 1856, the boy was christened John Charles, doubtless named for John Charles Fremont, then campaigning to be the first Republican president. A few days later on August 18, James and his friend, George Zinn, editor of the *Carlisle American*, served as delegates from Carlisle's East Ward to the first County Convention of the Union Party, where a slate of Union candidates was nominated for state and county offices in the fall elections.[28] Two weeks later a Fremont club was formed in Carlisle to rouse support for the 1856 Republican nominee under the slogan, "Free Men, Free Soil, and Fremont." James was elected president of the club.[29] Living and practicing law in Carlisle, the county seat, James was well aware of the currents of political opinion swirling around the country. As his later letters show, he firmly believed in the maintenance of the Union.[30]

John Charles Fremont. (*History of the Civil War in America*, John C. Abbott, 1863, CCHS.)

After the election in 1860 turbulence mounted. The *Herald* reflected much Northern opinion when it blamed the Democrats for the coming crisis in a late-November editorial:

> During the whole campaign, they endeavored to frighten the timid...by sounding alarms which they knew were false.... Let these pretended alarmists...now allay the storm they have raised.[31]

On December 20 South Carolina formally seceded from the Union. The seriousness of the situation was recognized in Carlisle. During Christmas week all of the town's papers carried the same message, signed by most of the town's business and professional men, calling for a general meeting of all concerned citizens at the County Courthouse:

> The community has been suddenly startled by the cry of disunion.... There are elements of trouble which are really threatening in their aspect.... [I]t behooves every community to meet and consult together about what is best to be done. Let us put off, for a moment, the armor of political warfare, and counsel together...whether we can do anything and what, to save the Union from its threatened destruction.[32]

Among the signers were not only James Colwell and many other members of the Carlisle bar, but also Editor Bratton of the *Volunteer* and other leading Democrats. That meeting resolved:

> That we cannot sanction the attempt of any State to secede from the Union, as the exercise of either a natural right or a constitutional remedy; and that it is the duty of the general government to regard it as a violation of the Laws of the United States.[33]

It was too late for resolutions. Mississippi seceded January 9, 1861; Florida followed on the tenth and Alabama on the eleventh. The January 10 issue of the *American Volunteer* reported the resignations of the first U.S. military officers to give up their commissions in order to return to the service of their home states.[34] State forces then seized the federal arsenal at Charleston, South Carolina, and other forts in Georgia, Alabama, and Florida.

Arguments raged in the Cumberland County newspapers. The *Herald* editorialized that the crisis was

> the full harvest of arrogant and aggressive policy by the pro-slavery men in Congress.... The secret of disunion is...the fact that the South has lost her power to dictate terms to the North.[35]

The Carlisle *American Democrat*, the pro-Union Democratic paper, referred to the "insolence and presumption" of South Carolina, "that insignificant state." Criticizing Buchanan, "the timid and iniflicient[sic][36] man who is in the presidential chair," the paper declared, "we ought to have *men* at the head of our government and not old women."[37] The *Volunteer* propounded the opposite view: "As our national troubles have been brought upon us by the Republican Party, we think it will be fortunate for that party in particular, if war can be prevented."[38]

UNION MEETING.

The community has been suddenly startled by the cry of disunion; and public sentiment in the South seems to give sanction to it. There are elements of trouble which are really threatening in their aspect, and the vast importance of peace and quiet, and the enjoyment of civil liberty under the banner of those Institutions which our fathers formed for us, is so dear to us all, that it behooves every community to meet and consult together about what is best to be done. Let us put off, for a moment, the armor of political warfare, and counsel together whether there is any better Government on the earth than that which we enjoy, and whether we can do anything and what, to save the Union from its threatened destruction.

The citizens of Carlisle and vicinity, without distinction of political opinions, are requested to meet together at the Court House, in Carlisle, on.

Saturday Evening, December 22,

at 7 o'clock, p. m., and express their opinions of the value of that Constitution which has so long protected us.

Announcement of a "Union Meeting" from the *American Volunteer*, 20 Dec. 1860.

Major General Thomas L. Crittenden.
(*Battles and Leaders of the Civil War*,
Grant-Lee Edition, CCHS.)

Major General George B. Crittenden,
C.S.A. (*Battles and Leaders of the
Civil War*, Grant-Lee Edition, CCHS.)

Senator John J. Crittenden. (Massachusetts Commandery Military Order
of the Loyal Legion and the U.S. Army
Military History Institute.)

One of John Crittenden's sons became a Major General in the Union army,
another a Major General in the Confederate army. The latter, George B. Crittenden,
had been Commandant of the Carlisle Barracks until February 1861.

Some still sought compromise. Kentucky Senator John
Crittenden, a strong supporter of the Union whose own family reflected the division in the country, proposed amending the Constitution to permit perpetual slavery in the South and the District of
Columbia and to allow its extension to territories south of the 36°30´
line. When Republicans would not accept extension of slavery to the
territories, Crittenden's proposals came to naught.

Another public meeting was convened at Carlisle's courthouse on
January 14, 1861, for all those favoring compromise and "some plan
of adjustment, such as that proposed by the Hon. J. J. Crittenden."[39]
The large meeting was attended by many leading members of the
Carlisle bar, among them former Judge Frederick Watts, the respected
senior lawyer in the county. Most of those in attendance favored
compromise, but opinions voiced at the meeting indicated the depth
of feeling and the breadth of division on the issue. A minority
strongly opposed extension of slavery into the territories. That
minority included former American Party Congressman Lemuel Todd
and former Whig Party State Assemblyman R. M. Henderson, and
Judge Watts's own son, William Watts, all friends of James Colwell.
Commenting on the meeting the *Shippensburg News* pointed out
accurately: "It is generally presumed...that the election of Abraham

AMERICAN VOLUNTEER.

JOHN B. BRATTON, Editor & Proprietor.

CARLISLE, PA., JAN. 10, 1861.

"Our Union, One and Inseparable!"
COUNTY MEETING.

The people of Cumberland county, who, in
the present national crisis, favor compromise
and conciliation, and are willing to accede to
some plan of adjustment, such as that proposed by the Hon. J. J. CRITTENDEN and his com-
patriots in Congress, are requested to meet in
the Court House, on MONDAY EVENING
NEXT, January 14, to give expression to their
views.
It is time the voice of the people should be
heard, for they are the rulers.
Signed by
A. S. SENER,
THOMAS CONLYN,
WILLIAM SPAHR,
J. ARMSTRONG,
and 148 others.

Announcement from the *American
Volunteer*, 10 Jan. 1861.

Lincoln is the actual cause of the disruption of the Union...but it is evidently a mere pretext." The actual cause, opined the paper, was "opposition to the growing influence of the North."[40] No compromise could change the census returns.

In any case, Southern political leaders had no interest in compromise. Delegates from seven seceding states[41] met at Montgomery, Alabama, on February 4, adopted a provisional constitution for the Confederate States of America, and chose former U.S. Senator Jefferson Davis as provisional president and former U.S. Congressman Alexander Stephens of Georgia as vice president.

On the same day delegates met at Montgomery, a Peace Conference convened in Washington. Delegates from twenty-one Northern and border states attended; none were present from the seven states that had seceded. For three weeks delegates sought a compromise, finally approving seven proposed constitutional amendments. Their work was in vain: the seven seceding states wanted no compromise and Republicans would accept none which permitted the extension of slavery to the territories.

As the seriousness of the situation became apparent, other voices for compromise were heard. The *Herald* supported some form of compromise similar to the Crittenden proposals. An editorial pointed out that giving the territories the option of voting for slavery would likely have little effect on the extension of the institution since geographical conditions in the territories were unsuited for plantation agriculture.[42] The *American Democrat* agreed:

> Perhaps our acquiescence in the plan proposed by Mr. Crittenden may save the country; and it would be consummate folly to risk all the perils and dangers that will follow, from *all* the slave states forming a Southern Confederacy, by the refusal.[43]

The paper noted that the five living ex-presidents of the United States, Van Buren, Tyler, Fillmore, Pierce, and Buchanan, all supported the Crittenden proposals. Lincoln "rejects all compromise." Asked the paper, "Is his wisdom greater than the combined wisdom of his predecessors?"[44] The *Volunteer* was far stronger. Its editorial repeated the long litany of Southern grievances against the North: restrictions on the expansion of slavery starting with the Missouri Compromise; the underground railway; efforts to abolish slavery in the District of Columbia; public criticism of slavery as a "sin" in violation of a "higher law"; publication of "incendiary papers, pamphlets"; extending the rights of citizenship to blacks; and "producing an insurrection at Harper's Ferry." "We believe," the editorial concluded,

> that the responsibility of a dissolution of the Union is justly chargeable to Northern fanaticism.... [A] compromise as brought forward by Mr. Crittenden is no more than the South has a *right to demand*.[45]

William M. Watts, Jr., taken at Louisville, Kentucky, December 1864. (A. A. Line copy, CCHS.)

When Lincoln was sworn in as President on March 4, 1861, his speech was moderate enough. The words were of conciliation, brotherhood, and "the mystic chords of memory," which, he hoped, "will yet swell the chorus of the Union when again touched...by the better angels of our nature." The words were also of determination, as he stated his intention to "hold, occupy, and possess the property and places belonging to the government."

The *American Democrat* reflected the opinion of many northern Unionist Democrats:

> Our view of the inaugural is that...the views therein are as conservative as could well be expected.... [W]e look upon it as a peace offering rather than a declaration of war.[46]

It was a time when men knew that the court of world opinion was judging the American Republic. "Is Democracy a Failure?" headlined an editorial in the *Carlisle American.*

Inauguration of Abraham Lincoln, March 4, 1861. (*Battles and Leaders of the Civil War*, Grant-Lee Edition, CCHS.)

> Among the many voices raised in Europe over the disaster of secession, amid the groans of sorrow, cries of indignation and tones of sympathy which reach us from many lands beyond the sea, there is one neither loud nor mocking, but which...is more torment-ing than all the other sounds combined. We mean that complacent "We told you so," of the friends of the old order of things...who have always predicted the downfall of the Republic...that Democ-racy is a false principle, and that, therefore, every Republic must be a failure.[47]

Of all the Civil War's political and military blunders, the worst may have been the South's decision to attack Fort Sumter. On April 8, 1861, Lincoln informed the governor of South Carolina that an attempt would be made to supply Fort Sumter with provisions only. When the message was passed to Montgomery, the Confed-erate cabinet convened. After discussion an attack on Fort Sumter was approved.[48] Until that attack the depth of Northern support for offensive action against the South was questionable.[49] However, when Southern guns fired on the fort April 12, 1861, and the national flag was hauled down in surrender the next day, the act provoked an emotional outburst of support for the Union through-out the North. In cities, country towns, and tiny villages, men and women, with rare exceptions, rallied to support the Union.

> A correspondent in Boston wrote, "The heather is on fire.... [T]here never was anything like it.... The whole population...seem to be in the streets with Union favors and flags." In Philadelphia "The assault on Fort Sumter started us all to our feet, as one man; all political division ceased among us from that very moment." Reported an Ohio man, "The West is all one great Eagle-scream."[50]

Bombardment of Fort Sumter. (*History of the Civil War in America*, John C. Abbott, 1863, CCHS.)

Carlisle reflected emotions in the North. "THE WAR; STAND BY THE FLAG," was the lead for the *Herald's* editorial on April 19, 1861. Forget all compromise, advised the paper, "until peace is conquered by the power of the Government.... [I]nsults and outrages cannot forever be heaped on the Stars and Stripes."[51] Declared the *Carlisle American*:

> This war is inevitable and must be fought to the bitter end.... [T]hat mongrel band...have begun the war and upon their heads be the consequences.... Arouse then Pennsylvanians![52]

The *American Democrat*, while still urging "conciliatory measures," made clear its opinion.

> We as good citizens...are bound to sustain our chosen rulers.... Shall rebellion go on and our people be slaughtered, and we raise no hand to prevent it? No! Never!.... [I]t is our duty to stand by the flag of our country to the bitter end.[53]

As might have been expected, the *Volunteer* was a rare voice blaming Lincoln and the North for the crisis. Headlining his editorial "Old Abe's War," Bratton wrote:

> Abraham Lincoln, the poor imbecile who occupies and disgraces the Presidential chair, has thought proper to commence a civil war.... [A]nd he arrived at the conclusion to drench the country in blood by civil war![54]

In an editorial headed "A Filthy, Treasonable Sheet" Edward Curriden, editor of the *Shippensburg News*, angrily responded to Bratton:

> If there is one sheet within the circle of the free States which deserves the condemnation of every honest heart, that sheet is the Carlisle *Volunteer*.... [T]hat sheet should receive the attention of Judge Lynch without delay.[55]

For Sumter must and shall be avenged.

Letterhead illustration dated 1862. (Manuscript Collection, CCHS.)

View of Harper's Ferry, after the demolition of the Government buildings. (*History of the Civil War in the United States*, Samuel M. Schmucker, 1865, CCHS.)

Events passed beyond the stage of newspaper editorials. On April 18, 1861, a force of one thousand Virginians advanced on the government arsenal at Harper's Ferry, defended by Lieutenant Roger Jones and a force of only forty-five men. In the face of overwhelming superiority, Jones burned and blew up what he could of the buildings, armory machinery, and supplies and evacuated the arsenal that night, marching thirty miles to Hagerstown, Maryland, the nearest railhead. There he took the train to Carlisle Barracks.[56]

Anger at the South found expression at another public meeting at the Carlisle Courthouse on Saturday afternoon, April 20. Perhaps editor Bratton of the *Volunteer* recognized widespread hostility to his views in Carlisle; for he interrupted the presentation of previously prepared resolutions at that meeting to offer a proposal that the County Commissioners establish a fund "for the support of families whose natural protectors have volunteered for the war," a proposal which was adopted by the meeting.[57] And in the next issue of the *Volunteer* he changed his tune, forgot "Old Abe's War," and editorialized under the lead "Our Flag":

> By the deliberate act of the rebellious states that have set up a government hostile to the Union...the first act in the bloody drama of fraternal war has opened.... The forces of the United States have been wantonly attacked, its flag shot down and dishonored.... [O]ur course is a plain one.... WE CAN KNOW NO PARTY BUT OUR COUNTRY—NO DUTY BUT OBEDIENCE TO ITS LAWS...NO ALLEGIANCE BUT TO ITS FLAG.... "AND MAY GOD PROTECT THE RIGHT."[58]

April 1861 was not a good month for John Bratton. George Zinn, editor of the Republican *Carlisle American*, was appointed the town's new postmaster in place of Bratton (as Republican editor Edward Curriden of the *Shippensburg News* was appointed the new postmaster of that town). And apparent disagreement with Bratton's views appeared closer to home; in the April 25, 1861 issue, the *Volunteer*'s editor announced that four members of his personal and business family had volunteered for the war, including two employees of the newspaper, one employee of the post office, and his own son, William Bratton.

Stand by the Union !

Democrats ! we have fought, in other times, to maintain the Union against the attacks of its sectional enemies. Now that we are in the midst of this bloody civil feud, let us stand by the old banner, under which we have marched to many a political battle. Let us not be heard crying, " The North against the South," or " The South against the North," but, " THE GOVERNMENT AND THE UNION !" It becomes our duty, our sacred, solemn duty, as citizens of a State loyal to the Government, to stand up for the maintenance of the authority of that Government. Let us be true to the covenant formed by our fathers, and discarding sectionalism of every sort, stand together for the vindication of the Constitution and the restoration of the Union.

" The Union, Oh ! the Union,
    So glorious and so pure !
We'll shoulder stand to shoulder,
    To keep our Union sure."

Bratton's editorial from the *American Volunteer*, 2 May 1861.

Robert Miller Henderson, c.1862. (Massachusetts Commandery Military Order of the Loyal Legion and the U.S. Army Military History Institute.)

Still trying to put himself right with his fellow towns-men, Bratton headed an editorial a week later, "Stand By The Union," declaring, "It becomes our duty, our sacred duty...to stand up for the maintenance of the authority" of the national government.[59] A wave of patriotic support for the national government swept Carlisle. The *American Democrat* referred to "the intense excitement of the past week," and reported of Dickinson College that "most of the Southern students have gone home or will probably go." Some Pennsylvania students at the college had already volunteered for service with the Union army.[60] They were not alone. Hundreds of Carlisle men volun-teered for military service to fill Pennsylvania's quota, among them James Colwell. Four companies of approxi-mately one hundred men each were organized in Carlisle within a week. One company, the Sumner Rifles, left for active duty on Saturday, April 20, 1861, a week after the attack on Sumter. When state and national authorities were overwhelmed with more volunteers than could be immediately processed,[61] Carlisle's three other volunteer companies had to practice marching and the manual of arms in Carlisle. One of those three companies was the Carlisle Fencibles. Electing their own officers, as was the custom, its members chose as captain R. M. Henderson, a lawyer and former member of the Pennsylvania House of Representa-tives. Chosen as first lieutenant was James S. Colwell; Ekuries Beatty, former editor of the *Herald*, was chosen second lieutenant. John Bratton's son and his former employees at the *Volunteer* and post office were members; so were several volunteers from Shippensburg, among them David Curriden, brother of the editor of the *Shippensburg News*.

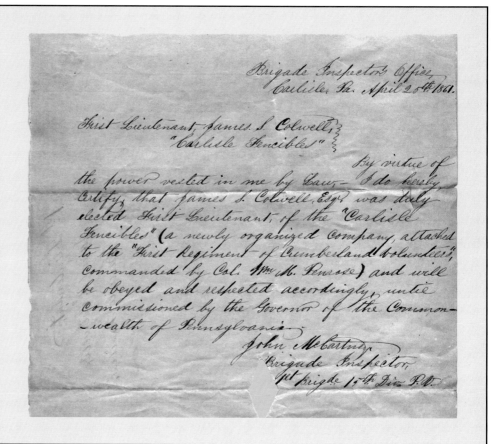

This hand-written appointment, dated 25 April 1861, reads: "By virtue of the power vested in me by Law,—I do hereby certify, that James S. Colwell, Esq. was duly elected First Lieutenant of the 'Carlisle Fencibles' (a newly organized company, attached to the 'First Regiment of Cumberland Volunteers,' commanded by Col. Wm. M. Penrose) and will be obeyed and respected accordingly, until commissioned by the Governor of the Commonwealth of Pennsylvania." The appointment is signed by John McCartney, Brigade Inspector. (Colwell Family Papers.)

"Rally to Your Country's Aid!.... Come, your country calls," read a letter to the editor in the May 1, 1861 issue of the *American Democrat*. "TO ARMS! TO ARMS!" was the headline for a clothing store advertisement in the same issue. "FLAGS! FLAGS!" advertised a manufacturer of flags and badges.

Carlisle's papers were unanimous in their feelings regarding the war. "[Southern leaders] have let loose the dogs of war upon the country.... [F]orce is necessary to cure their madness," editorialized the *American Democrat*,[62] while the *Herald* proclaimed, "The millions of the north...will know no half-way measures, until the supremacy of the government is successfully vindicated."[63] Wrote the *Carlisle American*:

> There is but one escape from the impending ruin. To swear devotion to our country, fidelity to the Constitution, and to live or die beneath the noble shadow of our country. Now is the time for Union men to prove their devotion to the Union.[64]

As the Civil War commenced, patriotism and an almost joyful attitude prevailed in Carlisle among its citizens. Wrote one of the members of the Sumner Rifles from camp at West Chester, Pennsylvania, where the company was in training, "We are in our glory now.—West Chester against the world. Hurrah! hurrah! for this brave land."[65] Impatience reigned at Carlisle where the three volunteer companies awaited their call to service. Eager to support the Unionist cause, the companies marched and drilled in the evenings. A reporter from the *Herald* visited the Fencibles one evening and was "surprised and gratified at their proficiency in drill."[66]

Contrabands coming into Fortress Monroe. (*History of the Civil War in the United States*, Samuel M. Schmucker, 1865, CCHS.)

Late in May of 1861, Carlisle residents, along with the rest of the country, learned a new term, "contraband," a euphemism for escaped slaves fleeing to the North. Fugitive slaves had fled their Southern owners and sought protection at Fortress Monroe, the large Union army base at Hampton Roads across from Norfolk near the mouth of Chesapeake Bay. When Col. Mallory, commander of Confederate troops nearby, sought return of his slaves, he was informed by General Butler, in command of the fort, that if he wished to take an oath of allegiance to the Union, his slaves would be returned to him in accordance with the Fugitive Slave Law, still the law of the land. Otherwise his slaves would be considered as contraband of war and would not be returned. The administration in Washington approved Butler's actions.[67]

Thus the term "contraband" entered the Northern vocabulary, and the thousands of runaway slaves who fled their Southern masters over the following four years became known as contrabands. Runaway slaves, fleeing owners in Virginia and Maryland, became common in Carlisle during the war. As early as June 1861 the *Herald* reported, "We hear numerous examples of biped contrabands in our own, and other counties" and wrote of a runaway slave knocking at the door of a local farmer requesting something to eat. (Carlisle *Herald*, 28 June 1861.)

After six weeks of waiting, the three remaining Carlisle companies were called to active duty. Their departure for camp on June 6, 1861 occasioned an emotional outpouring of civic fervor. An "elegant satin flag, mounted with gold fringe and tassels," and bearing the motto "May God Defend the Right," was presented to the Carlisle Fencibles by the ladies of the town, who asked James Colwell to make the speech presenting the flag to the company on their behalf. He did so, asking in their name that it "be consecrated to the noble leaders in that battle in which you are enlisted."[68] Then young girls from several of the town's public schools presented the company with "a neat little flag" with the words "God and our Country" inscribed on it. The girls, too, had an address, this one read for them by Capt. Henderson.

> The girls of the Borough of Carlisle, desire to express to you...the interest we feel in the successful issue of the noble cause which you go forth to defend.... Our hopes and prayers accompany you.... "None but the brave deserve the fair." Take this flag our little flag.... [O]n your return you will deserve wreaths of laurel.

Then, continued the newspaper account, all assembled sang "The Star-Spangled Banner" and

> The train moved off, the welkin rang with oft-repeated cheers.... [T]he universal feeling was that no sacrifice was too great, to save our country from the impious hands raised for its destruction.[69]

The flags, the tears, the flowers, the cheers, and the salutes of cannons continued at each village as the train moved through central Pennsylvania until it arrived in the evening at Camp Wayne in West Chester, Pennsylvania, where the recruits would train for the next six weeks.

Flags in the Carlisle home of William M. Henderson, c.1907. (A. A. Line, CCHS.)

On the left is the Adamantine Guards Flag. It belonged to one of the two companies of cavalry furnished by Cumberland County for the Civil War—the Big Spring Adamantine Guards. After the war the flag was kept by the Guards' captain, William E. Miller.

In the center is the banner of the "Carlisle Guards." This company was formed in Carlisle during the War of 1812. The blue silk standard was presented to the company during a celebration on the Public Square in 1817.

On the right is the flag of Company A of the 7th Penna. Reserves. It was made by Mrs. Samuel Alexander, wife of the general, and presented to Company A in 1861. The staff upon which the flag was fastened was taken from a Revolutionary War flag used by Carlisle soldiers. The flag was kept by Captain John I. Faller after the war.

James Colwell's Speech
June 6, 1861

On Behalf of the Ladies of Carlisle

It is said of a celebrated legislator of Athens that enacted a law that whoever remained neuter when great political questions were to be decided in the republic should be punished with the penalty of death. While we the professed champions of the liberty of opinion, liberty of speech & of action & surrounded as we are by the monuments of freedom, would condemn the severity of that law: yet we cannot deny that it has its foundation & origin in a true principle. If a foreign foe armed in battle array should invade your land, wasting & destroying your territory, pillaging your houses & burning your towns & villages, what man here with the soul of a freeman would say he had a right to remain at ease & leave to others to fight the battles of his country & protect his fireside? If there be such, the contempt of the good & the brave would rest on him forever. Yet no danger to republican institutions is to be apprehended from a foreign foe. Danger to a republic can only arrive from the supremacy of false principles at home—produced by faction ambition, ignorance, want of patriotism & a thousand other evils among the citizens themselves. Here is where the danger lies. How important then that all should examine & understand those

principles upon which rest the success & prosperity of the country & the perpetuity of her institutions. Hence we see it is the duty of all, old & young, male & female, to contribute, each in their peculiar sphere, to the advancement of those doctrines which they believe to be right, and to do honor to those who in every trial have proved worthy of the love, the confidence & the esteem of their countrymen.

Actuated by these sentiments, the ladies of Carlisle, ever foremost in a good cause, have prepared this beautiful banner to be consecrated to the noble leaders in that battle in which you are enlisted as soldiers. Of the time and merits of these eminent individuals I am not required on this occasion to speak. Their distinguished services are known to the whole county. The question—who is general Scott—is never asked

& needs no answer. That name is written among the brightest & greatest in the world's history and there it will remain written forever.

These ladies are no advocates of war unnecessary. Deeds of blood & the clangor of arms have no charms for them; but they delight to honour him who has periled his life not once nor twice but many times in his country's cause & who is distinguished in civil life as well as war. Who was it when the fierce storm of disunion was gathering fast & thick in a far off sister state & threatening to drench this glorious & happy union with the warm blood of brethren—who was it whom the iron hearted Jackson then in the presidential chair, selected & sent to calm the troubled elements and to whom Lewis Cap, Sec'y of War, wrote President Jackson has the fullest confidence in your judgment & discretion? Who was it but Genl. Scott? And President Jackson was not mistaken, he had put his confidence in the right man. Scott did go and with the olive branch instead of the sword rolled back those dark clouds of danger & returned in the sunlight of peace shining benignantly over all this broad & happy land.

Honor then to him who by his judgment & discretion saved the country from the horrors of civil strife & from being deluged with fraternal blood. Honor to the gallant old hero who has led your armies through two foreign wars, on foreign soil, & led them always to glory & to victory. Honor to the brave old Winfield Scott.

In the name of the ladies of Carlisle & on their behalf I present this banner to you the [blank] of Carlisle and commit it to your trust with full confidence that you will guard it as your standard in the battle now to be fought and by your earnestness show that you know & appreciate the importance of the high duty before you. I am sure you will leave no toil untried, no obstacle unsurmounted, to place at the [?] of state those tried patriots whose names are inscribed on it.

Endnotes

[1] *American Volunteer*, 5 November 1857.

[2] *American Volunteer*, 10 December 1857.

[3] *American Volunteer*, 25 February 1858.

[4] Carlisle *Herald*, 20 October 1858.

[5] *American Volunteer*, 21 October 1858.

[6] *American Volunteer*, 18 November 1858.

[7] *American Volunteer*, 17 February 1859.

[8] *American Volunteer*, 21 April 1859.

[9] *Carlisle American*, 15 June 1859; *American Volunteer*, 23 June 1859; *Shippensburg News*, 25 June 1859; Wing, *Cumberland County*, 265.

[10] Carlisle *Herald*, 26 October 1859, 2 November 1859, 9 November 1859; *American Volunteer*, 16 February 1860, 22 March 1860.

[11] *American Volunteer*, 9 February 1860.

[12] *American Volunteer*, 10 May 1860.

[13] *American Volunteer*, 17 May 1860.

[14] *Carlisle American*, 30 May 1860.

[15] *Shippensburg News*, 26 May 1860.

[16] *American Volunteer*, 28 June 1860.

[17] *American Volunteer*, 12 July 1860.

[18] *American Volunteer*, 19 July 1860. At the opposite end of the controversy, Wendell Phillips termed Lincoln "the hell-hound of Pro-Slavery.... [O]n the side of the slave power...for his pro-slavery character" during a July 4 abolition meeting. *Shippensburg News*, 28 July 1860.

[19] Carlisle *Herald*, 5 October 1860.

[20] *American Volunteer*, 18 October 1860.

[21] Carlisle *Herald*, 26 October 1860.

[22] *Carlisle American*, 10 October 1860.

[23] Carlisle *Herald*, 9 November 1860.

[24] *Carlisle American*, 7 November 1860.

[25] A common slate of electors was chosen by the two Democratic factions which agreed to combine their electoral votes if it would make a difference in the final outcome of the election.

[26] A few strongly anti-slavery Democrats refused to support the fusion ticket and voted for a separate Douglas ticket.

[27] Letter to J.G. Moody, 10 May 1834. The Colwell Family Papers.

[28] *Carlisle American*, 20 August 1856.

[29] Carlisle *Herald*, 3 September 1856. Although he was interested in political affairs, James was a homebody. He never himself sought political office; his lone attempt at an elected position was in 1858 when, with two young children and a third on the way, he ran for the local school board from the East Ward of Carlisle and was defeated by a vote of 192-134.

[30] JSC to AHC 4 July 1861 and 11 November 1861.

[31] Carlisle *Herald*, 30 November 1860.

[32] Carlisle *Herald*, 21 December 1860.

[33] Merkel Landis, "Civil War Times in Carlisle: An Address Delivered at Hamilton Library, Carlisle, Pa., February 12th, 1931," 3; in *Carlisle in the Civil War* (Carlisle, Pa.,: Hamilton Library and Historical Association, n.d.).

[34] *American Volunteer*, 10 January 1861. Of the 1,108 officers on active duty in the U.S. Army in 1861, 387 resigned their commissions to join the Confederate forces.

[35] Carlisle *Herald*, 11 January 1861.

[36] The rules of syntax, punctuation, spelling, and capitalization were less rigorously applied and less consistently followed in the mid-nineteenth century than they are today. As long as the

intent is clear, quotations are not corrected or conformed to modern usage in this book. Here "iniflicient" was probably a typographical error for "inefficient."

37 *American Democrat*, 2 January 1861.

38 *American Volunteer*, 10 January 1861.

39 Carlisle *Herald*, 11 January 1861.

40 *Shippensburg News*, 23 January 1861.

41 By 4 February 1861, South Carolina had been joined in secession by Mississippi, Florida, Alabama, Georgia, Louisiana, and Texas. Virginia, Tennessee, North Carolina, and Arkansas would later join them.

42 Carlisle *Herald*, 8 February 1861.

43 *American Democrat*, 30 January 1861.

44 *American Democrat*, 27 February 1861.

45 *American Volunteer*, 7 February 1861.

46 *American Democrat*, 13 March 1861.

47 *Carlisle American*, 20 March, 1861.

48 Robert Toombs, the Confederacy's first Secretary of State, warned Davis against the attack on Fort Sumter: "Mr. President...you will wantonly strike a hornet's nest which extends from mountain to oceans, and legions now quiet will swarm out and sting us to death. It is unnecessary; it puts us in the wrong; it is fatal." Pleasant A. Stovall, *Robert Toombs* (New York: Cassell Publishing Company, 1892), 226. A detailed account of the actions by both Union and Confederate political leaders in the period immediately prior to the attack on Fort Sumter is contained in Bruce Catton, *The Coming Fury* (Garden City, N.Y.: Doubleday & Co. Inc., 1961).

49 Horace Greeley, publisher of the New York *Tribune*, editorialized only days after Lincoln's victory in November: "If the Cotton States shall become satisfied that they can do better out of the Union than in it, we insist on letting them go in peace." New York *Tribune*, 9 November 1860. Two months later he repeated his advice: "Wayward sisters, depart in peace," he told the South. Quoted in Morison et al., *Growth of the American Republic*, vol. 1, 613.

Abolitionist Wendell Phillips told a Boston meeting that he considered himself a disunionist and hoped the slave states would leave the Union as soon as possible. Carlos Martyn, *Wendell Phillips: The Agitator* (New York: Funk & Wagnalls Co., 1890), 306. New York City's Democratic mayor, Fernando Wood, suggested that New York become a free and neutral city and deal with North and South on an equal and friendly basis, 199, citing the New York *Herald* of 8 January and 12 January 1861. The whole crisis was Lincoln's fault, not the South's, complained James Gordon Bennett, editor of the powerful New York *Herald*, on 10 April 1861.

50 Henry Steele Commager, ed., *The Blue and the Gray* (New York: Bobbs-Merrill Company, Inc., 1950), vol. 1, 40-44.

51 Carlisle *Herald*, 19 April 1861.

52 *Carlisle American*, 17 April 1861.

53 *American Democrat*, 17 April 1861.

54 *American Volunteer*, 18 April 1861.

55 *Shippensburg News*, 20 April 1861.

56 Ibid.

57 Carlisle *Herald*, 26 April 1861.

58 *American Volunteer*, 25 April 1861.

59 *American Volunteer*, 2 May 1861.

60 *American Democrat*, 24 April 1861.

61 When the war started, the U.S. Army totaled 16,000 men; 183 of the Army's 198 companies were stationed in the West. Training facilities, the organization for supply, and the general administration of the Army were completely inadequate to cope with numbers on active duty which rose to about 1,000,000 in the North and perhaps half that number in the South. Catton, *The Coming Fury*, 120. See also the concise summary headed "Numbers and Losses" in Morison et al., *Growth of the American Republic*, vol. 1, 634-636.

62 *American Democrat*, 1 May 1861.

63 Carlisle *Herald*, 3 May 1861.

64 *Carlisle American*, 24 April 1861.

65 Carlisle *Herald*, 10 May 1861.

66 A regular army sergeant had been detached from duty at the Carlisle Barracks for a few weeks to instruct the raw recruits. Carlisle *Herald*, 17 May 1861.

67 The story is told in full in John G. Nicolay and John Hay, *Abraham Lincoln: A History*, vol. 4 (New York: Century Co., 1886-1914), 386-395.

68 Undated handwritten draft of speech by James Colwell. The Colwell Family Papers.

69 Carlisle *Herald*, 7 June 1861. The same issue carried news of the death of Senator Stephen A. Douglas, who had publicly and unfailingly supported Lincoln since the outbreak of hostilities.

CHAPTER 3

"A Sense of Right and Duty"

Illustration from a printed announcement for the 1905 annual reunion of the survivors of Company A, 7th Penna. Reserves. (Manuscript Collection, CCHS.)

Article from the *American Democrat*, 19 June 1861.

Correspondence of the Democrat.

FROM OUR ARMY CORRESPONDENT.

CAMP WAYNE,
June 15, 1861.

Mr. Editor :—According to promise I now give you the first letter from Camp Wayne—as your own special correspondent at this place. The dreary weather of the morn of our departure from old Carlisle clung close to us as a wet garment all the day, and the first sight we had of West Chester was muddy streets and falling rain, with a thick dark night closing upon us; and that we might taste soldiers fare immediately we were taken from the cars into the West Chester passenger depot and our quarters pointed out to us on the rough plank floors. Not a blanket, a bit of bread or cup of cold water was offered to a single soldier to comfort him in the dreary place. But thanks to our noble Captains, we did not tarry in the car house, as in a few minutes we were ordered by squad and company to the best hotels, and there the most of us fared for the next forty-eight hours on the best in the land.

On Friday and Saturday, (June 7 and 8.) we repaired our quarters at Camp Wayne, so that by the eve of our second day here we were all enabled to "bunk in tent" as bold soldiers only can, and the commissary having supplied the companies according to regulations. your Carlisle boys did in truth, for the first time in their lives, partake of soldiers rations on Sunday (June 9) following. And here we have been ever since in good style serving as guard, police, drilling, &c., not going out without a pass.

All have been examined—*a la mode* regular service. Capt. McCartney's company was sworn in on the 8th inst., Capt. Todd's on the 10th, and Capt. Henderson's on the 11th. Many indeed were the compliments paid the "Carlisle Boys" for good appearance, cleanliness, &c., by the board of examiners, the 'Carlisle Fencibles' bearing off the palm in every instance.

At Camp Wayne the Carlisle Fencibles were sworn in as Company A, 7th Regiment, Pennsylvania Reserve Corps. Fourteen of Pennsylvania's early Civil War regiments became known as the Pennsylvania Reserve Division, as they are consistently referred to in histories of the Civil War. They were so named because for seven weeks, until sworn into Federal service, they were part of the newly created Reserve Corps of the Commonwealth of Pennsylvania, trained and supported by that state. James's regiment, the 7th Pennsylvania Reserves, was officially sworn into Federal service as the 36th U.S. Infantry on July 27, 1861.[1]

☞At a meeting of the officers and men of the Carlisle Light Infantry, Carlisle Fencibles, and Carlisle Guards, held at Camp Wayne on Tuesday the 18th of June; on motion of Maj. L. Todd, Capt. R. McCartney, was appointed Chairman, and Lieut. J. S. Colwell, Secretary.

Maj. L. Todd submitted the following preamble and resolutions, which were unanimously adopted, with three cheers and a "Tiger" for the Ladies of Carlisle.

WHEREAS the Ladies and citizens of Carlisle and vicinity, have kindly and generously presented the three companies here assembled with Havelocks, Towels, &c., &c. Therefore

Resolved, That we tender to them our sincere thanks for their timely and opportune gifts, and that we will treasure up the memory of their kindness as a sure testimony of their humanity and loyalty of our people.

Resolved. That a copy of these proceedings signed by the officers of the meeting, be sent to the newspapers of Carlisle for publication.

R. McCARTNEY,

J. S. COLWELL, Sec't'y.   Chairman.

Article from the *American Democrat*, 26 June 1861.

The strains of separation were immediately felt by James and Annie. Impelled by patriotism to sustain the Union, James had volunteered within a week of the attack on Fort Sumter. At forty-eight he was assuredly the oldest of all who left Carlisle on June 6, 1861. Twenty years older than Annie, he was strict, authoritarian, and set in middle-aged ways.

Heretofore largely dependent on her older husband, Annie was left at home with four young children, the eldest of whom was six. Born in Baltimore, she sympathized with the South, felt little moral repugnance toward slavery, and was not persuaded of the need to use force to prevent secession. More significant, however, was her anger that James had deserted her and volunteered for army service without consulting her, charges she repeated for months. In her first letter to James she suggested only half-jokingly that "this terrible war was only a diabolical plot enacted between Jeff Davis and Lincoln to deprive good wives of their husbands."[2] Regarding James's volunteering for active duty, she wrote:

> Your cousin Dr. Mahon of Balt. asked me if you had gone for the glory of the thing. Feeling rather indignant, I replied that your motives were purely conscientious, but that you & I differed widely in regard to your taking so active a part.... I feel thankful that those conscientious motives have been dormant for 7 years.... I trust they will be restored to the same happy state and remain so forever.[3]

MUSTER ROLL OF THE CARLISLE FENCIBLES.

The following is a complete list of the "Carlisle Fencibles." This Company is now at Camp Wayne, West Chester.

Captain— R. M. HENDERSON.

1st Lieutenant— Jas. S. Colwell.

2d   do   E. Beatty.

1st Sergeant—John D. Adair.

2d   do   W. M. Henderson.

3d   do   S. V. Ruby.

4th   do   Jos. B. Haverstick.

1st Corporal—Wm. R. Holmes

2d   do   William W. Harper.

3d   do   Charles B. Goddard.

4th   do   Isaac B. Parker.

MUSICIANS.

Wm. A. Monyer.

Van. B. Eby.

PRIVATES.

Lewis Bosh,	Jacob Landis, Jr.
Charles Bliss,	Sam. A. M'Beth,
William Bratton,	Chas. H. Mullen,
Charles Brechbill,	James H. Moore,
J. E. Burkholder,	Jacob L. Meloy,
W. Burkholder,	John Morrison,
James Barton Jr.	John A. Natcher,
D. D. Curriden,	D. R. B. Nevin,
J. J. Cuddy,	William Nevel,
Jacob Cart,	John Otto,
W. F. B. Dixon,	E. W. B. Phillips,
Isaac Elliot,	W. L. Spottswood,
John W. Elliott,	R H. Spottswood,
W. A. Ensminger,	Marion Sipe,
Leo. W. Faller,	A. Brady Sharpe,
J. H. Greason,	Thomas Sharpe,
Wilson H. Gould,	Wm. B Sites,
J. A. Gardner,	Sam'l C. Smith,
John T. Harris,	David Spahr,
W. H. Harkness,	J. G. Spangenberg,
Chas. Harkness,	George Strohm,
J. L. Halbert,	Charles A. Spicer,
J. H. Hendricks,	J. C. Schuchman,
R. P. Henderson,	Jos. B. Thompson,
Edgar. W. Hays,	G. H. Vautleberg,
J G Heiser,	George H. Welsh,
J. S. Humer,	W. M. Watts, Jr.
J. W. Humer,	Jno. L. Waggoner,
H. L. Hecker,	Chas. Wonderlich,
J. R. Kenyon,	George Wilders,
Sydney Kempton,	George Williams,
Wm. Zimmerman,	J. W. Haverstick.

Muster Roll from the *American Democrat*, 19 June 1861.

A few days later she wrote, "Mr. McClure [James's law partner] spent yesterday evening with us.... I can't get over the notion that he should have gone instead of you."[4] In September she wrote, "Oh I do wish you had never gone," and again declared her unhappiness "because you left me without talking about it."[5] Later that month Annie wrote that she had cried all one morning. "Oh I do wish you had never gone for I'm afraid I'll never be happy again."[6] A few weeks later she referred to her "dear husband who left her without saying beans whenever President Lincoln asked for 75,000 men. There are three big tears which I enclose as a memento from an aching heart."[7] In another letter she clearly expressed her feelings about James's army service: "I must contradict you in regard to being a Lieut.'s wife. I am a lawyer's wife."[8] To that letter James replied:

Detail of Annie's letter of 15 November 1861 showing the blotches of three tears.

So you are not a Lieutenant's wife. If I were a colonel or a general perhaps you would like it better. Well I am sorry on your account that I am not. But never mind. Perhaps there are happy days in store for us.[9]

James defended himself vigorously; initially he wrote in a condescending manner:

I feel sorry that you permit hard thoughts to possess your heart at our separation.... I did it from a sense of right and duty.... [M]y dear wife, the North is right and the South wrong.... [P]osterity and the whole civilized world will so decide. Of this I have no doubt[10]

Now I am sure my own Annie would not wish me to come back with dishonour, and thus bring disgrace on her and our children. No, she is too noble, too good, too true, too loving for that.[11]

As he realized the depth of her unhappiness, his letters became more understanding:

I hope...you will scold me no more, but that rather you will forgive my many faults.... My whole effort in this world is to make you as happy...as...is in my power.... It is not worth while to enquire at this late day whether I was right or wrong in entering into the present movement.... I did it with the best motive in the world. I have no hostility against the south.... [T]his war is not in behalf of Lincoln... but it is to sustain the government.... I do not see how I could get out of the service without bring[ing] disgrace and dishonour on myself & my little family.[12]

Two months later he wrote again, "Perhaps I was wrong to leave you & them. If so I hope you will forgive me. It cannot be helped now."[13] In his next letter he wrote, "Wify you must restrain your tears and crying or your eyes will become dim & lose their light."[14]

Annie's letters revealed other cross-currents and divisions within her family and other families in Carlisle. Her older brother, George, and younger sister, Minnie, were in Carlisle when James left for camp. Expressing his sympathy for the South, George argued heatedly about the war with William W. Eells, minister of the Presbyterian church they attended in Carlisle. Wrote Annie, "George finally told him they had better not discuss the subject he [Eells] being rather ultra."[15] In another letter Annie reported a heated political discussion: "George, Minnie & Cousin Annie Miller were at loggerheads."[16] George later sought a commission in the Union Army. "Genl. Cooper has given him a position in the Commissary department," Annie wrote, "but Genl. Curtin won't sanction it. Why nobody knows."[17] James replied,

> It is very probable that the reason Cameron refused to confirm George was that somebody charged him with being a secessionist. I have been told that he was considered in Baltimore as inclining that way at the commencement of the trouble & you know how strong Minnie's feelings were that way when she first came on.[18]

Another of Annie's brothers, Ban (John Bannister Hall), married and living in Baltimore, was "a red-hot secessionist."[19] When he became a father a few months later, he and his wife nicknamed their baby boy "Beauregard" in honor of the Confederate general.[20]

Annie's cousin, Sallie Gibson Anderson, wife of a Confederate army officer, was in Carlisle when the war started. She was forced to remain in Carlisle for two months until she was able to rejoin him by taking a train to Tennessee en route to their home in South Carolina.

Rev. William W. Eells, pastor of Second Presbyterian Church 1855-1862. (Courtesy of Second Presbyterian Church.)

Captain George Gibson. (Massachusetts Commandery Military Order of the Loyal Legion and the U.S. Army Military Institute.)

Sallie Anderson's uncle was General George Gibson, Quartermaster General of the U.S. Army. Annie reported, "The old Genrl. is very angry" at Anderson, who had received his education at West Point and then deserted the Union. (AHC to JSC 20 June 1861.) Annie continued in the same letter that Sallie Anderson "would rather go the battlefield with her husband," than return to her home in Carlisle. Sallie's brother, Union Captain George Gibson, later reported of his sister "that when we get sick in Fort Lafayette," she might return to the North. (AHC to JSC 16 September 1861.) Fort Lafayette was the prison in New York harbor where traitors and those suspected of disloyalty were confined.

Two other cousins of Annie's, Mary and Ettie Ege, residents of Centreville, Virginia, just across the Potomac, also were in Carlisle when the war started and were not able to return home. Annie wrote a few months later that they "have gone to Richmond, their house and property all destroyed near Alexandria."[21]

The war divided other families. Annie reported that Roger Jones, who had led the forty-five Union soldiers from Harper's Ferry as the Virginia militia closed in on the arsenal, and who was actually a cousin of Robert E. Lee,[22]

> is very uncomfortably situated—two brothers in the Southern army, all his friends living in Virginia & most of them in arms and he not able to go there on account of his late action at Harper's Ferry.[23]

William Penrose, a fellow member of the Carlisle bar who had been elected lieutenant colonel of the 6th Pennsylvania Reserves, was torn between his wife and his desire to serve the Union. Prone to frequent bouts of illness, perhaps occasioned as much by domestic political differences within his family as by actual illness, Penrose spent prolonged periods at home in Carlisle rather than with his unit in camp.

When Annie wrote that Mrs. Ege, wife of her first cousin, Galbraith Ege, had failed to invite her to a social affair in Carlisle, James replied that he could "not imagine what had induced Mrs. Ege to treat you as she has done by not inviting 'our house'" and reported that he had seen Galbraith Ege recently and he appeared "very friendly."[24] It is possible that James may have understood that Annie's outlook on the war and the sympathy which George and Minnie had expressed for the South were perhaps responsible for Mrs. Ege's attitude.

Galbraith Ege made several trips east from Kansas to lobby in Washington for a general's commission. When Annie said jokingly to him, "I hope you won't return with too many honors so we'll be able to recognize you," he replied, "Child, I'm rather old for that but hope to come back with many crowns in my pocket." (AHC to JSC 9 July 1861.) He may well have done just that, for he never received a commission, but became instead sutler to the army garrison at Fort Leavenworth, Kansas. (Carlisle *Herald*, 14 February 1862.)

COL. W. M. PENROSE.—This gentleman was, on Saturday last, selected as Lieutenant Colonel of the 6th regiment of the Pennsylvania Reserve Corps, now on duty at Camp Curtin. This is a good selection, and we feel convinced that should an opportunity offer, Col. P. will discharge his duty ably and heroically.

News note from the *American Democrat*, 26 June 1861.

James wrote to Annie in August of 1861 that "Penrose went home about a week before we left Camp Tenally sick. I understand the people of Carlisle do not think there is much the matter." (JAC to AHC 31 August 1861.)

Annie reported that Mrs. Penrose "hopes the South will last and thinks her husband's day of retribution is coming." (AHC to JSC 8 July 1861.)

James wrote from camp a few weeks later that the general opinion in the army was that Mrs. Penrose was a "secessionist." (JSC to AHC 19 August 1861.)

When Penrose resigned from the army in December 1861, Annie wrote James, "I wish I could induce you to resign as Penrose has done." (AHC to JSC 16 December 1861.) Local reaction to Penrose's resignation was not entirely favorable; some thought his resignation was due to his wife's secessionist views. Annie wrote further in the same letter: "Penrose remembered that in marrying he ought to consult his wife's happiness as well as his own. She says that neither one of them care what the people think for he has done what she desired. He & Kate Sharpe had a fight before he left last time. He told her that 'he made more in his office than by soldiering.'" Kate Sharpe was the wife of Brady Sharpe, another prominent Carlisle lawyer, serving as a private in James's Company A.

Sympathy for the South found little favor among the new recruits. Local papers often printed letters from men at camp. One soldier's letter to the *Herald* referred to former postmaster and *Volunteer* editor John Bratton as "that utterly disgraced old public functionary." Writing under the pseudonym "Sumpter," the author wrote that Bratton

> cannot refrain from venting all the venom of malignity on those opposed to him.... [H]is elegant weekly is not appreciated in this neighborhood, and would do better if transferred to some spot in "Dixie".... Does not his whole course look as if...he was trying to see how near a man can go to treason without its actual commission.[25]

Like many professional families in the town, James and Annie had house servants; but with their husbands gone the town's wives had to cope alone with domestic duties, some of which had previously been their husbands'. Annie "purchased 3 pairs of chickens which I attend to entirely myself just because <u>you</u> used to do that."[26] She planted beets, hoed corn, and "found that hoeing in hoops was not very convenient."[27] Even with help in the house, Annie's days were full caring for the four small children. Frequently she noted that she was writing at one o'clock in the morning or before breakfast since those were the only free times she had.[28] James wrote frequently to ask that Annie make him clothes, shirts, undershirts, and drawers. After the regiment moved from training camp, Annie, like other wives and parents in town, frequently sent boxes of food to James containing chickens, occasionally a ham or turkey, butter, jam and jelly, and at James's special request, a few of his bottles of rare old whiskey.

Finances were another matter with which wives had to deal. Since Army paymasters visited regimental camps at infrequent intervals and paydays were unpredictable, money was a matter of concern; James made arrangements with a local bank for Annie to draw such funds as she needed. The paymaster first came to the 7th Pennsylvania Reserves on August 13, 1861, but James wrote that he had sent all he could spare from that first payday to R. P. McClure, his partner, to pay a debt he owed in Carlisle. In the same letter he advised her to use paper money whenever possible: "I would not use the specie only when you cannot avoid it.

The house owned by P. Spahr on S. Pitt Street (now #145) where Annie and her children were living in 1861-62. (CCHS.)

Specie may become very scarce."[29] The paymaster came again on September 26, 1861, and
James sent $100 home. Thereafter money
problems eased somewhat as the paymaster
came every six weeks or so and James regularly
sent funds to Annie. Annie managed well on the
money she had, never borrowed from the bank,
and reported, "I use the specie as little as possible."[30] They had employed two servants at
their Carlisle home, but Annie wrote in the fall
that she would dismiss one of them to save
money.[31]

She received rent payments from James's
tenant in Shippensburg[32] and from time to time
McClure paid her amounts due James from the
partnership. She also dealt with legal correspondence received by James in Carlisle, which she
either forwarded to McClure in Shippensburg or
held for him, since he came often to the county
courthouse.

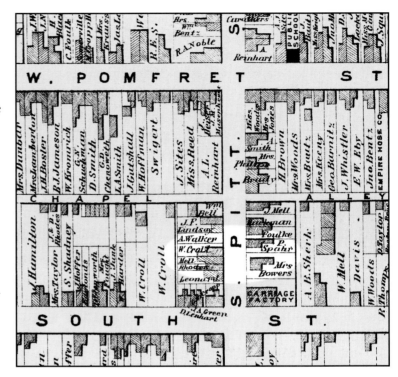

Detail of a map of Carlisle from the 1872 *Atlas of Cumberland County*
by F. W. Beers & Co. Annie Colwell and her children lived on the east
side of the second block of South Pitt Street in a house owned by P.
Spahr. She mentions her neighbors the Crofts and the Rhodeses in
several of her letters.

Their letters were full of advice for each
other. Wrote Annie, "Have you shaved any? Do
you wear that horrid flannel shirt all the time....
Do you wear that blue coat.... [H]ave you any
[blankets]? Beware of rheumatism."[33] He wrote
her to speak to their neighbor, Mr. W. Croft, if
she needed help with the vegetable garden; Croft had promised to find
someone to assist her if necessary. He advised her to be sure the two
older children said a lesson every day.

The war was always present in Carlisle since the town was the site
of a major army base and was situated on the main railroad line used by
troops moving to the western Virginia theater of operations. "Yesterday
several regiments passed through & also through the night I heard engines," Annie wrote in early July.[34] Three weeks later she reported that
two thousand men from Patterson's Division, which had come up from
western Virginia, were encamped at Carlisle:

> Yesterday after we dined I was in the yard & two very hungry
> fellows passed & I invited them in to dine. They had not eaten at a
> table for three months. They are waiting for pay of which they
> have never received a cent.

She asked them questions about the war, "but they were so Dutch I
couldn't understand them."[35] John, their precocious five-year-old, visited
neighbors' homes as well as military encampments in and around Carlisle.
John brought some soldiers "in to tea this afternoon and seemed perfectly
delighted at offering them hospitalities," wrote Annie.[36]

First Battle of Bull Run. (*History of the Civil War in America*, John C. Abbott, 1863, CCHS.)

On July 11, 1861, James came home to Carlisle on a week's leave, returning to Camp Wayne on July 18 amid rumors that the regiment was to move within a few days. When those orders came, they were urgent. Following the rout of Union forces at the first Battle of Bull Run on July 21, 1861, and fearful that Confederate troops would move on Washington, the War Department quickly ordered more troops to Washington.[37] James's regiment left Camp Wayne the following day, July 22, spent one night in Harrisburg, passed through Baltimore the next day, and arrived at Washington at one o'clock in the morning of July 25. After encamping for a week at Meridian Hill, two or three miles north of Washington, the regiment moved again to a permanent site six miles northwest of the city at Tenallytown, not far from the Potomac.

As the extent of the rout at Bull Run became apparent, the panic in Washington was reflected in the increasingly frantic telegrams sent to Pennsylvania Governor Curtin by the War Department on the day of the battle:

"Get your regiments at Harrisburg, Easton and points ready for immediate shipment, lose no time preparing. Make things move to the utmost."

"Forward all you can tonight.... Press forward all available force."

"Let me know how your regiments are moving. What have you started and how fast will they move?"

"Tomorrow wont do for your regiments. We must have them tonight. Send them tonight. It is of the utmost importance."[38]

Not all were enthusiastic about the war. In early August, local papers reported that upon their arrival at Washington, twenty-three men in the Carlisle company led by Captain Robert McCartney, former Cumberland County Sheriff, refused to be mustered into federal service.

"Disgraceful" and "Deserters" declared the local papers; the *American Democrat* and the *Herald* printed the men's names.[39] Soldiers in the ranks were not the only ones reluctant to risk their lives; McCartney himself resigned on August 21, 1861.[40]

Local papers reported the Union defeat at Bull Run in full, inspiring among some only a greater determination,

> a feeling of patriotic ardor...rose superior to all the humiliation inspired by the defeat.... [T]he masses are ready by thousands and tens of thousands to rally and fill up the broken and diminished ranks of the army.[41]

Bull Run brought home to Annie and James the fact that soldiers were fighting a real war and that some were dying. The war made them reflect on their own relationship and revealed the depth of their religious faith. "I never knew how much I loved you, nor how entirely dependent I am on you for all my earthly happiness," wrote Annie, who continued,

> I do beg of you to help me pray for your speedy return home & as the united prayers ascend every day to the throne of Grace we may hope that a Father of love may have pity on his erring children.[42]

Another letter continued in the same vein:

> Now my dear Husband do please take care of yourself & we will trust that Providence has foreordained that you shall be restored to us for I know I never can be happy without you.[43]

The war, wrote James, who rarely waxed poetic,

> has taught me how much I love you my dearest Annie, and how badly I could get along without you. It seems to me that my earthly happiness is bound up in you and your welfare and your love.[44]

James too expressed his faith in the Almighty: "If Providence is on our side we shall prosper & need have nothing to fear. If he 'is for us who shall be against us?'"[45] In another letter he wrote, "My dear Annie be of good cheer. There is a providence that guides and protects us. I feel that we shall be together again."[46]

For many months James was consistently optimistic as to an early end to the war. "I hope my dear wife," he wrote in August, "that this difficulty will be ended before a year."[47] A month later he repeated his opinion that he would be home "not over a year from the time I left and perhaps a great deal less."[48] Later the same week he wrote, "The news here is that the Southern army cannot be held together much longer without another battle or victory."[49] A few weeks later he wrote, "they are whipped now, unless the Lord fights their battles."[50]

In mid-August, Annie, feeling lonely in James's absence, left Carlisle for two and a half months, first visiting his sister Nancy Hayes

---

The Deserters.

Last week we mentioned the fact that a number of Capt. McCartney's men had left the service and returned home. Since then, Col. Roberts, to whose regiment they belong, has published an order announcing that the following named persons had deserted from the service of the State of Pennsylvania. The following is the order of Col. Roberts, which we publish for the *benefit* of those concerned.

HEAD QUARTERS.
1st Regiment Penn'a Reserve Corps.
Naval School, Annapolis, Md., Aug. 1, 1861.
NOTICE IS HEREBY GIVEN THAT

Lewis Forber,	Carlisle, Cumb., Co., Pa.		
Henry G. Beidler,	"	"	"
Jacob Hipple,	"	"	"
Henry Hipple,	"	"	"
Max Karge,	"	"	"
Henry Linnikuhl	"	"	"
John W. Lamison,	"	"	"
Anthony Moore,	"	"	"
Wm. McDonald,	"	"	"
Wm. Richey,	"	"	"
David Richwine,	"	"	"
Lewis Long,	"	"	"
John Donnelly,	"	"	"
Harrison Kelley,	"	"	"
George Chambers,	"	"	"
John Bennet, Papertown,	"	"	
Jacob Sowers, Plainfield	"	"	

Hugh Finley, Concord, Franklin Co., Pa.
John Boyer, Mortonville, Chester Co., Pa.
Members of Company H.
David Baker, Papertown, Cumb. Co., Pa.
Jacob Boggs, Thornburry Trape, Pa.
George Cramer, Carlisle, Cumberland co.
Thomas Bell, (musician,) Carlisle, Pa.
Members of Company I.
Deserted from the service of the State of Pennsylvania, from the First regiment Pennsylvania Reserve corps, while the said regiment was stationed at Camp Carroll, Baltimore. No reward is offered or will be paid for their apprehension, because *better men* are *offering.* These men had been well fed, well clothed, and *paid off on that day.* No reason for their *desertion* can therefore be given, save *cowardice;* and this notice is only inserted to prevent annoyance to recruiting officers, and in order that their fellow-citizens may understand their conduct when they *supposed themselves near the enemy.* By order of
R. BIDDLE ROBERTS,
Colonel commanding.
Chas. B. Lamborn, Adjutant.

Notice published in the *American Democrat*, 7 Aug. 1861.

and her family at Middle Spring, a few miles north of Shippensburg, and then moving into Shippensburg to stay with another of his sisters, Jane Phillips. The Hayes's young son, Edgar, was a private in James's company. Like many Civil War soldiers, he caught a fever, perhaps malaria, at camp in the heat of early August. The fever lingered on and was the subject of concern and much correspondence between James, Annie, and Edgar's parents. When he failed to improve after two months, he was discharged and returned home in late September, where he rapidly improved.[51]

Edgar Hayes was fortunate. Sickness and disease killed more soldiers in both armies during the Civil War than died in battle. In September and October 1861, three of Company A's soldiers died in camp from illness. A soldier in another of the regiment's companies died of an accidental gunshot wound. (*American Democrat*, 2 October and 22 October 1861; and Carlisle *Herald*, 11 October and 18 October 1861.)

Carlisle soldiers continued to die before they ever met the enemy in battle. Lt. Augustus Zug, who had entered active service in the summer of 1861 with the first of the Carlisle companies, died in February 1862 of tuberculosis contracted while in the army. (Carlisle *Herald*, 28 February 1862.) Three weeks later Company A's orderly sergeant, Will Henderson, brother of Captain Henderson, the company commander, died at home in Carlisle of sickness contracted while in army camp. (Carlisle *Herald*, 21 March 1862.)

DEATH.

The most saddening thing to happen in a camp of young soldiers is for a companion to die in the Hospital. Charles A. Brechbill, (private company A,) died in the field hospital of the Seventh regiment at Camp Tenally, between twelve and one o'clock on Saturday morning, (Oct. 12.) His company was here at the time, and did not expect his death. And such were the circumstances that had not some of his friends been at hand on Saturday evening, he would have been buried without any funeral rites at all. Thus has gone from among us one of decided courage—brave to a fault—a warm friend, and an excellent companion.

Excerpt from an article in the *American Democrat*, 23 Oct. 1861.

Camp life had a few lighter moments. In one letter James wrote, "While I write some of the men are having a jolly time outside. It is a beautiful moonlight night and some are mimicking the bawling of a calf, some the grunting of little pigs, some cats etc.... By turns they are singing songs, comical & serious. And there are some remarkably good singers in the regiment. One night...I...found a squad of men sitting on a caisson with music books singing as if for life by note, the different parts & doing it well." (JSC to AHC 13 September 1861.)

On August 23 James wrote that he had been offered a position as aide on the staff of Major General George A. McCall, commander of the Pennsylvania Reserve Division, but had declined the position.[52] Second Lieutenant Beatty of the same company accepted the position, leaving Company A short one officer for some months.

Erkuries Beatty. (D. Scott Hartzell Collection, U.S. Army Military History Institute.)

Pickets in the woods. (*Harper's Pictorial History of the Civil War*, Guernsey and Alden, 1866, CCHS.)

On August 26, 1861, James's regiment marched fifteen miles upriver to the Great Falls of the Potomac where they remained for two weeks on advance picket duty, guarding against a Confederate crossing of the upper Potomac. The regiment came under fire for the first time from Confederate forces across the river, and a piece of shrapnel slightly wounded one of the men in James's company. Pickets exchanged rifle fire intermittently across the river, apparently killing one Confederate soldier. James wrote:

> I do not approve of firing on pickets for the mere fun of the thing. It seems like a barbarous mode of warfare & accomplishes nothing. A man may be killed occasionally, but it neither strengthens one side nor weakens the other, nor does it tend to hasten the conclusion of the war.[53]

The regiment returned to Tenallytown on September 9 and remained there until October 9 when they moved across the Potomac to a camp near Langley, Virginia, where the Pennsylvania Reserve Division constituted the extreme right wing of the Union army.

Larger issues of the war were not forgotten by the local press or by Annie and James Colwell. The matter of European opinion was much on the minds of thoughtful people in America. When William Howard Russell, correspondent

> Another account of James's regiment's first conflict was written home by one of the Confederates. Typical of the hearsay reports and misinformation on both sides of the conflict is the description of this minor affair by South Carolina soldier Richard Wright Simpson in a letter dated 5 September 1861: "[W]e heard the booming of cannon and the rattle of small arms. I think one hundred guns were fired. That evening they came back stating that they had surprised the Yankee forces at the water works, killing some 7 or 8, and that they had succeeded in destroying the works which supplied the city of W[ashington] with water. They never lost a man. The Yankees ran like dogs without firing a gun." [54]

to the London *Times*, reported the rout of Union troops at Bull Run, his account of the battle found its way back across the Atlantic. Although truthful, his account so angered Northern opinion that Russell ultimately had to return to London when he found doors closed to him in Washington. Annie wrote to James on August 22, 1861:

> I'm afraid Mr. Russel is injuring us with England & France by his letters ridiculing the conduct of our troops at the Manassas battle. If those countries recognize the southern Confederacy I do wish you could come home, for I'm afraid we would be beaten.[55]

James, who remained an optimist, replied that he did not "think the recognition of the South as a government by England will change the final result."[56]

Local papers debated the question of slavery. The *American Volunteer*, fervently Democratic although temporarily suppressing its pro-Southern, anti-Republican opinions, raised a question for which no one yet had an answer. Under the headline, "WHAT SHALL WE DO WITH THEM?" editor Bratton wrote:

> Suppose the war for the preservation of the Union...should...be diverted into a war for the abolition of slavery, what, we ask, would we do with the slaves after we had them?.... How then can we employ the four millions and more of half barbarians the Abolitionists propose to foist upon us? Our own free blacks are already a heavy expense to the people."[57]

When Annie wrote that she did not consider Lincoln "competent to fill his present position,"[58] James replied at length, in a serious vein, and with foresight:

> But you don't think him competent.... I care nothing about Lincoln individually.... [I]t is the government that I hold must be maintained.... [O]ld general Scott says he is not a party man & did not vote for Lincoln but he considers him a man of genius, a very able man...of great ability, fidelity and patriotism.... [T]hat is the judgment of every man of ability, almost, democrats as well as republicans, except those democrats who have or had secessionist proclivities.... I doubt whether we ever had a president against whom his enemies could find so little fault as the present one.... And if he finishes as he has begun history will pronounce him one of the ablest and best presidents we have ever had.[59]

Perhaps the largest issue of all was not slavery, success on the battlefield, or the maintenance of the Union, but the question as to whether American democracy, a novel concept of government among the nations of the world, could survive. "Democratic institutions are indeed on trial in the United States," editorialized the *Carlisle American*:

> We can hardly blame the aristocracy of Great Britain for seeking to derive from our present national troubles an argument against the ballot and the extension of suffrage, and equal representation.... It may be in the interest of the titled aristocracy of Europe to see the

Southern Confederacy triumph, but for the landless millions [in their countries], no event so deplorable could happen, short of their own reduction to Slavery.[60]

A thoughtful editorial, reprinted by the *American Democrat* from the Louisville *Democrat*, addressed this issue, as it discussed a recent article in the *London Quarterly* entitled "Democracy on Its Trial":

> "The great republican bubble in America has burst," is the style and now let us rejoice, is the sentiment. [The article] undertakes to search out the philosophy of the failure, and finds it in the rule of the people.... [I]f the United States, which was "once our rival"...had not broken down, aristocratic rule would have fallen before the example.... That awful Republic has committed suicide.... It no longer lives to shake the nerves of those who rule by the "grace of God".... General suffrage in America is a demonstrated failure.

Concluded the *American Democrat*, "We shall see if the democracy will not vindicate itself yet."[61]

Life in camp continued in its routine way. The Pennsylvania Reserve Division was constituted into three brigades. James's 7th Regiment became a part of the 2nd Brigade under the command of Brigadier General George Meade. Reviews of the troops became commonplace in the fall of 1861 and early winter of 1862. General George McClellan, in charge of the Union armies after the retirement of old General Winfield Scott, enjoyed the opportunity to parade in front of the assembled regiments and receive their cheers.

The Pennsylvania Reserve Division was made up of three brigades. The 1st Brigade was commanded by Brigadier General John Reynolds, the 2nd by Brigadier General George Meade, and the 3rd by Brigadier General Edward Ord. Meade, Reynolds, and Ord became three of the most highly respected Union generals in the war. Meade became commander of the Army of the Potomac, leading it at Gettysburg. Reynolds became a corps commander and served under Meade at Gettysburg where he was killed. Ord became a corps and army commander and was commander of the Army of the James at Appomattox. [62]

General George G. Meade. (*Civil War Illustrations*, reprints, Carol Grafton, 1995.)

The men of Company A were not fond of the marches and long periods of standing in the ranks which were required. Letters to the *Shippensburg News* from "Quantico," a soldier correspondent, conveyed something of their feelings:

"During that day we marched not a fathom less than twenty miles and during the whole thirteen hours of the time were on our feet.... We arrived at our camp, finally, perfectly exhausted, and with blistered feet and damaged heels, unanimously voted big reviews a humbug." (*Shippensburg News*, 30 October 1861.)

"When the Major or Brigadier General are favored with the visits of some particular friends, of course a big review must be had. This is as necessary as dessert to a dinner. 'It is fine fun to the boys, but death to the frogs,' as Mr. Aesop would say." (*Shippensburg News*, 25 January 1862.)

Quantico was a pseudonym for David Nevin of Shippensburg, a lawyer and Princeton graduate serving as a private in Company A, who was later appointed second lieutenant in the regular army and transferred to another regiment.[63]

Leo Faller, a private from Carlisle in Company A, wrote home after a January 1862 review: "There was a great many ladies there to see it, and no doubt but what they were very well pleased with the arrangement. But the boys did not like it any too well for we had to stand in mud up to our ankles...and at each step we sank in mud up to our shoe tops."[64]

David Robert Bruce Nevin, the correspondent "Quantico." (Civil War Library & Museum MOLLUS Philadelphia, Pa.)

Many officers had servants with them in camp who purchased supplies, cooked, and laundered for them, matters which officers had to provide for from their own pockets. Both officers and men, however, were now finding a new source of domestic servants. Wrote "Anthony," a soldier correspondent for the *American Democrat,*

A new thing to us is a contraband in Camp. The Band boys of the 7th have now a negro boy, perhaps fifteen years of age in their employ as cook. He is (or was) a Virginian slave, and brought into Camp by members of Company H.[65]

As the months went by, many contrabands were employed by the army's officers and men as domestic servants.

Annie urged James to have a picture made. James managed to get into Washington and reported:

I did intend once when I went to Washington to have my ugly self taken and fixed up & get my hair cut & beard trimmed & moustache shaved for that purpose, and when I went to Brady's his instrument was out of order & I had to return without it.[66]

On Saturday October 19, inexperienced officers led inexperienced Union troops across the Potomac at Ball's Bluff near Edward's Ferry, twenty miles upstream from Washington, climbed the bluff under Confederate fire, and received heavy casualties. About two hundred men were killed or wounded (including Colonel Edward Baker, a U.S. Senator and close friend of Lincoln) and seven hundred captured before remnants of the brigade were able to straggle back across the Potomac. James wrote Annie on October 29, "The fight at Edward's Ferry was a terrible slaughter, and entirely without any object.... Where the fault lies does not appear to be very well settled yet."[67]

Back in Carlisle Annie urged James to get leave to visit home for Thanksgiving or Christmas. She expressed her belief that James could "easily obtain a furlough to visit your bad wife & four hopefuls."[68] Unfortunately for them both, Captain Henderson, also a lawyer and commander of James's Company A, was chosen to serve as judge advocate for two general court martials at the time, and James was unable to obtain leave since two officers could not be absent from the company at the same time.

On November 20 outside Washington, McClellan held a grand review of the troops which was extensively described in the Carlisle newspapers. Annie wrote James:

> A thought crossed my mind on reading the account of your grand review that how many millions of human beings have all their earthly happiness wrapt up in those 70,000 men & how many will return just as they went? Some never—others will contract diseases from which they will not entirely recover.... I drove the thought away by asking Heaven's over-shadowing wing to be always over you.[69]

As winter came on, James wrote that he had fashioned a crude furnace by digging down eighteen inches at one corner of his tent, covering the fire in the hole with a flat stone, and constructing a flue to the outside of the tent to carry off the smoke. James also reported that his regiment had gone out foraging, although his company was excused, having been on picket duty the night before. The wagons "went some six or eight miles and got some wheat, oats, corn, etc."[70] In a subsequent and missing letter, James must have expressed his disapproval of stealing food from the local Virginia farms, for Annie wrote that she had bought him "a mammoth chicken as a reward for your remembrance of the 8th Commandment in not partaking of the chickens of the foraging party."[71]

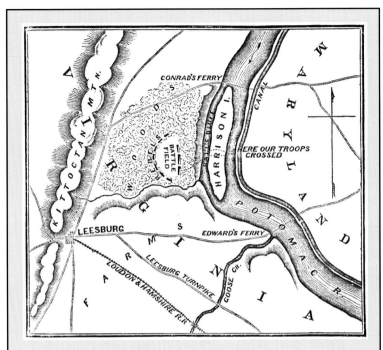

Map of Ball's Bluff and vicinity. (*History of the Civil War in America,* John C. Abbott, 1863, CCHS.)

In a perceptive letter to the *Shippensburg News* Quantico referred to the "horrible, blundering butchery at 'Ball's Bluff,'" and continued:

> "There is something wrong someplace, and the rank and file are beginning to manifest their disapprobation by whisperings and innuendos.... We have underrated...our adversaries. They are bold, brave determined men, who will fight desperately for the cause they have espoused.... [W]e have too many selfish stupid military men on our side...who originally joined for pecuniary or political motives, and who have at heart no more patriotism than a school of snails." (*Shippensburg News,* 2 November 1861.)

Quantico was ahead of his time. It would be months before Northern opinion came to realize that Confederate troops were "bold, brave determined men," willing to "fight desperately" for their cause.

This is a sketch of the place we live in,

Drawing by Leo Faller of Company A, showing his tent at Camp Pierpoint in Fairfax County, Virginia. Neighboring tents are those of Henry Hite [Hyte] and Marion Sipe. These tents had log sides and canvas tops. This drawing is part of a letter written by Faller to his sister on 15 December 1861. (Manuscript Collection, CCHS.)

December 13 was their wedding anniversary. Both referred to it in letters. James, an unemotional man, wrote Annie after receipt of her letter:

> You speak of the anniversary of our marriage. This reminds me that every Sunday the band plays two or three times as a church call to collect the soldiers for preaching. And one of the tunes they play is Do they miss me at home. Do you recollect when & where we heard that soon after our union.... Sometimes when I listen to the tune I find myself wiping a tear from my own eye.[73]

On December 20, 1861, the 7th Regiment's 3rd Brigade went out foraging and encountered determined resistance from Confederate troops near Dranesville. In a sharp encounter the Pennsylvania troops routed the Confederates. The 2nd Brigade, of which James's 7th Regiment was a part, had been in camp; but when news of the battle reached them, they hastened thirteen miles to the battlefield only to find the fight over when they arrived. The forced march back to camp left them exhausted, having marched twenty-six miles in six hours.

A day or two later, after weeks of anticipation, James's request for leave was finally approved and he was home in Carlisle for Christmas. The *Herald* reported that "We were greatly pleased to see at home on yesterday our esteemed friend and fellow citizen, Lieut. Jas. S. Colwell."[74] After ten days at home James returned to camp on December 31. "Everything is quiet here and has been ever since I left," he wrote Annie.[75] But in the camps outside Washington, a purge of incompetent officers and promotion of qualified officers and men from the ranks to replace them was under way.

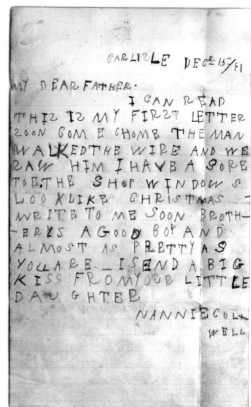

Letter written by young Nannie Colwell to her father, James Colwell in December of 1861. (Colwell Family Collection.)

By now the men were well able to judge the performance of their officers, whatever the pre-war social position and popularity of those officers might have been. When John Adair, the well-liked orderly sergeant of Company A, was promoted to lieutenant, the enlisted men of the company purchased him a sash, sword, and belt. Wrote Private John Faller, "John is a nice little fellow and we all wish him good luck wherever he goes. As an officer and gentleman he cant be beat." The regiment's colonel presented the sword to Adair in a ceremony attended by company members.[76]

When Private David Nevin was promoted to lieutenant, his thoughtful letters, under the pseudonym Quantico, no longer brought news of Company A to the local readers of the *Shippensburg News*, although he continued writing under the same name from the new regiment to which he was posted. "Typo," a pseudonym for D. D. Curriden, the paper's other soldier correspondent and the brother of the paper's editor, wrote of Nevin that he left the company "with

John Faller. (D. Scott Hartzell Collection, U.S. Army Military History Institute.)

David D. Curriden, the correspondent "Typo." (Shippensburg Historical Society.)

the love and esteem of all his comrades, who...rejoice in his promotion. He will make an officer of whom any body of men may be proud." (*Shippensburg News*, 22 February 1862.)

A soldier's letter to the *Herald* noted, "No less than four captains have resigned and as many lieutenants promoted to their places. In six instances orderly sergeants have been promoted."[77] Three enlisted men from James's Company A were appointed lieutenants early in 1862. As the winter dragged on amid snow, freezing spells, rain, and mud, men and officers spent most of their time inside their tents warmed by makeshift stoves. The warmth attracted other creatures. Wrote James in March, "As I write I can hear the mice skipping through my tent at a rapid rate. They are become very numerous and seem to enjoy themselves hugely."[78]

As 1861 gave way to 1862, Carlisle newspapers engaged in heated arguments about slavery and the progress of the war. When initial suggestions surfaced suggesting the use of black troops in the Union armies, the *American Volunteer* reprinted an editorial originally appearing in the Democratic New York *World*:

> "*The Secesh are upon us! Ho! niggers to the rescue.*" Can it be believed that there are American freemen dastardly enough to raise a cry like that?... If we must look to the poor, blind, creeping African to help vindicate our birthright...there is no word of scorn too low for us.... [W]e may as well at once advertise our degeneracy to the world.[79]

With little to do the men turned to pranks in their spare time. Carlisle private Leo Faller wrote home that the "Collaest Joke we have here was a private from the fourth Regt stealing a goose from Gen Mead while he was on guard at the Gen Quarters. The General found the man out and told him he did not want to see him about his Quarters again. The General did not want to punish the man for it was too good a rig on himself."[80]

A week later Bratton erupted again, comparing the Carlisle *Herald* to "a very sickly but very foul skunk," and characterizing its management as "creeping, cringing, crafty sycophants, whose pockets are pregnant with the wages of political prostitution, and who gather their editorials from the streets and gutters as a ragpicker does his rags."[81] In turn the *Herald* wrote of the *Volunteer*'s editor, "We knew we were dealing with a knave, but were not quite prepared to hold a controversy with a fool."[82]

Furious controversy persisted in the local papers. Railing at the Abolitionists, the *Volunteer* editorialized that their object "in commencing this war was robbery and the abolition of slavery, and nothing else. Not a mother's son of them care a prostitute's curse for the Union."[83] In an angry editorial the *Shippensburg News* responded, referring to the "scurrilous attacks of that vile traitor sheet, the Carlisle *Volunteer*."[84] The *Carlisle American* joined the brawl: "There is one comfort, however, that [the *Volunteer*] cannot do any serious damage in the community, being regarded as a sort of *secesh* and treated with the respect which characters of that sort receive from loyal citizens."[85] *The Volunteer* responded by calling the *Shippensburg News* "a dirty little smut machine."[86] Possibly the invective in the *Volunteer*'s columns was a deliberate attempt to increase circulation through the shock value of extreme language.

Contrabands fleeing north were one facet of slavery. Bratton predictably blamed abolitionists for inducing slaves to flee their masters and encouraging them to seek their fortunes in the North. A "vile and vicious" horde of ex-slaves would soon overrun the state, "one-half of whom will cheapen and degrade labor, and the other half fill the jails and alms-houses of the Commonwealth." The same editorial quoted a story in the Philadelphia *Ledger* reporting the arrival in that city of ninety-seven escaped slaves and commented: "What these poor creatures are to do in a place like Philadelphia, already over-crowded with unemployed white labor...it is impossible to conjecture."[87]

When Congress, at Lincoln's urging, enacted a law providing for the abolition of slavery in Washington, D.C. with compensation for their owners, the *Carlisle American* called the act a sign "of the Genius of the Age, as well as Christianity...a record of progress in this country of liberal ideas." The country would henceforth "stand as the representative of freedom and progress."[88] "There can be no permanence in human slavery," the paper editorialized three weeks later, "there can be no permanence in a Political Government which is founded on such a bitterly bad fallacy."[89]

The *American Democrat*, less strongly opposed to Lincoln's actions, accurately described the views of most Americans and offered a prescient forecast of the debate over slavery:

The Result of Secession.

JULIUS.—"Is your massa Union or Session?
SAM.—"Why he's Session."
JULIUS.—"Den I pitys yer—you was as good a leben hundred dollar nigga as eber I see— an' now yer aint wuf wun cent!"

Illustration from a Civil War era envelope printed in New York. (Manuscript Collection, CCHS.)

Ours is a government of *white* men, made for the benefit of *white* men, and any Quixotic attempt...to raise the negro to an equality with the white man...will only have the effect to hasten the day of his destruction. Reader, ponder over this question, for it is one that is rapidly coming up for solution, and will be more momentous in its consequences than any that has yet come before the American people.[90]

Yet if the country didn't know what to do about the slaves, opinion was slowly hardening in the North that the institution must be ended, as a soldier's letter to the *Herald* made clear:

Large numbers of "contrabands" seek their liberty by entering our lines.... I most earnestly hope that before the weapons employed in this deplorable war shall be "beat into ploughshares," the accursed institution of slavery, which indisputably has brought about the disastrous events which affect our country, will have been extinguished, blotted out.[91]

On the larger question of prosecution of the war, impatience at Union inactivity was widespread. "Forwards March," was the headline for a January story in the *Herald*.[92] The *Carlisle American* exhorted, "The battle of liberty must be fought now or never.... It must be inaugurated by destroying the power of slave treason in the South,"[93] and quoted approvingly a speech by Secretary of War Stanton: "The purpose of this war is to attack, pursue, and destroy the rebellious enemy and to deliver the country from the danger menaced by traitors."[94] The inactivity of George McClellan came under criticism. McClellan was becoming the favorite of those in the North who sympathized with the South and, accordingly, the target of those favoring immediate, vigorous prosecution of the war. Not unexpectedly the *American Volunteer* took up the defense of McClellan, blaming Abolitionists for

endeavoring to destroy the reputation and character of McClellan. With this crowd nothing seems to be right, unless it be the unconditional emancipation of the slave.... Greeley and that horde of restless Abolitionists who should have been hung for their opposition to the laws long ago, still cry, "onward, onward."[95]

In the war at large a Union tide was flowing. In the first three months of 1862, Union troops gained victories at Mill Springs, Kentucky; Forts Henry and Donelson in Tennessee, capturing fourteen thousand Confederate troops in the latter victory; and Roanoke Island, North Carolina, gaining full control of the North Carolina coast and closing a marine back door to the Confederacy.[96] On February 24 Harper's Ferry was once more occupied by Union troops; the same day advancing Union forces entered Nashville. On March 8 Union troops won another battle at Pea Ridge, Arkansas, forcing Confederate troops to withdraw from that state.[97] Only McClellan's troops in northern Virginia remained inactive, a matter which brought increasing criticism both from Northern Republicans and from the ranks of the army as well. "E.," another soldier correspondent, wrote the *Herald* on March 4 that "in reference to the army of the

Major General George McClellan. (*Battles and Leaders of the Civil War*, Grant-Lee Edition, CCHS.)

Potomac, M'Clellan is still working out his 'masterly inactivity' plan."[98]

Union victories prompted a heady dose of optimism in Carlisle and throughout the North. James had always been confident of the war's early end. "If we don't meet with some very serious reverses," he wrote in February, "I think the war will be over before the end of the year from the time we started."[99] A few weeks later he added, "I am of the opinion there will be one or two severe battles in Virginia, & if we are successful the rebellion will be pretty well subdued."[100]

In March 1862, as spring arrived, the armies began to move. James's optimism reflected the confidence in Carlisle and throughout much of the North that the war was near an end. The country would soon learn whether the rebellion would be subdued after "one or two severe battles in Virginia."

> Carlisle newspapers wrote as though victory might be taken for granted. The *Carlisle American*, for example, editorialized: "At length we are enabled to congratulate our loyal countrymen on the prospect of an early and complete overthrow of the Slaveholders' Rebellion. The signs of the coming day are too many and too sure to be doubted." (*Carlisle American*, 22 January 1862.)
>
> Other papers offered similar optimistic predictions: "The night of doubt and uncertainty is followed by the daylight of victory. The power of rebellion is effectually broken in the South and West.... [W]e should not be surprised to hear within a month of the total collapse of the Rebel Government." (*American Democrat*, 19 February 1862.)
>
> "Our faith is...that the conspiracy will virtually be put down by the opening of Summer, and the authority of the Government in the rebel States completely restored at the end of the year 1862." (Carlisle *Herald*, 28 February 1862.)

Endnotes

1 Samuel P. Bates, *History of the Pennsylvania Reserve Corps, 1861-5*, 3 vols. (Harrisburg, Pa.: B. Singerly, 1869), vol. 1, 540-541, 720.

2 AHC to JSC 20 June 1861.

3 AHC to JSC 20 August 1861. Annie closed the letter, "Now good bye my own husband. Always forgive me for everything I say or do wrong & write to me very often."

4 AHC to JSC 26 August 1861.

5 AHC to JSC 30 September 1861.

6 AHC to JSC 30 September 1861.

7 AHC to JSC 15 November 1861. The letter itself is stained by the blotches of three tears.

8 AHC to JSC 14 December 1861.

9 JSC to AHC 19 December 1861.

10 JSC to AHC 19 June 1861.

11 JSC to AHC 23 June 1861.

12 JSC to AHC 4 July 1861. With respect to her unhappy letter, Annie subsequently wrote that she regretted having sent it: "It was written from the impulse of the moment. Please destroy it." AHC to JSC 29 June 1861. Apparently James did as

she wished; the letter was not found among the others.

13 JSC to AHC 24 October 1861.

14 JSC to AHC 29 October 1861.

15 AHC to JSC 25 June 1861.

16 AHC to JSC 8 July 1861. Cousin Annie Miller had grown up in Carlisle and had little sympathy for the South.

17 AHC to JSC 2 November 1861. Annie may have meant Pennsylvania Governor Andrew Curtin, or Secretary of War Simon Cameron, who held a Pennsylvania state militia rank of general.

18 JSC to AHC 11 November 1861. At loose ends for months, George finally found a job in New York in December 1861.

19 AHC to JSC 9 July 1861.

20 AHC to JSC 31 October 1861.

21 AHC to JSC 2 November 1861.

22 Catton, *The Coming Fury*, 333.

23 AHC to JSC 20 June 1861.

24 JSC to AHC 7 January 1862.

25 Carlisle *Herald*, 21 June 1861.

26 AHC to JSC 14 June 1861.

27 AHC to JSC 20 June 1861.

28 On a Monday, for example, she wrote, "I have risen this morning quite early so that I shall have time to write before breakfast, for as this is the farmers washday I shall have no time till night." AHC to JSC 8 July 1861.

29 JSC to AHC 17 August 1861.

30 AHC to JSC 22 August 1861.

31 AHC to JSC 16 September 1861.

32 The miller, John McLeaf, was actually a tenant of James, renting the house and small mill outside Shippensburg which had been left him by his father, and paying rent for the premises. His son was in the 7th Regiment's Company A, the company of which James was first lieutenant.

33 AHC to JSC 20 June 1861.

34 AHC to JSC 8 July 1861.

35 AHC to JSC 27 July 1861.

36 AHC to JSC 31 July 1861.

37 A good summary of the Battle of Bull Run is contained in Catton, *The Coming Fury*, 448-465. A dramatic description of the rout of Union troops and their ensuing flight from the battlefield is

contained in Russell, *Diary North and South*, 254-285.

[38] All quoted from J. R. Sypher, *History of the Pennsylvania Reserve Corps* (Lancaster, Pa.: Elias Barr & Co., 1865), 93-94.

[39] *American Democrat*, 7 August 1861; and Carlisle *Herald*, 9 August 1861.

[40] Annie wrote, "I hear that McCartney is tyrannical & 40 of his men have left and won't serve under him." AHC to JSC 31 July 1861. Two months later James wrote Annie, referring to "Captain McCartney who has resigned, and gone home, and the people of Carlisle will scarcely speak to him, or to his son who has deserted and gone home to his wife." JSC to AHC 30 September 1861.

[41] *American Democrat*, 24 July 1861.

[42] AHC to JSC 27 July 1861.

[43] AHC to JSC 15 August 1861.

[44] JSC to AHC 7 July 1861.

[45] JSC to AHC 13 September 1861.

[46] JSC to AHC 7 August 1861.

[47] JSC to AHC 4 August 1861.

[48] JSC to AHC 2 September 1861.

[49] JSC to AHC 5 September 1861.

[50] JSC to AHC 30 September 1861.

[51] William F. Fox, *Regimental Losses in the American Civil War* (Albany, N.Y.: Albany Publishing Company, 1889), 526-527, reports Union battle casualties at 110,000 and deaths from disease and other causes at 249,000.

[52] JSC to AHC 23 August 1861.

[53] JSC to AHC 28 August 1861. His opinion came to be shared by most soldiers throughout both armies: whatever their officers' orders, pickets rarely fired on each other in earnest unless an attack was underway, and customarily warned opposing pickets when they were about to commence firing in earnest. For fraternization between Union and Confederate soldiers see Randall C. Jimmerson, *The Private Civil War* (Baton Rouge, La.: Louisiana State University Press, 1988), 164-175.

[54] Richard Wright Simpson letter, Guy R. Everson and Edward W. Simpson, Jr., *Far, Far from Home* (New York: Oxford University Press, 1994), 69.

[55] AHC to JSC 22 August 1861.

[56] JSC to AHC 2 September 1861.

[57] *American Volunteer*, 5 September 1861.

[58] AHC to JSC 7 November 1861.

[59] JSC to AHC 11 November 1861.

[60] *Carlisle American*, 18 September 1861.

[61] *American Democrat*, 29 January 1862.

[62] Succinct histories of the careers of these officers may be found in Stewart Sifakis, *Who Was Who in the Union* (New York: Facts on File, 1988).

[63] Leo and John Faller, *Dear Folks at Home*, ed. Milton Flower (Carlisle, Pa.: Cumberland County Historical Society and Hamilton Library Association, 1963), 8. In this book are forty-three letters from two young soldier brothers written home to their family in Carlisle during the war.

[64] Leo Faller letter of 15 January 1862 in *Dear Folks at Home*, 48.

[65] *American Democrat*, 16 October 1861.

[66] JSC to AHC 4 November 1861.

[67] JSC to AHC 29 October 1861.

[68] AHC to JSC 2 November 1861.

[69] AHC to JSC 29 November 1861.

[70] JSC to AHC 4 December 1861.

[71] AHC to JSC 14 December 1861.

[72] John Faller letter, 5 January 1862, *Dear Folks at Home*, 46.

[73] JSC to AHC 19 December 1861.

[74] Carlisle *Herald*, 27 December 1861.

[75] JSC to AHC 31 December 1861.

[76] *Dear Folks at Home*, 53, 55.

[77] Carlisle *Herald*, 27 December 1861.

[78] JSC to AHC 4 February 1862.

[79] *American Volunteer*, 19 December 1861.

[80] Leo Faller letter, 15 December 1961, *Dear Folks at Home*, 39.

[81] *American Volunteer*, 26 December 1861.

[82] Carlisle *Herald*, 10 January 1862.

[83] *American Volunteer*, 30 January 1862.

[84] *Shippensburg News*, 22 February 1862.

[85] *Carlisle American*, 26 February 1862.

[86] *American Volunteer*, 6 March 1862.

[87] *American Volunteer*, 3 April 1862. Benjamin Quarles, *The Negro in the Civil War* (New York: Russell & Russell, 1953) and James M. McPherson, *The Negro's Civil War* (New York: Pantheon Books, 1965) both discuss in detail the life and activities of blacks, both in and out of uniform, during the Civil War.

[88] *Carlisle American*, 23 April 1862.

[89] *Carlisle American*, 14 May 1862.

[90] *American Democrat*, 30 April 1862.

[91] *Shippensburg News*, 22 March 1862.

[92] Carlisle *Herald*, 10 January 1862.

[93] *Carlisle American*, 8 January 1862. In late January the *Shippensburg News*, briefly reviewing various magazines, as many of the weekly papers were wont to do, reported on the February 1862 issue of the *Atlantic Monthly*, noting briefly, "This Magazine for February is one of the best numbers recently issued. It opens with the 'Battle Hymn of the Republic.'" Set to the tune of "John Brown's Body," the words and music yet stir hearts and echo down the corridors of American history. *Shippensburg News*, 25 January 1862.

[94] *Carlisle American*, 26 February 1862.

[95] *American Volunteer*, 27 February 1862.

[96] Descriptions of these engagements may be found, among many other sources, in Bruce Catton, *Terrible Swift Sword* (Garden City, N.Y.: Doubleday & Company, Inc. 1963), 138-139, 148-160, 167-171. It was at Ft. Donelson that U. S. Grant achieved permanent fame when he delivered his famous "unconditional surrender" reply to an inquiry from the Confederate general as to the terms he would offer for the fort's surrender.

[97] William L. Shea and Earl J. Hess, *Pea Ridge: Civil War Campaign in the West* (Chapel Hill, N.C.: University of North Carolina Press, 1992) contains the best detailed description of this battle.

[98] Carlisle *Herald*, 7 March 1862.

[99] JSC to AHC 13 February 1862.

[100] JSC to AHC 23 March 1862.

Letters 3:
June 1861 – February 1862

Notes from the author, David G. Colwell

Fifty-four letters were selected for inclusion in this book. In the Colwell Family Collection there are 179 letters: 47 AHC (Ann Hall Colwell) letters and 132 JSC (James Smith Colwell) letters. While Ann probably wrote about as many letters as James, none of her letters from December 31, 1861 to August 26, 1862 were saved, with the sole exception of her letter of February 1, 1862. Probably the missing letters were lost at some time during James's hurried trip to catch up with his company in late August and early September, 1862. The last 11 AHC letters were probably found in JSC's effects when he died, or arrived at Company A after his death and were returned.

There are perhaps 20-25 other missing letters. In various surviving letters other missing letters are referred to, which were not found in the trunks which came from Carlisle. There are also references in the surviving letters to other letters which were written and mailed but were never received and must have miscarried in the mail.

It proved impossible to be entirely consistent in the transcription of these letters. The rules for written English were clearly less strict then than they are now; and the authors of these letters applied those rules less rigorously and less consistently then we would today. Spelling and the use of punctuation, capitals, and paragraphs varied within a single letter and from one letter to the next. A change of thought in the written letter might be marked by a period (.), a comma (,), a dash (—), or simply by a space. The next thought might or might not start with a capital letter. A major change of subject, for which we would start a new paragraph, might be indicated by a somewhat longer space or dash on the same line, or by a new unindented line, or by nothing. Except for the initial paragraph of a letter new paragraphs were almost never indented. Decisions as to whether clauses or phrases should be treated as parts of other sentences, as separate sentences (sometimes without verbs), or even as the beginnings of new paragraphs were therefore frequently made arbitrarily.

In addition some word or phrases were indecipherable, even with frequent and painstaking use of a magnifying glass. Letters written in pencil have faded, particularly where they were folded. A few letters were cut or torn, and the hand-writing of the authors was sometimes illegible. In this regard AHC was worse than JSC.

When I started this project, I thought I would clean up the letters. As I continued, I concluded that the spelling and punctuation didn't matter very much as long as the meaning was clear. There are therefore a minimum of corrections. In spite of the difficulties, I do not believe that the intended meaning of anything written in these letters has been changed in any important way.

JSC to AHC, June 10, 1861

My Dear wife

I wrote you a few lines on Saturday morning which I hope you received ere this. Spent last night in camp first time. Had a soft pine board for a bed my blouse folded for a pillow & part of a blanket for covering. It felt a little hard but not so bad as one would suppose. We were offered as much oat straw as we desired but the company with half dozen exceptions have concluded to sleep on the boards. I have no doubt that is the better way.

We have abundance of provisions of excellent quality except sugar & coffee, which is not the best. The variety is not extensive—fresh beef, smoked shoulders, beans, rice, potatoes, bread, crackers, salt, pepper, vinigar etc. I have not discovered yet how we are to use the vinigar. Presume we will learn by & by. I have been very well since I last wrote. Did not get to church yesterday being officer of the day. If I had you and the children here I would be right well contented. I have met a number of the citizens. The[y] seem very kind, though they have sent no pies, cakes, etc.

I suppose that you have heard that the 1st Regiment Penna. Reserve has been formed here. Biddle Roberts Pittsburg Colonel. Capt. McIntyre of this place Lieut. Col. L. Todd Carlisle Major. We are not in this regiment, Capt. McCartney's co. & Todd's are.

I forgot to mention before I left that I was taking the Press & Tribune. They are paid up till the 1st of June. You can take them on, or if you do not want the Tribune (I believe you don't read it) you can pay from 1st June and [or] discontinue it. I think you would like the Enquirer better than the Press.

I would like if you could make me two undershirts of that best unbleached muslin. No collar or band at the neck merely hemmed or bound below the neck like an undershirt. I do not know how you will get the length of the sleeves. You will have to guess as near as you can so that they will come just to the top of the wristband and wide enough for the hand to go through easily. Please excuse me for troubling you with such particular instructions.

Major Todd who leaves for Carlisle today will return next Friday or Saturday, and I presume will carry back anything if the package is small as I presume he

James Colwell's walnut secretary desk, now in the possession of David Colwell in California. In James's first letter to Annie he asks for a newspaper cutting in one of the drawers. Photo taken by David Colwell.

will have a number of them. I believe no clove bag was in my trunk. I have not unpacked it yet having left it in town. Please send it & an extract cut from a newspaper relating to cooking. You will find it in the desk in one of the drawers inside at the left corner. You can enclose that in a letter.

I hope you will all get along charmingly & try to make yourselves comfortable. If Minnie leaves; do not hesitate to write to sister Libby. She will come with pleasure. Please kiss all the children for me, and tell John, Nan & Daisy they must be good and do everything you tell them.

I am exceedingly anxious to hear from you and expect a letter today or tomorrow. Direct your letters care of Capt. Henderson, Camp Wayne, West Chester, Penna.

Best respects to Minnie & George if he is with you.

> Truly your affect. husband
> J.S. Colwell

AHC to JSC, June 14, 1861

Friday evening

My very dear Husband,

Mr. Harkness kindly sent me word twice today that he would carry a letter so I avail myself of the politeness although I have nothing excepting very domestic news to write for this morning I mailed a letter to you. On examining the Herald this afternoon I came across a letter from Camp Wayne & also a notice of the entire company of "Carlisle Fencibles" whereupon I took a comfortable cry to myself just by seeing your name—ain't I a baby? Soon after Mrs. Johnston came and I suppose my doleful manner must have induced the remark, she said I was the most desolate person she knew which so entirely agrees with my views that you must excuse my disagreeable letter this time. To do Mrs. J. justice she heartily approves of your conduct thereby agreeing with Mr. Watts.—You see you have two!!

Mrs. Penrose was to see me a few evenings ago—she thinks her husband will remain at home. Miss Martha tells me say to you that she carries a flag for us. Elize bids me say she carries a palmetto.

We have had a long season of dry weather—the cistern is dry. Our landlord mended the step yesterday and promises faithfully to make the wash-house next week.

I have purchased 3 pairs of chickens to which I attend entirely myself just because <u>you</u> used to do that. Ys day's papers anticipate a battle very soon. I do hope it will be the last—the blunder at Vienna is much gloried over South.

I am very glad you are so comfortable, I hope you will enjoy yourself & take good care of your health for your life is more precious to me than all the gold and glory this world could afford. I sometimes think I have been too careless and ungrateful regarding the bless-

ings of my past life & now God is punishing me. I hope for future good.

My dearest husband don't be angry with me but I feel so choked up this evening. I know t'will all be over in the morning & my next letter will be more cheerful & when you write about coming home I will be the very happiest woman the world ever knew. Cousin Henriette has been up this evening, 'tis a great relief to her to have Will in your company. She hopes he don't drink.

I notice by the papers that Lincoln has been trying the balloon, I should think it would be rather a dangerous operation if <u>rebels</u> hear about. They would have a good chance.

John is beginning to anticipate the 4th of July, all the cents which Uncle George gives up for shooting crackers. They all talk a great deal about you. Nan has quite a patronizing air in her care of Daisy & Brother holds long conversations about his Da Da.

Good night my darling husband, always think very kindly of me just as you used to when I was good.

> Ever your attached wife
> Annie

Don't forget to write regularly.

AHC to JSC, June 20, 1861

Carlisle June 20th /61

My ever dear Husband,

Your two very welcome letters were received with great pleasure & re-read many times for whenever I feel low spirited, I fly upstairs and go over them again to re-assure myself that I still have you—so please don't forget to write me as you heretofore have done every other day for 'tis such a comfort & I would be miserable without my letter & conclude at once that this terrible war was only a diabolical plan concocted between Jeff Davis & Lincoln to deprive <u>good</u> wives of their husbands & thereby try their tempers not a little.

Mrs. Robt. Henderson & Beck kindly brought me up a letter of May Hayes relating to her visit to Camp Wayne. It was very gratifying for she entered into particulars so satisfactorily. She mentioned you and the other gentlemen looking particularly <u>nice & clean</u> and I knew you must have had a <u>white</u> collar on. Now I want you to write me just how <u>you</u> look—have you shaved any? Do you wear that horrid flannel shirt all the time or only in the morning? Do you wear that blue coat when you go to town or look as a civilian?

Thinking of military matters reminds me that George has applied for a Captaincy in the <u>regular</u> army to be attached to the commissary department, his knowledge of business being such he is better qualified for that than for active service. If Genl. Cooper's answer is favorable he will not go to California as he would prefer a certainty. Poor Charley don't know what to do. His business has resulted unfavorably and he hopes that the California correspondence will be encouraging.

Mr. McClure was down two days this week. Today letters for the firm arrived from Phila. for the collection of bills for Knight & Co. from Clark & Son. I enclosed them for Mr. McC. by Mr. Drake as you desired.

Sallie Anderson got off on Monday. The Gorian [?] family who are her travelling companions to Tennessee are red hot secessionists & say they have paid their final visit to Baltimore unless she secedes. They will have a good talk. About four hours after her departure a letter from her husband came from whom she had not heard for five weeks owing to delays.

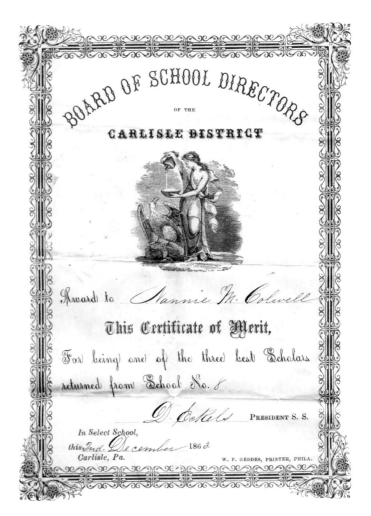

School Certificate of Merit for Nannie M. Colwell, oldest daughter of James and Annie Colwell, 2 December 1863. (Colwell Collection, CCHS.)

On Wednesday morning the children went to school at 7 & 1/2 o'clock and I at 9 to the examination which passed off very creditably both children and scholars requitting themselves well but I think both Mrs. Lynn and the children felt called upon from a sense of duty like other patriots—to sing Yankee Doodle with uncommon emphasis. I returned home with a terrible headache ever since and the adventures of Yankee Doodle have been ringing through my head ever since. The children are now in the 1st class—John hopes you will make some comment on this distinction.

George is laid up with a sore heel which is and has been very painful but Dr. Harmon says it is doing so pretty he'll be up in a day or two. Cousin Margaretta was up this evening. She says Mrs. Mahon was the originator of the plan to order Sallie away—such impertinence! There was a shade of melancholy attached to her departure which made me feel very sad. Jack Ransom has resigned. The old Genrl. is very angry. Roger Jones is very uncomfortably situated—two brothers in the Southern army, all his friends living in Virginia & most of them in arms and he not able to go there on account of his late action at Harper's Ferry.

On Thursday afternoon I planted out red beets, hoed the corn & weeded the garden but I found that hoeing in hoops was not very convenient for I would occasionally come in contact with an adjoining hill of corn. The next morning I arose early, went to market, bought wretched beef and 14 lbs of elegant butter at 9 cts a lb, worked it all over & packed away—ain't I turning out a worker. But indeed my dear husband I can't sit still any time & sew for I'm imagining all sorts of things about you. I'm told that Ike Parker would like to enjoy camp life 7 years. May Henderson and I came to the conclusion that you would all return as fat as Alderman. She is really brave hearted & enviable in that respect and just as pretty as she can be.

Cousin Galbraith is off again to Washington—such energy surely ought to be rewarded. If not he will return shortly to Kansas. Raymond Stevenson is clerk for something I've forgotten at Chambersburg—$80 a month. I told Mrs. Beatty of the good things her husband had received from Mrs. Prince & I also told her I hoped I would be able to tell him of many more nice things he would get. She and Katie Sharpe sent blankets—have you any? Beware of rheumatism.

Our baby has 5 teeth & is as sweet as possible, walks with one hand. Daisy is a real boy [or hog] & misses her Papa's knee & the carrying down to dinner. She is a winning little puss. Nan is my chief companion, & promises to be a fine girl & tries to do what I tell her. John is making collections of old locks, screws, hinges, & nails to learn a trade during vacation. Today I overheard a conversation between him and Viena— "Mama always does what she says for she promises me a cent even if I am bad I get it"—so I'll take the hint and put in a promise in future.

I do want you to come home so much, my own dearest husband. Do come as soon as you can. Write me very often. The friends in Shippensburg Mr M.C. says are well. A kiss and a very good night from your sincerely attached wife.

Annie

JSC to AHC, June 23, 1861

Camp Wayne
West Chester 23 June 61

My dear wife,

I have received your letter of the 20th inst. [meaning current month], also your note accompanying the jar of pickles & the night shirt. The latter was particularly illegible from the vinegar which nearly all leaked from the jar and saturated the shirt. I received also your letter of Friday evening by Mr. Harkness.

Your letters are always looked for with great anxiety. I would like to receive two or three every day. But there is such a strain of unhappy feeling, and wretchedness runs through some of your letters, that the perusal fills me with sadness. You say that you are the most miserable woman in the world. My dear, dear wife, why should you be so? Have you not a husband who loves you better than all else in this world and who holds your best interests and that of our little children before everything? My absence should not make you so miserable. I am only about 100 miles from you and how many are separated for years. You say if I only would say I was coming home it would make you the happiest woman in existence. Now I am sure my own Annie would not wish me to come back with dishonour, and thus bring disgrace on her and our children. No, she is too noble, too good, too true, too loving for that. I feel that I will be with you before a great while and hope that we will live many happy years together.

You mentioned in one of your letters that you were talking of coming on with Mrs. Watts. I advised you to postpone the visit, but I have begun to look on the visit as a certainty and felt considerably disappointed when you subsequently wrote that you had abandoned the idea.

You speak of rumors of our being sent from here. We hear these rumors but know no more of their truth or falsity than you do. I do not think, however, that we will be sent away for two or three weeks at least. If you would wean baby, you could come here without much inconvenience and perhaps it might do you good. It is said that the citizens of West Chester are going to give us a dinner on the 4th of July & that we are to have a grand parade etc. That might be a very good time to be here. You could get no better company than

Mrs. Watts. Mrs. Sharpe I believe is coming on soon perhaps this week or next. I do not know that any others are coming but it is probable they will. When you are coming, let me know before and I will make arrangements for you. I suppose Minnie & George could get along with the children for three or four days. I know sister Libby or Jane would go down if you would write to them.

If we remain here three months I expect to be in Carlisle within that time, but if we should be ordered away within a short time, I may not get there for some time. I presume you have received all my letters, but a number of letters between this and Carlisle have been lost I am told. I would like if you would write always how much money you draw out of bank as I must make arrangements to replenish when the deposits are nearly withdrawn.

The pickles you sent are very nice but I have no use for the night shirt and will return it. I sleep in my flannel shirt, I have one muslin night shirt here & have never worn it. I know of nothing that you could send me. If we stay here I might use my slippers. If we leave I suppose I will have no use for them.

I will probably send this by Mr. Christ Long. He will leave camp soon after five o'clock tomorrow morning. I would like to send the children something, but cannot get to town in time at 5 1/2 o'clock when the cars leave.

John and Nan ought to say a lesson every day during vacation, commencing at the beginning of their old book, and go regularly on. It will prevent them from forgetting what they learned and will enable them to progress easier when they commence school again. Tell them I am very glad that they have been promoted to a higher class and I hope they will be good children and try to learn so that they may not be at the foot of the class. They must do everything Mama tells them and not quarrel with each other as bad girls & boys sometimes do.

I might write you much more but I have not the time, and it would hardly interest you much. I hope I will have the pleasure of seeing you before a great while. Give my best regards to George & Minnie. Try to keep up your spirits and get fat. I fear you are dwindling away. I remain your sincerely attached husband

    James

JSC to AHC, June 26, 1861

Camp Wayne West Chester
26 June 1861

My dear Annie,

The last letter I received from you was by Mr. Harkness. I wrote Sunday night and forwarded by Christian Long with the shirt. I presume you received it. Capt. Henderson announced suddenly this afternoon that he was going home and left immediately. He will return in a day or two. I had no time to write you by him after I knew he was going. I presume he will call to see you. I was up all last night on duty and do not feel for writing a long letter.

I believe I did not write you that I was at church on Sunday last in town at the court house, that being the Presbyterian place of worship at present, their church undergoing repair. I also heard a sermon in the afternoon in camp from Mr. Newton, the Episcopal clergyman.

There have been quite a number of persons here from Carlisle at different times. I forgot to bring my old bible that I have always carried with me wherever I have gone for the last 20 or 25 years. I left it in my office. You might get it out and send it down by someone.

I still hope you are getting along better and feel more contented. It grieves me to think that you are miserable and unhappy. Do try for my sake to amuse yourself, and enjoy yourself and don't give way to despondency. It does you great injury, and makes me unhappy. Still I would rather that you would write your true feelings just as they are and not deceive me by expressing sentiments you do not feel. I only desire that you endeavor to make yourself as comfortable as possible and enjoy yourself as well as you can, always bestowing your best affections on me. Now do not deem me selfish. I have only your happiness and best interest at heart. I am expecting a letter from you. Perhaps I may not write you again this week, but do you write at every convenient time.

Best regards to Minnie & George and do not forget me to Nan, John & Daisy. I expect to see them all good children when I return.

    I remain your true
      and devoted husband
        James

JSC to AHC, July 4, 1861

Camp Wayne
West Chester 4 July 1861

My own dear wife Annie,

I have been more sad since my last than any time since my arrival in this place. You cannot imagine what a weight your letter of the 2nd lifted from my heart. It was handed to me today just after our arrival on the ground where the celebration took place. As soon as I could get relieved, I sought a place to sit down & devoured its contents, and oh, what joy it brought to my heart. It was like my own wife, and I cannot thank you too much for it. I hope now we understand each other & that you will scold me no more, but that rather you will forgive my many faults. I know I err frequently but it is nearly always an error of the judgment & not of the heart. It gives me pain to do anything that may bring unhappiness or even anxiety of mine to you. My whole effort in this world is to make you as happy & comfortable as, under all existing circumstances is in my power and if you will only not permit your affections to become estranged I think we will be very happy. It is not worth while to enquire at this late day whether I was right or wrong in entering into the present movement. It may be that I should not have done so. I did it with the best motive in the world. I have no hostility against the south, and this war is not in behalf of Lincoln or any other man, but it is to sustain the government. And if Jeff Davis had been elected president and was endeavoring to preserve this union, I would have been found aiding him with all efforts. But whether I am right or not, I do not see how I could get out of the service without bring[ing] disgrace and dishonour on myself & my little family, and my prayer and hope is that I may be saved from any act of that kind.

The great parade & dinner is over, and a laborious time we had of it. We were out at half past 8 o'clock A.M. and paraded & marched & stood for inspection & review from that till 20 minutes after 12 o'clock. When we arrived on the ground selected for the orations etc. having marched through most of the streets in the town and stood for more than an hour in one place in the hot sun for review and inspection, a number of men fainted in the ranks, ten in one company. Our company had one only who became sick & was obliged to

sit down a while and after joined in the ranks. I stood it very well & do not feel much tired tonight.

We had a good dinner, cold beef, ham and other things as much as we could eat. The address I did not hear, being engaged in pondering over your letter & enjoying its contents. I also received a letter from Mr. McClure at the same time I received yours which gave an account of his stoppage at Carlisle and visit to you.

I have seen Mrs. Beatty at camp and out at the celebration, but have not called on her which I intended to do every day, but somehow could not get it accomplished. I have also seen Mrs. Graham & the judge. The latter was with us at a gentlemen's party at a Mrs. Buckwalter's last night. The last I saw of him was climbing in at a window in his hotel—the Green Tree, about 12 o'clock m. last night. There are quite a number of visitors here from Carlisle. I have named most of those with whom you are acquainted.

O how I would like to see you. I hope to have that pleasure next week or the week after. I will if I can conveniently get permission. I am tied here and cannot get away without leave, which I have no doubt I can get unless something should turn up of which we are not now aware.

I was vaccinated, as was the whole camp some days ago, mine has taken the doctor says. I wish you could have been here today. You would have seen some 1500 or 1800 soldiers together on a march, and thousands of citizens from the town & county, and probably a great many from other places. There were two or three small enclosures fenced off in which we dined, and the people gathered round to see the animals feed, and watched us with great interest while we were eating. I must say here that the Carlisle Fencibles are the crack company here for good behaviour & for proficiency in drill. We are attached to the 7th regiment and have been assigned the post of honour every time we have parades. But as you do not like that subject I will drop it.

Now I hope my dearest Annie that you will endeavour to keep up your spirits & enjoy yourself as well as you can. I would like to be with you beyond all other things, but let us have patience and all will be well. Write me as often as you can as nothing affords me so much pleasure as your letters excepting those that scold. I do not know by whom I shall send this or whether by mail, as I may not see any of those who are about to leave in the morning. My space is occupied and I must now bid my dearest Annie adieu for this time. I remain your devoted and loving husband

James

JSC to AHC, July 7, 1861

Camp Wayne
West Chester 7 July 1861

My Dear Wife,

My letter of yesterday was cut off very abruptly, it being called for a little sooner than I expected. Perhaps I will have time to write a bit the more this time.

I was at church today and heard a sermon from the presbyterian clergyman. It was exceedingly warm and I had great difficulty in keeping awake. I saw some little girls paddling along so innocently & happy that I could have taken one up and kissed her for Daisy, so much did she remind me of her. Often when I see little children it reminds me of our little darlings, their innocent prattle being so similar in many cases.

We have very little variety in camp life. Almost the same scenes pass before our eyes every day, and almost the same to eat each day.

Yesterday I was at the Brandywine with a squad of men to bathe. It was a pretty long walk—from 3 1/2 to 4 miles & back. We went out in the morning taking provisions along & remained out till the afternoon.

Mr. & Mrs. Miller arrived here yesterday evening, or rather they arrived in town. Mr. Miller was in camp last night, I saw Madame Miller in town today. The visitors all give the same account of the extreme dullness of Carlisle. The lawyers are doing nothing although nearly the half of them are absent. If we had all remained at home, we would have starved all together.

I hardly know what to say to you about my going home. I did expect I would be able to see you the last of this week or next. But we received an order that we were to have officers drill tomorrow and to be continued. This may prevent me from going for a week or two longer. I should like to see you beyond all other things now since you have promised not to scold me. It seems to me that my coming here has done one thing that I had some idea of before but not the same realizing knowledge that I have now. It has taught me

how much I love you my dearest Annie, and how badly I could get along without you. It seems to me that my earthly happiness is bound up in you and your welfare, and your love. If I should lose that then all would be a blank. How could I get along? is a question impossible for me to fathom. O my dear wife bestow on me your love while life lasts and I will strive always to deserve it. You cannot imagine how utterly miserable I was before I received your last letter. I did think that others were poisoning your mind to such a degree that possibly you might forget me.

If you can you might get another shirt or two made for me to wear when I go home & to bring with me. The two old ones I brought along are giving out. As you have never said anything about getting any money out of the bank I am afraid you are using all your specie. You ought to save that as much as possible by getting a note changed every opportunity as I have an idea gold and silver will become very scarce after a while. You can get the small notes which will answer your purpose nearly as well as the specie.

How I would like to see you and have a talk with you. If I cannot get to Carlisle I think you will have to come here. If brother was weaned you could come without much trouble. But I hope I shall be able to get to Carlisle for a day or two sometime this month if not this week. I have not received any letter from you since Thursday now more than three days. I hope to get one tomorrow morning.

I was glad Libby was down to see you. I know she will go down and remain with you whenever you desire it. While George & Minnie are with you she thinks it would be increasing your family unnecessarily, and she could be of no use to you, and you will not be lonesome while they are in the house. Besides I suppose it is a throng time at Mr. Hayes' and probably they would like her to stay with them at present. But whenever you are left alone she will go.

I hope you are getting along comfortably and are happy. To know that you are will afford me more happiness than any news you can send me or anything else. To make you so shall be my every endeavour although you may differ at present from me as to the means to be used.

I remain your ever loving husband

James

AHC to JSC, July 8, 1861

Carlisle July 8th /61

My very dear husband,

I have risen this morning quite early so that I shall have time to write before breakfast, for as this is the farmers wash-day I shall have no time till night. Your letters by Messrs Duffield & Henderson came duly received and of course you know how very welcome they were but I must confess when the latter told me his special business in Carlisle at this time I felt considerably disappointed for I had begun to consider your being here to recruit for a couple weeks a certainty. Mr. Haverstick had apprised George of the necessity of enlarging the companies & told him he would give Robt. Henderson a hint about sending you for that purpose. Therefore I counted on it as a certainty but I'm now looking forward to seeing you at any rate very soon.

Last Friday I had a presentiment of your taking me by surprise, so I hastened to the parlor window & peeped through the shutters for 1/2 hour thinking every footfall was certainly yours.

Yesterday several regiments passed through & also through the night I heard engines. The president's message seems to be hastening matters. I hear a good deal of southern movements and am so uneasy so that [if] you are only kept at Camp Wayne & fight imaginary battles I'm satisfied. Annie Ege thinks there is a possibility of John Smead's being ordered to this garrison shortly. John Hays is off to Washington to get a commission in the regular army. Cousin Galbraith is Colonel at last of a mounted troop. In a letter from a secession cousin of mine last week there is a particular desire to know in which regiment you were so patriotially enlisted. If you receive any letters from that quarter you need not answer for they are so silent [?] as not to shake hands with any who voted for Lincoln.

Mr. Roberts has sent for Ben R. to go out in Sept. Ben's health is bad so Cousin Margaretta urges him to stay. I saw Kate Sharpe at ch[urch] yesterday. She appears much better satisfied with the military arrangements than when she went to West Chester. I suppose the patriotism of the 19 officers and 16 captains of the regiment is superior to any feeling of disappointment at Sharpe's rapid promotion. You see I have not in-

Annie Colwell attended the Second Presbyterian Church on the south-east corner of Hanover and Pomfret Streets, c.1865. (A. A. Line, CCHS.)

cluded my own husband for I have no ambition regarding him in this matter & still hope to have him stationed down next Miss Martha's with the closed shutters flung wide open & the old shingle as large as life without any military appendix. My own dear husband I'm only writing this, & don't intend to talk one word of it when you come.

We had quite a political discussion at Miss Martha's steps on Friday evening. She says she will hang out a flag because she is in a nest of secessionists. Mrs. Penrose hopes the south will last and thinks her husband's day of retribution is coming. Miss Virginia Lyons & I took more conciliatory grounds while George, Minnie & Cousin Annie Miller were at loggerheads.

I hope you will be able my dearest husband to read this. I'm in such a hurry. The children are all well and talk much of your coming. Ever your own affectionate wife

Annie

I took Daisy to church one Sunday. During the sermon whilst I was giving my undivided attention to

Mr. Eales she crept through the under part of the pew to Mr. Miller's and the first we knew was the white head popping up.

JSC to AHC, July 29, 1861

Washington City
29 July 1861

My dear Annie,

I wrote to you on Friday I believe it was but have not heard a word from you since I saw you. I hardly expected to hear from you before this but I hope to get a letter from you today or tomorrow. I always feel anxious to learn how you all are & where you are.

We are in the same place as when I last wrote, from two to three miles north of Washington, out 7th street beyond the park. It is said we have one of the best camps about the city. We are much more confined here than at Camp Wayne. I have not been out of camp since we arrived except on Friday when we march[ed] to Washington to the arsenal to get our arms exchanged. The distance is variously estimated at 4 1/2 to 5 1/2 miles which we marched in the morning and waited all day without a bite to eat getting home about sundown.

We are as much cut off from the world here almost as if we were at the Rocky Mountains. I scarcely ever see a newspaper and know nothing of what is going on in the country although within three miles of the capitol. I don't know where Penrose's Regiment is although it came to Washington the day before we did. I don't know where Todd's Regt. is. It arrived at Baltimore a day or two before us. In it are McCartney's and Crops companies. You will perceive this is written in pencil. The facilities for writing with pen & ink are not very great. I write this sitting on the ground in my tent with my trunk for a writing desk. Mr. Beatty & I have a tent together but being a small one it crowds us considerably.

A couple of Shippensburgers were to see us yesterday & Saturday, Mr. Cox & Mr. McPherson. I understand Rev. Mr. Harper & several others from Shippensburg are expected here this week. I presume we will not have as many visitors from Carlisle as we had at Camp Wayne. We have had no person to call on us from Washington except a few acquaintances & we do not expect any.

I have no idea how long we will remain where we are. It was the current report before we left Camp Wayne that our regiment with four others of the Penn. V.R.C. were to be under the command of Genl. McCall. I have seen by a stray paper that he has been assigned to the Department of Alexandria. It may be that we will be ordered there shortly. Wherever I am ordered I am prepared to go, and there is no service I would as willingly engage in as in the defence of Washington City.

And now my dear wife I must again say farewell. Remember me with kindness to our dear little children. Tell John & Nan & Daisy again & again from me to be good children & remember do everything you tell them. Write as often as you can. I fear I shall not be able to write as often as I did from West Chester, but will as often as I can. Direct to me Co. A, 7 Regt., Penna. Vol. Res. C., Washington City, D.C.

Your ever affect. husband
J.S. Colwell

AHC to JSC, July 31, 1861

Carlisle   July 31st 1861

My very dear good husband,

Oh, I cannot tell you how thankful I felt for your letter which I received this afternoon, for I was feeling so anxious that my heart almost grew sick as the mail time came round, so please write as often as possible telling me how & where you are. Please never eat anything which a stranger gives you for fear of poison; these returning volunteers tell us that food was frequently poisoned which was offered them at Charlestown.

John brought two soldiers in to tea this evening and seemed perfectly delighted at offering them hospitalities & when I think of your ever being placed in the same situation I feel as though nothing was too good for them. John's military enthusiasm is at a high pitch; he tells me that in addition to his duty of bugler he has assumed that of drummer for another Co. for he is bound to be a soldier. The inducements to run at large are very great since the encampment so I have to devise many plans to keep my boy at home. He has noble traits of character but he requires careful training.

Sister Jane & Mr. Craig were down in a buggy this morning & remained till after dinner. They report all well in Shippensburg. Miss Jane Galbraith was buried on Saturday. Charly McClure mentioned having seen you.

I send you by this mail today's Inquirer & as you so seldom see a paper perhaps you would like me to send it regularly. I am sorry you are kept so closely confined for I was hoping that all these people from town were thrown together so that it would be more like home. Todd's Regt. are near Annapolis at the junction of the road. I hear that McCartney is tyrannical & 40 of his men have left & won't serve under him. Speaking of reports yesterday I was on the street & Mr. Harkness informed me that your Co. had gone within 10 miles of Manassas, which excited me so much that George made it his business to go down town to inquire into it & discovered no foundation for the report. Everything almost seems to devolve on McClellan & I do pray that an all seeing God may give him wisdom & control his movements. I read it with a great deal of interest the opinions of the press regarding Genl. McCall's ability & past experience, but I hope you won't be sent to Alexandria as you intimated.

My dearest husband my whole being seems wrapt up in this movement where you are concerned & I cannot express my solicitude regarding you, but I can look to a Higher Power & rely on his strength & <u>know</u> that not even a sparrow falls to the ground without his knowledge. If this war was only among the things that are past & we were all united & happy in the enjoyment of peace. Nan Daisy & James are well & very good. Nan is my little comforter.

My darling husband good night; write as soon as you possibly can & always think of me as your sincerely devoted wife

Annie

I can't leave this space without filling it up with kisses. If you think you will go away I could leave the baby at Cousin W. Lossoners [?] a day in B. & go to see you for a few hours. I cannot give you up. Thursday of next week I propose going to Shippensburg.

AHC to JSC, August 12, 1861

Middle Spring
Aug 12th 1861

My very dearest Husband,

Your news of the 7th inst reached me on Saturday & I do assure you I was very anxious to get it for I had not heard since Tuesday. I was sorry to hear you had such an uncomfortable time in your late military experience, but very glad to know that you were still well & had not seen the enemy & I do sincerely hope you never will for I shall be more anxious than ever then.

Another comforting assurance for which I must thank you doubly my own Husband—that in the midst of all your duties you still find time to think of us at home. Indeed I cannot realize that you are away for any length of time, & often find myself picturing you in your red gown & slippers in the old rocking chair, beside the children & me, in our little nursery. A few nights ago I dreamed that I was in the midst of the battle. The weapons used were long rods such as the one we have on top of the wardrobe, for chastising purposes, & I figured as Pocohontas between you & the enemy. I think little Brother must have been kicking me in the back just then for the sensation in sleep was similar to a scourging.

Middle Spring Presbyterian Church, home church of James Colwell and his ancestors. (CCHS.)

Have you got anything to protect your neck from rain? I regret so much that we could not get the silk oilcloth cape. It troubles me very much that you belong to the Brag [?] Co for I'm afraid you'll be put front—but we must rely entirely on God. He has said "as our day is so shall our strength be." His strength is perfect in our weakness. Have you a chaplain in your regiment? By the Prsbyn I notice that both Drs. Scott & Leyburn have resigned to go south. Yesterday I heard a sermon by Mr. Hays at Middle Spring.

The weather is still very warm yet it is drizzling today. Vienna has gone to live with Cousin Margaretta for a few weeks. I will put up the tomatoes in our garden for winter. They are particularly fine & they promise to be quite a buy in market selling for 25 cts per bushel. I was very sorry to hear of Edgar Hayes' sickness. I [hope] it proves nothing serious & he has recovered ere this. Dr. Mahon & his wife are here from Baltimore. John is enjoying himself very much constantly on his feet & bare-footed too from morning till night. He says he does love <u>Rarbert</u>. Nan makes a great many tea parties with the shells. Daisy tells Aunt

Nancy to make soup like Mrs Croft, & she enjoys everything Aunt Nancy gives her; dear little brother James is very fond of walking alone & can nearly walk the length of the entry without assistance. A letter from Minnie reports the house being well fastened up. George is still in Carlisle.

If you should be so unfortunate as to get sick won't you send for me? In that event I would not hesitate about leaving James. Let me hear from you as often as possible. All send love. Good-bye my own precious Husband. I am ever your sincerely attached wife.

Annie

AHC to JSC, August 20, 1861

Middle Spring
August 20th 1861

My dear Husband,

I received your letter of the 16th inst. & feel truly glad that your health has been universally so good through the many changes of weather in the last two weeks. I hope you will always be fortunate enough as to get under some shelter in time of storm when you are on duty. But I don't like these picket guards at any rate. It must be some new regulation to have the officers go on such duty.

I received by Mr. Long a dirty shirt of yours & three pairs of stockings. Are your stockings getting pretty thin? I sometimes hear of persons going where you are & could send you any thing. I will wait for advices before I make you more flannel shirts. Your adventure with the secession cavalry must have been quite exciting. I hope all your adventures will terminate as happily.

Your cousin Dr. Mahon of Balt. asked me if you had gone for the glory of the thing. Feeling rather indignant, I replied that your motives were purely conscientious, but that you & I differed widely in regard to your taking so active a part. At the same time I could not suppress a thought that such extravagant love of country was certainly very powerful so as to make every other feeling subordinate to it, but I feel thankful that those conscientious motives have been dormant for 7 years at any rate & I trust they will be restored to the same happy state & remain so for ever. Methinks I hear my Husband say "you are in a bad humor." No indeed I aint, but I would like to have a husband to talk to just now, & if he don't get a little teazing occasionally he'll grow too fat.

I spend my time very pleasantly in the country. On Friday afternoon we went over to Mrs. Robt. McCune's to tea. Sister Molly is staying there now. Sister Nancy & Mr. Hayes both had cramps that night but have recovered. The children are very well & enjoy themselves very much. John thinks he could live on corn all the time. We all do justice to the corn field. Daisy is getting very fat. Nan won't get fat despite of her stuffing which I think so very ungrateful. James is a darling fat boy. I do wish you could see him. He is always laughing & showing his two big butter teeth. Sister Nancy had a letter from Edgar last week. I hope he will rapidly regain his strength.

I have no news to tell you excepting domestic. Mrs. Creigh has died since I left home. Have you seen anything of George yet? He expected to be in Washington last week. I have not been in town since I've been up. Yesterday we heard Mr. Hays preach. How do you like your chaplain? The proper person in such a position would be very useful. Now good bye my own husband. Always forgive me for everything I say or do wrong & write to me very often.

Ever your sincerely attached wife

Annie

The children & I have [been] making excursions very often. I put on an old wrapper of Sister Libby's & can almost swim. They are waiting on me now. I wish you could see the mermaids.

JSC to AHC, August 22, 1861

Camp Tenally
Washington City, D.C.
22 August 1861

My Dearest Annie,

I received yours of the 19th inst. on my return from picket duty. It seems to me that letters are a long time getting here & going to you. You say you had not heard from me since Monday evening previous. I have written since here three times every week. I presume you will receive the letters.

We had an exceedingly wet night the last night we were out; it rained at intervals the whole night & at times tremendously. I fortunately had a shade again but my feet were as wet as they could be all the time.

It cleared off the next forenoon and became very pleasant. What seems very extraordinary is that although I have been out three wet nights I have taken no cold. The first night I was wet to the skin all night, and my clothes remained wet till dried the next day by the sun and my own animal heat. The other two nights my feet were wet in the same way. And yet I have not caught a particle of cold, and never was in better health than since I have been in camp, with the exception of the complaint I had when I saw you at Harrisburg, which stuck to me for a couple of weeks.

It was during that time we had the march from Camp Harvey to this camp. It appears someone reported that I was very much fatigued. I was tired it was true, and so was every one else I have no doubt. A number gave out & had to leave the ranks on the road. I am well persuaded that I could have march[ed] back to the place we had left the same afternoon without much inconvenience. The day was excessively warm & we took the middle of the day which made it pretty hard work.

We had a grand review yesterday by Genl. McClelland & the President and most of the cabinet. I presume you will see an account of it in the daily papers, if you see them. Genl. McClellan complimented us very highly. It is nearly breakfast time & may not have time to write more after breakfast. Give my love to all friends and believe that I remain your always devoted husband

James

P.S. Do you ever hear from your friends in Baltimore? The Baltimore secessionists it appears are quite elated at the success of the rebels at Bull Run.

You ask if there is anything I want. I will need five or six pairs of woolen stockings, two or three flannel shirts and as many pairs of drawers. It will be time enough to get them. Perhaps you cannot get the flannel in Shippensburg. If you do not go to Carlisle soon perhaps you could go to Chambersburg & get it as sisters Jane & Nancy & Martha Craig frequently go. I want heavier flannel than the shirts that were made in Carlisle, and all wool but not too rough. I think the drawers ought to be good strong flannel like wire. And I would prefer grey flannel if you can get it or a dark colour. If you could get home made stockings they would be the best. I thought I could get these

View of the Carlisle Deposit Bank (where Annie did her banking) and Saint John's Episcopal Church, taken from the tower of the First Presbyterian Church, c.1873. (A. A. Line, CCHS.)

things in Washington, but a Captain informed me yesterday that he had hunted Washington all over & could not get a flannel shirt. Some opportunity may offer for sending them down—if not they can be sent by express.

I sent an order to Mr. McClure to get the money from Rheem & some other persons. If he gets it he will pay it over to you. But you can draw on the Carlisle Deposite Bank for what you want, and get the money in Shippensburg.

Take care of yourself & make yourself happy. Bring up our children as well as you can. Tell them for me it is their duty to obey you in everything, my own dear wife.

Your loving husband
James

JSC to AHC, September 5, 1861

Great Falls, Md. 5 Sept

My dear Annie,

We are still here & do not know how long we may remain. We have had some excitement since I last wrote. The night of the day I wrote or rather the next morning at 1 o'clock we were ordered to march up the river 25 men each out of 3 companies. We march up about three miles and laid there till about dawn when the men were scattered along the bank of the river but nothing was observed. After some time some 50 or sixty volunteered to cross over one branch of the river to an island. I did not go as I thought it a useless trip. Over they went into the water up to their necks some places. They returned all safe.

Yesterday morning we were surprised by the firing of cannon in the neighborhood. I was up in camp which I believe I informed you was about 1/4 of a mile or more from the river where there are several buildings there & the colonel and a number of officers with the reserve were quartered there. I was told by some of our men that the firing was by our own cannon who were practicing. I thought from the sound & direction that it was not, but as others said they knew it was, I gave it up. After some time the rush of men came into camp & the news flew like wild fire that the enemy were shelling the building down at headquarters from 3 batteries posted on the other side of the river. The call was to arms immediately and in a few minutes we were all under arms and then I heard what had happen.

Just after breakfast they unmasked their batteries & commenced a brisk fire with shell & solid shot some from rifled cannon, & the shell and balls flew thick & fast into & around the buildings, with no other damage than the partial destruction of the houses & injury of one man although there must have been from 100 to 150 persons in & around those buildings, men, women & children. W. Harper of Shippensburg was the only one struck. He was wounded on the arm with a piece of shell. It is nothing serious being only a flesh wound which will be well enough in a few days. We could do nothing. Our guns would not reach their batteries. We have no rifled cannon. The Col. sent for some & four rifled cannon arrived in the afternoon but too late. The enemy had left or at least moved out of sight.

Since about last Thursday we have had beautiful weather, till last night when it rained slightly and this morning it commenced right fast & has been raining incessantly ever since (about 2 PM) and looks as if it might rain a week. The news today are that the enemy on the other side have moved to other posts, which is probably true.

Cole Watts came here on Monday with several others to enlist. His father was at Camp Tenally yesterday after him and he was sent back. It seems that he had run off without permission. The news is here that Sallie Anderson has returned to Carlisle within a few days. Can it be true? If is it portends something eventful. The news here is that the Southern army cannot be held together much longer without another battle or victory.

I must now close. My paper is all done and too rainy to look for more. I do not know whether I can get a postage stamp or not. I hope you and the children continue well & enjoying yourselves. Mr. McClure did not get any money for you. You will have to draw on Carlisle Deposite Bank for what you want, unless McCleaf has some for you. I remain your true & devoted husband

James

I have returned from church & learned that a man will probably be sent to Washington tomorrow morning with letters & bring back our mail. I hope I will receive at least two. Continue to direct your letters to Washington as heretofore, always putting on the Regt. and Co and McCall's division. I understand a division postmaster will be appointed in a day or two. His business will be to send in & bring out from Washington all the letters of the division. I do not know how often we will get a mail but I hope you will continue to write as promptly as you have done the last two weeks.

I have not the least idea where we are to go nor when we will start. There is a rumor that we are to guard the railroads running through here on down south. That will be a tiresome task. But whether it is a rumor started in camp I have no means of knowing. It may be true or it may not. A great many of the officers and men have gone today to visit the battlefield of Bull Run which is said to be about five miles from where we are. There is great appearance of rain this afternoon. It will make it very unpleasant, if it does, as our

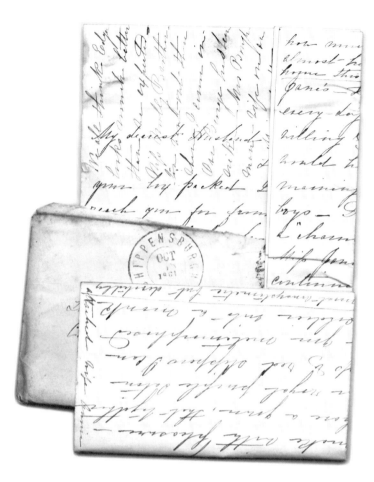

quarters are. Major Todd has just passed along. He is looking very well and says he is with the exception of a slight return of rheumatism.

> I remain
>> Your sincerely afft.
>>> husband
>>>> James

AHC to JSC, October 3, 1861

Shippensburg Friday
Oct. 3rd 1861

My dearest Husband,

Last night we got your box packed. I hope it will reach you for from Edgar's account you must be almost in a state of destitution. The remainder of the stockings I will send again. The light blue pair Sister Molly knit & Sister Libby the other two. If you think the shirts not warm enough I could make of the drawers' flannel which I think you will find comfortable. The pillow case looks odd. I'm afraid your dreams will be rather sombre. The little bucket of butter I hope you will enjoy. Edgar tells me it is rather a rarity. Don't throw the bucket away as it will be useful; if not to yourself, you can return it to me by Mr. Long or someone & I can fill it for you again.

My only regret is that Mr. McClure did not get a larger box so as to put in more apples. The next time you shall have more. He looked so funny fixing the things. Everything had to be just so. You will perceive that your shirts have each three pockets, two on the left side so as to keep any system from creeping into your heart for now as you have her located so near Camp Tenally you might grow too systematic.

I received yours of the 29th inst & as you gave me such a good scolding I shall be on the stool of repentance this week. I would have returned you the money by the box but was afraid it would miscarry. I only gave Sister Nancy $20.00 promising to give her the rest again. She wishes you to say how much a week & told me to ask you. I have only given Sister Jane $15. for I do not know when we will go home, but when Mr. McClure gives me some money I can send you as much or the whole amount if you wish. I forgot to mention in my last letter that McCleaf sent me $10 more making $30 which I have from him.

We were in the country 7 weeks & four days. I as well as the children enjoyed our sojourn there very much. They were all as kind as possible but I know we were some trouble for they had great difficulty getting servants. We are very comfortably fixed now at Sister Jane's. The children go to school every day with Mary. Nan was very willing & anxious to go, but John would have much preferred remaining in the country with the boys. Daisy is pronounced to be a "charming likeness of you" by Miss Jane Wilson. Little James continues to be a very good boy.

In regard to a gown, if you decide to have me make you one 7 feet long I think it will be very nice to sit in whilst you are writing me good long letters, but in bed I should think a comfort most suitable. Whichever you desire I will make with pleasure. If you have a gown, that together with your royal purple satin night cap & red slippers I can imagine your metamorphased from a soldier into a monk.

We all think Edgar looks much better than we expected. Miss Molly Bertherton went out there when I came in. Our George has been sick. Mrs Broughman—wife of an officer of the Adamantine Guard—left here to go to her husband last week & expected to be confined there but she was so frightened at the report of a battle that she returned on Monday. Write soon. I

learned to make butter & can churn now. I have looked in vain for you this week so I'm afraid you stood your examination bravely. If Mr. McClure had only gone instead of you. When you next write tell me how much you love me once more. I almost hear you say "you baby." Do try & come home this fall. Always write 3 times a week.

Ever your most unsystematic but devotedly attached wife

Annie.

AHC to JSC, October 15, 1861

Shippensburg
Tuesday Oct 15th /61

My dearest Husband,

I have just received yours of the 13th brought by Mr. Earnshaw with whom I am very much pleased. He was so gratifying in every particular about you & gave me a many sided picture of camp life. All the time he was talking Daisy was whispering in my ear "Mama is this Papa?" & when he was leaving she ran to the door & called to him "I'm going to write a letter to my Papa" & has been scribbling a long time with that intention. He says he has a furlough till the 1st Nov so you can't get your stockings till then.

So the box had reached you at last. I'm so sorry that I did not make the shirts off the same piece as the drawers but after a deliberate consultation with the sisters we concluded it would be too heavy. You have said nothing lately about the bag & gown. So I have concluded to make both as they will always be useful. The beige lining of your "Hamel cloak" will make a nice lining for the bag & then you know the association will be so pleasant excepting that putting your feet into it will be rather unsentimental.

When I heard of your movement into Virginia I was in a very bad humor for I thought you would not get home soon but your letters of yesterday & today have cheered me up & when I read of your probably being home this fall I was elevated almost to the seventh heaven. I am making you a night cap. Indeed I do think you are so good to try to come home. You we all want to see. I think John must have been dreaming about camp life last night. His first remark in wakening this morning was "Oh! Mama Camp Wayne is just like a fair excepting there were no ladies in carriages."

Last Thursday evening we were at a little party at

Miss Jane Wilson's. I see a good deal of Miss M.C. Reynolds. I like all the people here very much excepting Miss Alice Cresnell. The judge is elected again. They will all be judges now for a long while. The young men who are raising the military Co here are succeeding very well. Mr. Earnshaw thinks he will take a good many back with him. The new Co. is called the "McClure Light Guards" in honor of our unpatriotic friend but indeed he is very clever in offering to do anything he can for me. He told me he had some money for me. Mr McCleaf has just been here & gave me $75.00 for which I gave him a receipt on his rent, also a receipt for the $30.00 received some time ago. I will take good care of it & not squander it these busy times. He has been very sick. His throat was lanced. He can scarcely speak.

James has been sick with diarrhoea for some days. I have a great deal of solicitude regarding him whenever he is not perfectly well. Nan & John are at school. Sister Jane received your letter yesterday. This is a lovely day. I hope you are enjoying one equally as fine. Write very often. Your letters make me feel young. Now & ever your fondly attached wife.

Annie

JSC to AHC, October 29, 1861

Camp Pierpont, Va
Near Washington D.C. 29 Oct

My dear wife,

Your letter of the 25th inst was received in good time, & Oh what a sad, sad, sad letter it was. I hope you will be in better spirits when you write your next or rather that you were in better spirits when you wrote your last. For I trust you have written since & that letter is now in Washington or at least on the road. I do not know, as is usually the case, when the mail will go in, but as we go on picket tomorrow morning to be out 24 hours I thought a mail might go before we return or if we had returned before I would have time to write especially as it is reported that we are to have a grand review of two divisions Genls. McCall & Smith including 25,000 men.

There was a review of Genl. McCall's division today. We went out at 8 o'clock A.M. & were on our feet till one P.M. at which time we go home. It was a grand spectacle, 10,000 or 12,000 men in one body with bayonets gleaming in the sun. The day was most pro-

pitious. It could not have been finer for the purpose. There were very few ladies present, those being articles which are very rare in this part of the country. There were however a few ladies, Mrs. Meade the wife of our General and Mrs. McCall it was said and Mrs. Green wife of our surgeon & a lady friend of hers a Miss Sykes of Georgetown and a few others that I know nothing of. I was introduced to Mrs. Green & Miss Sykes. These ladies it is said came on for the propose of seeing the grand review which was to have been of 3 divisions some 30,000 men, but for some reason the two divisions could not come.

I was wishing you had been here to see the grand sight and also that I might get a sight of your bright eyes. But wify you must restrain your tears and crying or your eyes will become dim & lose their light. I don't know whether I ever informed you that McCall's division is divided into three brigades, 1st Genl. Reynolds, 2nd Genl. Meade, & 3rd without a general as yet commanded by Col. McCalmot.

And so you hardly suppress envy of Martha Craig's husband. The nice dear little soul, I am glad you got out to see them. I suppose they are very proud of their baby. By the way I have often tried to think what the name of our youngest is. I know the first name is James, but the 2nd I have never been able to make out satisfactorily. Please tell me if you think of it.

The fight at Edward's ferry was a terrible slaughter, and entirely without any object. There was no intention to cross. Genl. McClellan had not ordered it & did not wish it. And Genl. Banks had not ordered it. Where the fault lies does not appear to be very well settled yet, at least not by the public. Great as our loss in killed & wounded was, it is ascertained that the rebel loss was much greater.

Write soon my dear wife & believe me ever your loving husband

James

JSC to AHC, November 4, 1861

Camp Pierpont Va.
Near Washington D.C.
4 Nov 1861

My dear wife,

My last letter was sent yesterday, but no mail was brought out owing to the fact that our carrier did not get into the city till after the office was closed—it being Sunday. It was sent after today however & this evening I had the gratification of receiving yours of the 31st ult. It was truly in a different spirit from your previous letter & I must say I felt more comfortable. I do not know whether any mail will go in tomorrow, but I thought I would write a few lines to you at any rate. If it does not go tomorrow it probably will next day.

This afternoon I took quite a stroll through some of the camps. I went to Genl. McCall's headquarters which is about 3/4 of a mile from our camp. Saw Mr. Beatty there. We went from that to the Bucktails' camp & near a couple of Vermont Regiments & a Maine regiment and made our way to the 4th Penna. I saw Mr. Earnshaw who returned last Saturday to camp. I also saw "Ike Parker" who is a lieutenant in this regiment, Doct. Brisbane also who is Lieut. Colonel. The latter treated us to a bottle of wine. I returned to camp in time to read your very acceptable letter by the light of day. It is all quiet still but there are rumors of an advance to be made soon but when or where does not seem to be fixed by madame rumor. I judge we are waiting for intelligence from the naval expedition before moving & movements here will probably be controlled by events there.

You requested me in one of your letters to have my photograph taken the first opportunity—but not in uniform. But you did not say in what costume I should be. I presume in the flannel shirt & drawers you made. I have no clothes but uniform except an old vest. I can put that over my shirt. I did intend once when I went into Washington to have my ugly self taken and fixed up & got my hair cut & beard trimmed & moustache shaved for that purpose, and when I went to Brady's his instrument was out of order & I had to return without it. I will say however it would have been in uniform. If you desire a picture not in uniform, you have a better one now than I can get taken again.

I think you will have some trouble getting all the children on one plate. You would get better likenesses by having them separate. I would like exceedingly to get a glimpse of them as well as of you.

It is well enough you did not send the stockings by Dr. Rankin. It is doubtful whether I would have got them. You had better not send them, I think. I have sufficient to do me all winter. It is difficult as well as expensive for anyone to get out here. I suppose

Abraham Lincoln. Copy of a carte de visite. (CCHS.)

Edmond told you that they asked him $25 for a horse to come out. He got one for $4 by telling the man he was going to a New York Regt. on the other side of the river from here.

I am still my dear Annie your affectionate husband

James

JSC to AHC, November 11, 1861

Camp Pierpont Va.
Near Washington D.C.   11 Nov 1861

My dear Annie,

I was delighted this evening at the receipt of two letters from you dated the 7th & 8th inst. respectively. I presume you have been somewhat disappointed by this time at not receiving one from me today but it is no fault of mine & I trust you will receive one tomorrow morning. I wrote last Friday night & gave it to the mail-man on Saturday morning who informed me it would go to the post office that morning. I learned in the evening it had not gone. As we were promised a mail daily I thought of course it would go on Sunday morning, and I therefore did not write by Mr. Conlyn who left yesterday morning for home and I suppose reached Carlisle this morning. The mail did go this morning, but my letter is dated back on last Friday the night it was written.

I have no news later for you except that the paymaster was here today & paid us off. The good news from the fleet you will have in the newspapers.

I am glad to have at last your reason for hating Lincoln vs. Davis. I am not going to quarrel with you about it but wife don't you think there are some preconceived notions still lurking in your "precious bosom." I am not going to say where you got them but I think I know. You do me wrong when you charge that I exchanged Lincoln for you. Why I had you as my sweet wife long before I knew there was such a man as Lincoln. And I am sure I would not exchange my wife for all the Lincolns that could stand in a row. But you don't think him competent. It would not make any difference to me if he was not competent. For as I have often told you I care nothing about Lincoln individually, more than any other honest man, but it is the government that I hold must be maintained.

Now I advise you to read what old general Scott says on retiring from the command of the army. He says he is not a party man & did not vote for Lincoln but he considers him a man of genious, a very able man, and says that he has agreeably disappointed him, "He is a man of great ability, fidelity and patriotism," and untiring zeal & conscientiousness. In fact he could say no more praise. And that is the judgment of every man of ability, almost, democrat as well as republican, except those democrats who have or had secessionist proclivities, in other words Breckinridge democrats, and many of the ablest of them say the same.

I doubt whether we ever had a president against whom his enemies could find so little fault as the present one, notwithstanding there was never a time that required so great ability & sagacity to carry on the government as the present. And if he finishes as he has begun, history will pronounce him one of the ablest and best presidents we have ever had. Now if you will observe the next person who says the president is not fit, you will find his or her sympathies are with the south, if you scrutinize closely, notwithstanding he may say he is a union man. That is enough for the present on the Lincoln subject.

I am glad you are in such fine spirits & are so happy. I do contemplate a visit home, but as I wrote you I have no idea when it will be. Captain Henderson is on a court martial now & is absent every day. He says the court may & probably will last three or four weeks. As one commissioned officer must always be with the company I need not try to get off while the court sits. Mr. Beatty you know is always away.

I will send you about $30 by "Parke" Henderson. I would send more but I want to send Mr. McClure about $130 to pay Mrs. Irvin what I owe her. You can pay

Bentz his whole bill. You need not pay for the coal for a couple of months. After paying Bentz you will have over fifty dollars left. If I sent thirty you will have eighty. By the time that is done I think you will have more. If not you can get some out of Bank. Do [you] want to get a hog & quarter of beef.

It is very probable that the reason Cameron refused to confirm George was that somebody charged him with being a secessionist. I have been told that he was considered in Baltimore as inclining that way at the commencement of the trouble & you know how strong Minnie's feelings were that way when she first came on.

I must close,
　　　　your devoted husband that loves you
　　　　　　"as much as ever"
　　　　　　James
I forgot to say that if any letters come for me open them. If they relate to law business send them to Mr. McClure any others forward to me. The Prothonotary Benjn. Duke Esq. goes to Shippensburg every Saturday and will take anything to Mr. McClure.

Very Truly etc.
J. S. Colwell

AHC to JSC, November 15, 1861

Carlisle　Nov. 15th /61
My dear Husband,

I did not write in the beginning of the week thinking that from the tenor of a previous letter & from what Wm. Penrose said that every train might bring you & even after I had retired I would start up at the sound of carriage wheels thinking you might come that way. On Wednesday I received your two letters so I concluded to comfort myself till the court-martial would be over although Mr. Penrose told George that there was only a little "pushing" necessary for you to obtain leave which has proven itself in his case for he has visited home four or five times in three months. But today's letter has extinguished almost the last ray of hope & I will try not to set my heart on it any more & I will remember this among the many disappointments which make up my wretched life.

Mrs. Beatty was visiting me some days ago & I told her I was expecting you home so she no doubt has written to her husband to come.

I don't think the papers indicate an advance move-

Annie's letter of 15 November 1861 with tear stains. (Colwell Family Collection.)

ment excepting some New Jersey Regiments. The news from the fleet is very encouraging but I should think an additional force would be required down there to maintain our position but if the 7th Reserve is wanted I would much rather not maintain it. Sister Libby has been sitting beside me knitting & listening to my remarks on the war, the Government & infatuated officers without saying anything. She is a good deal better than I but then you know she has no dear husband who left her without saying beans whenever President Lincoln asked for 75,000 men. [There is a splotch on the page.] There are three big tears which I enclose as a memento from an aching heart.

Charley spent Monday with me on his way to Chicago. He expects to have Lizzie & the baby out there in three months. He is very much opposed to George accepting an office under Government. Adam Holliday & his wife are going to live in Chicago. Business is quite brisk there. I don't know whether Cousin Galbraith has received the Brig. Genlship. but he has received another young daughter in his family.

Our baby is sick tonight. I think he is constitutionally more delicate than any of the others. He is cutting 4 back teeth. Nan has two eye teeth to be drawn. I have taken her twice to the dentist's but she refuses to have them touched. Neidrich would like to give her ether but I'm afraid of making her nervous. John re-

quires constant watching. With your consent I would like to board some clergyman for a year who would manage & teach John. Daisy is still a little darling. I have school every evening directly after tea.

I have a bad headache tonight. I don't care about getting a hog & quarter beef. I am glad to pay Bentz. I don't want to contract any more bills & since my return here have been paying as I go. Good night. I will try & be more cheerful next time. Our pets are well excepting James.

> Ever your attached wife
> Annie

Sally Biddle told me of her visit to camp & also if she had known you were there would have sent for you. Write very often. Don't forget. Please don't be provoked at me but always remember my many weaknesses & forgive them.

JSC to AHC, November 15, 1861

Camp Pierpont Va
Near Washington D.C. 15 Nov 1861

My dear Annie,

I have not received any letter from you since I last wrote. I suppose that is because you did not receive any from me for a longer time than usual. But remember that was no fault of mine. The letter was written ready to go but no mail left camp.

I write now to let you know that I have not forgotten you for I have nothing of interest to communicate. Everything is quiet here. We had another heavy rain last night. It rained nearly the whole night. As I was officer of the day I had to stay up most of the night and although in my tent it was not very agreeable, still not so bad as being Officer of the Guard when I had to be out all the time. I have had no fire yet in my tent. If you were to sit on the balcony till bed-time, then make your bed & sleep there all night you might get some idea of what it is like. Yet I have experienced but slight inconvenience from it as yet.

The news of the operations of the fleet are more favorable than could have been anticipated and if success continues with us the war cannot be very long.

Notwithstanding the cheerlessness of my tent I had a very pleasant dream night before last. I thought I was at home not the old "our house at home" but the real present home of you & me. I had just arrived and saw your sparkling eyes and Nan with her little dancing eyes as glad as she could be and John standing off showing his two front teeth pretending not to care much but evidently as glad as any body. And poor little sedate Daisy taking it as calmly as a May morning but apparently as happy and self contented as a philosopher. James Hall I thought was very shy of me & did not seem to comprehend what it all meant. And last of all there was myself I thought happier than any of you and exceedingly glad to see you all. But I awoke and it was all a dream.

Mr. Parker Henderson has not left yet and I don't know when he will as he don't seem to know himself. I presume however he will go some day when I will send the letter which has been written for two days already. I have not heard whether Mr. Beatty has succeeded in getting his furlough. His quarters are about a mile from us. I saw Mr. Earnshaw about a week or ten days ago. His regiment is about 1/2 mile from our camp. "Ike" Parker is in the same regiment and "Bill" Brisbane is lieutenant colonel of the same. I shall hope to receive a letter from you tomorrow evening & another very soon thereafter.

I remain most sincerely
your true & faithful
husband
James

AHC to JSC, November 19, 1861

Carlisle Nov 19th 1861

You are a dear precious husband for writing me so regularly even when I was so irregular, but when I'm dispirited I can't write & my epistle would by no means be agreeable. But I'm very much disappointed in not seeing one word in your last three letters about "coming home" for that is the burden of my song. I heard nothing of the sweeping assertion which you mentioned in connexion with Mr. Penrose, & I don't believe it at all. His wife told me on Saturday what a warm feeling her husband has for you. But whether he said it or not 'tis no more nor less than what many others think & he has proven very clearly that his attachment must be very strong for his family by coming so often.

As you mentioned Mr. Sharpe I think with him it is different. He left only a wife & labored under a temporary abberation of mind in consequence & left only because others did. But we are discussing a subject of which you have always known my opinion so we will forget the past & build air-castles for the future, but I hope they will not all prove airy.

Mr. Beatty visited me this evening & handed me your letter enclosing $35.00 for which accept my thanks. In anticipation of it I paid Bentz the full amount of his bill $87.00 today. Mr. Beatty speaks encouragingly about the ending of the war or first the return of the Volunteers. He was also very gratifying in particular regarding your precious self even to the toasting of your feet at the "California furnace." He thinks you will get home. I hope by Thanksgiving. I think he looks very well. I was very glad to see him. Tomorrow will be your grand review.

What lovely nights we have. Last night in my dreams the town was being blown up & I was fleeing with our four babies out of the reach of Secession. The Kentucky body guard who are encamped here are creating quite a sensation among the young girls. Julie Watts gave a dance last week. Annie Hepburn another last night & Mrs. Biddle's in anticipation. I am sorry to tell you that Betsy Parks is going to die. She has a large tumor in her stomach & is very ill. Old Mrs. Ross is unaccountably all bruised up & Aunt Ege sick, so poor Cousin Henrietta has her hands full. The Episcopal Ch[urch] is almost finished—quite ornamental. George talks of sailing to California shortly.

View of the north-west corner of the Public Square taken from W. High Street. The three-story stone building on the left is the Washington Hotel, owned by Henry Glass from April 1859 until it burned in April of 1861. The church in the background is Saint John's Episcopal Church. The tower was built during the fall and winter of 1860-61. (Charles L. Lochman, Robin Stanford Collection, CCHS.)

Nan, John, Daisy & James are in perfect health. Young Mr. Goodyear is fully installed in your office. Mr. McClure was here tonight. Goes up tomorrow. I'm so glad to think that the War will soon end. But will you ever be happy & live quietly in a house & just have four youngsters & one Annie Colwell to review?

I was glad to hear Mr. Beatty say that you had not moved onward. Is the Court Martial over?

My dearest Husband good bye. I will always be your sincerely attached wife

Annie

AHC to JSC, December 16, 1861

Carlisle Dec. 16th /61

My dear Husband,

This afternoon I relinquished the idea of Shepley's house & told him so. He assured me that the rent would not be raised during three years, & the house not sold except in case of death or some unforeseen extraordinary cause. I was very sorry that you did not approve of the movement because it was a rare chance of getting a pleasantly situated house at so cheap a rate. Just think Mrs. Blaney's is $150.00 & not so desirable & you have misunderstood Mrs. Biddle's motives. She would prove an excellent neighbor, & then most important of all the children would have different associates. I would not rent it without your approval because husbands & wives should always try to please each other in taking any important steps in life.

Your reminiscences of our married life in yesterday's letter were sweet, sad & touching. I read them over & over again when alone & blotted out the unhappy days with my tears. My dearest husband if you had not gone to this hateful war I could have blessed you till my last hour, but it has cost me so many bitter tears & nights that indeed believe me I would have almost given my life to have prevented your going. Then I would only have remembered you as so good & domestic. Now I shall be afraid at the slightest pretext you will be off.

I wish I could induce you to resign as Mr. Penrose has done. He wrote telling his wife last evening & she is happy. He has remembered that in marrying he ought to consult his wife's happiness as well as his own. She says that neither of them care what the people say for he has done what she desired. He & Kate Sharpe had a fight before he left the last time. He told her that "he made more in his office than by soldiering." My husband don't call this a scolding. It is not. As this is the last of the year I will try to bury all my misery in oblivion if you would only manage to get home & then I would begin the New Year with many good resolutions & try to keep the "angel over my right shoulder" in view all the time.

I have been reading Mr. Chase's views on the conclusion of the war by midsummer /62. They seem plausible, though I meet & talk with a great many doubting spirits. When you come home I will try to make you so happy that you will never go again. Don't you think you can spend Christmas with us?

This morning Beck Henderson & Willie & Webbie were here. She is such a dear sweet girl & so good too. I hope your butter wont be spoiled this warm weather. I suppose you will have received your little box before this reaches you. I have nearly one of your wristlets finished. Oh I do hope you can get a furlough soon for I'm sure we can make you happy. Won't you forgive whatever you don't like in this letter?

It is very late. I must say good night. Ever your devoted wife

Annie

All the children are well. John is contemplating writing another letter. Sister Libby is well. This weather is perfect. Providence seems to smile on the Volunteers. Again good night. Hoping that you are enjoying a good sleep at this time I remain your attached wife who wants you to write as often as possible.

JSC to AHC, February 9, 1862

Camp Pierpont Va
9th Feby 1862

My dear Wife,

I received yours of the 6th inst. yesterday evening. I wrote you on the 6th enclosing ten dollars, which I hope you have received. Your dollar note came safely for which I am much obliged.

I hardly know what to tell you to send in the box, but I suppose some sausages & puddings, butter etc. would be best. I presume there are no new smoked hams cured this winter. If there were I would like to have a small one of 10 to 12 or 14 lbs not any larger. About 10 lbs sausages & 5 of puddings. If you get a ham then not so much sausage & pudding. Do not give yourself any trouble to get a ham for I do not care much about it, I only mentioned in case you have one.

You might send some pies. I know you can make as good ones as Mrs. Henderson, & two or three quarts of cranberries, good sound ones. I think we can cook them here very well. We have a pretty good cook. You might send a turkey not a large one but I don't care how fat so that it is not too poor, also a couple of chickens if you can get fat ones, but no poor ones or Shanghies. That will be enough to send. I rather think too much. If you could get small wooden boxes to put each thing in separately and enclose the whole tightly in one larger box it would answer. The tin things are very good but rather expensive. Then the small boxes should not be pine or things will taste of it. I hardly know how you can fix pies that they will not break without going to too much expense, and we must keep an eye on that.

Every pound of butter ought to be wrapped in a cloth. The butter you sent rusted the bucket wherever it touched. I suppose the salt in the butter was the

Market day on the Public Square (where Annie attended market), looking down N. Hanover Street, c.1862.
(Charles L. Lochman, Robin Stanford Collection, CCHS.)

cause. It did not damage it much but made it look to disadvantage. We had [to] only shave off a very thin slice.

As you cannot get ready to send the box till after next Saturday morning's market, before that I will write you again.

I know the getting the boxes & packing and marking is a great trouble having no man about. The last one was not very distinctly marked. The boards ought to be planed off before marking. When the last one came, a number of other ones came with it and the man turned it over several times looking at the directions and said there was none for me.

I guess you had better not trouble yourself about a ham, or if you do let the turkey & chickens go. Cook all except cranberries. It will be early enough to send the things Monday week.

I remain your affect & troublesome husband

James

CHAPTER 4

"The Battle Fearful and Terrible"

Transports on the Potomac. (*Battles and Leaders of the Civil War*, Grant-Lee Edition, CCHS.)

With high expectations in the North of an early end to the war, McClellan finally took the offensive. Moving his army by water to the peninsula between the York and James rivers in Virginia, he planned to advance on Richmond via Yorktown and Williamsburg, rather than by marching overland south from Washington. In a three-week period in March and early April 1862, more than a hundred thousand men were transported to Virginia by ship, as the Peninsula Campaign commenced.[1]

Routine drills, picket duty, warm tents, and food packages left behind, the Pennsylvania Reserves moved too. On March 10 the regiment left camp and marched to Hunter's Mills where they spent two days repairing the railroad, cut in several places by retiring Confederate troops. On March 13 they were ordered back to Alexandria. The Reserves encamped at Alexandria for three weeks, guarding the capital while troops moved by ship to the Peninsula. James wrote Annie, "I have not the least idea where we are to go nor when we will start."[2]

Camp scene near Washington. (*Battles and Leaders of the Civil War*, Grant-Lee Edition, CCHS.)

When bridges on the line of march were found to be destroyed by heavy rain, the regiment was forced to spend two days and nights marching and counter-marching, passing one night in such heavy rainfall that they could neither sleep nor dry out. Typo, the correspondent, described this march in a letter to the newspaper headed "Camp Misery." (*Shippensburg News*, 22 March 1862.)

General George Meade, a veteran of more than twenty years in the army, wrote his wife, "I do not think I have ever seen a much harder march than the one from Hunter's Mills."[3]

At Alexandria the regiment received the army's new shelter tents: a piece of canvas stretched over a ridge pole with the edges secured to the ground. Two, or at most three, could sleep under the canvas. The soldiers called them dog tents. We still call them pup tents.[4]

General McCall. Copied from a carte de visite in a Colwell Family photo album. (Colwell Family Collection.)

THE MOVEMENTS OF THE PENNSYLVANIA RESERVES CORPS.

SCENTS AND INCIDENT ALONG THE ROAD AT HUNTER'S MILLS.

THE ENCAMPMENT.

Special Correspondence of the Inquirer.

HUNTER'S MILLS; Monday, March 10, 1862.

The Pennsylvania Reserve Corps, commanded by Brigadier-General George A. McCall, left their camp this morning, at half-past one o'clock, on their march to Hunter's Mills, in accordance with orders received from the head-quarters of the Army of the Potomac. So soon as the order was received by the General, the troops were immediately put in readiness.

War news from the *American Volunteer*, 20 March 1862.

In Carlisle, Annie again succumbed to depression and anger at James for having left her. In response to what must have been a particularly unhappy letter from her, James wrote early in April:

I am sorry that you sometimes feel very bitter toward me for having come. That is one of the things I cannot understand. I can conceive how you might be sorry & grieved at me and regret it but why you should be embittered against me is past my comprehension unless you are a secessionist. I hope & trust that these moments are very brief & of rare occurrence.[5]

Two days later James wrote in response to another letter, "I could hardly get a furlough now and I presume my resignation would not be accepted at this time if tendered."[6] Their feelings about each other, however, remained strong: "It is almost three weeks since I saw your bright little eyes. How I would like to be where I could see them now," he wrote not long after returning to camp from his Christmas furlough.[7] "I sincerely wish the war was at an end and I was home with her I love above all others," James wrote in early March.[8] A few days later he wrote again, "I hope and pray your dream will be realized in all its extent. And then I shall stay with you always till you consent I shall go."[9]

As battle approached, fatalism and trust in the Almighty, derived from James's Presbyterian faith, were an integral part of his outlook:

> We expect orders every day, and I have no doubt they will come before many days. You ought not to be grieved by accounts of what the reserves are going to do.... They may be in some battles and some may be destroyed. But we must put our trust in providence. He can preserve us in all circumstances. And we cannot escape his will by any course of our own.[10]

The 7th Reserves finally left Alexandria on April 11, marched to Centreville, to Manassas Junction, and then a further twelve miles to Catlett's Station where they remained from April 17 to April 28. On April 29 they marched again, encamping at Falmouth, across the Rappahannock River from Confederate-held Fredericksburg, where they were about fifty miles from both Washington and Richmond. Lincoln ordered McDowell's corps, of which James's regiment was a part, to maintain position there to protect the capital from any swift strike by Confederate forces concentrated at Richmond. James received his first extensive views of the northern Virginia countryside, well foraged over by two hungry armies. "This is a completely poverty stricken country," he wrote in mid-March, "and still it might be middling good if properly cultivated. I think they are a shiftless set as the New England aunt in Uncle Tom's cabin observes."[11] Marching through Virginia near Manassas James wrote:

> In fact it is a beautiful country all around here.... [O]n the south side it seems to be poor while on the opposite side it seems naturally to have been good but impoverished by bad culture. At present the country is desolated. The fences for miles all gone, most of the houses deserted, and many of them destroyed. How the secesh have suffered here for their disunion principles.[12]

A few weeks later he described the area near Fredericksburg: "This country is so dilapidated and ruined. There is scarcely anything in the cultivated portions except the forest to redeem it."[13]

> James was not the only Company A soldier struck by the poor condition of the Virginia countryside. Typo wrote the *Shippensburg News*, "I have often thought, as I looked out upon the once beautiful but now desolated landscape stretched out before me, how favored by Providence has been the delightful valley of Old Mother Cumberland—'a land flowing with milk and honey.'" (*Shippensburg News*, 8 March 1862.)

Union success continued; Union troops took control of New Madrid, Missouri and nearby Island No. 10 in the Mississippi River. In a bloody two-day battle at Shiloh Church, Tennessee, on April 6 and 7, Confederate troops, nearly victorious after the first day's fighting, were forced to retire, and their commander, General A. S. Johnston, was killed. Combined casualties totaled nearly twenty-four thousand men, five times those at Bull Run and by far the heaviest casualties of the war up to that time. Most of the Union troops involved were from the West; the full cost of the war had yet to come home to the Atlantic seaboard states. On April 25 Union naval forces under Farragut took New Orleans.

While James's regiment marked time at Fredericksburg, McClellan's troops moved slowly towards Richmond. Norfolk fell on May 10. James became more confident of an early end to the war:

> I do not think now that the rebels will make a determined stand in Virginia.... It is just ten months since I left home.... I hope that the expiration of the twelve months will see it ended...& we are all safe at home. It may be a month or two more, but not longer unless our army should meet with serious reverses which might prolong the war.[14]

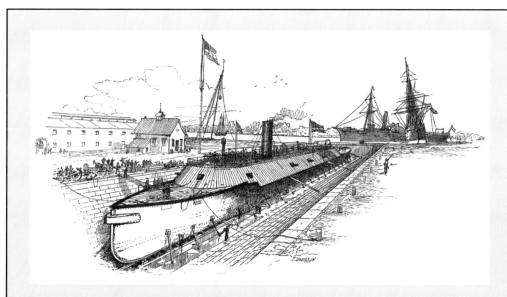

Remodeling the "Merrimac" at the Bosport Navy Yard. (*Battles and Leaders of the Civil War*, Grant-Lee Edition, CCHS.)

McClellan's troops entered Yorktown on May 4 to find that the Confederates had evacuated it the previous night. When Lincoln landed at Fort Monroe two days later, McClellan, only thirty miles away, informed the President that he was too busy to see him. Lincoln himself then prodded old General Wool, Union commander at Fort Monroe, to attack Norfolk which fell May 10, forcing Confederate sailors to scuttle the *Merrimac* so she would not fall into Union hands.[15]

Treasury Secretary Salmon P. Chase, who accompanied Lincoln to the Peninsula, called the trip "a brilliant week's campaign for the President, for I think if he had not come down, [Norfolk] would still have been in the possession of the enemy and the *Merrimac* as grim and defiant and as much a terror as ever."[16]

A few weeks later he wrote Annie in an equally optimistic vein: "And if some reverse does not occur for the Union armies the war cannot last very long."[17] A few days later, following the fall of Norfolk, James wrote Annie from camp:

> The news of the surrender of Norfolk arrived between 10 & 11 o'clock, and made a wonderful excitement. The men had all retired but got up & sent cheer after cheer from one camp to another. The bands were playing all around as far as one could hear.[18]

Local papers reflected similar optimism. "The last dying throes of Secession are becoming more and more apparent every day," proclaimed the *American Democrat* in early April.[19] After the fall of Norfolk the same paper declared, "We believe this to be the beginning of the end; the general break-up has now commenced."[20] In late April under the heading, "The End At Hand," the *Shippensburg News* declared,

> The crisis of the rebellion has been reached. Unless a great victory and the destruction of one of our great armies is achieved by the confederates within the coming two weeks, the doom of the rebellion will have been pronounced.[21]

The North had yet, however, to come to grips with the matter of slavery. Lincoln had successfully promoted bills to abolish slavery in both Washington and the territories, and the institution was increasingly seen as an evil which had to be eliminated. What would become of the slaves, poor, uneducated, owners of little more than the clothes on their backs, was not clear. In a message to Congress on March 6, 1862, Lincoln proposed government-compensated emancipation in any state which would undertake gradual abolition of slavery, a proposal aimed at the border slave states. Though Congress approved his proposal, no state initiated such a program, and there was as yet no unanimity in the North about abolition. On March 29 Wendell Phillips, the well-known abolitionist, was mobbed and driven from a stage in Cincinnati when he proclaimed himself both an abolitionist and a disunionist who favored the South leaving the Union. "The mob...pelted him with rotten eggs and stones [and] finally came down and made a rush at the stage," at which point he disappeared. While much of the anger was generated by his support for disunion, the mob's cries after the "nigger Wendell Phillips" made clear their lack of sympathy for the slaves.[22]

Bitter denunciations in Carlisle's newspapers exacerbated local differences over policy. The *Herald* described the editor of the *Volunteer*:

> This man Bratton is as cold and heartless as a snake—invulnerable to personal attack, because literally without friends. His political course has rendered him obnoxious to all loyal men.[23]

The *Volunteer* returned the compliments in its next issue, calling the *Herald* "that utterly degraded, abandoned and filthy paper, the Carlisle *Herald*," and terming the article in question the contents of a "stagnant

GLORIOUS NEWS!

Monday morning brought us glorious news. New Orleans, the telegraph informed us, had been captured by the Federal army! This is indeed, cheering intelligence, and all classes of men are congratulating each other on this signal triumph. This will be followed up by other victories very shortly. McCLELLAN is now punching the Rebels at Yorktown, and will soon, we doubt not, give them a severe trouncing. Then "On to Richmond!" With New Orleans and Richmond in our possession, the war must come to a speedy termination, and our country again united. God speed the day.

Article from the *American Volunteer*, 1 May 1862.

and putrid stomach.... [T]he sediment of the sewer and the perfume of the muskrat combined."[24]

At Falmouth the Pennsylvania Reserves passed several quiet weeks. James wrote Annie his opinions of Southerners with whom he sometimes came in contact, "The people are utterly & ignorant of everything."[25]

> All the boasting of Southerners that they can never be conquered is senseless bombast.... The Southerners are by no means as difficult to conquer as Northern men.... And this is not self-aggrandizement, as I am neither a North-man nor a South-man, but a Pennsylvanian.[26]

He was contemptuous of the South. "The Virginians," he wrote, "whether from slavery among them or some other cause, are 'a shiftless set.'" In subsequent letters he wrote again: "But they...actually seem to think it is impossible for yankees to whip southerners and it will require repeated drubbings to bring them to their senses." "Hatred of the Yankees is the predominant power.... They have no cause except the belief that they are superior & that the northerners are an inferior race of beings."[27] Such Southern opinions of the North exasperated James and he in turn wrote of the straits to which some Southerners had been reduced in equally scornful terms:

> The F.F.V.'s [First Families of Virginia] have come down wonderfully in the matter of pride or self-respect.... The misses Washington that I wrote you about some time ago...have been taking washing for the yankees, and the misses Moncure, daughters of Judge Moncure, one of the F.F.'s living here after we left camp, came with their donkies and gathered up the old cast off dirty clothing to take home.... What do you think of Southern honor now.... Southern chivalry and southern honor is played out. They must stop their boasting.[28]

On May 24, as General Johnston, commander of Confederate troops in the Richmond area, retreated, Union troops reached Mechanicsville, four miles from Richmond. But orders for McDowell's corps to move south on Richmond were canceled when Thomas J. "Stonewall" Jackson commenced a brilliant campaign in the Shenandoah Valley. Fearing an invasion of Maryland and a drive on Washington itself, Lincoln ordered most of McDowell's troops west to pursue Jackson.[29] McClellan, whose slow advance up the Peninsula had given Jackson time to mount his campaign in the Shenandoah Valley, was furious at the orders directing part of McDowell's troops to the valley, terming the action, "hypocrisy, knavery & folly."[30]

The siege of Richmond began favorably enough for the Union troops, with a vicious engagement on May 27 at Hanover Court-House north of Richmond, where Union troops drove back Confederate troops in disorder and captured seven hundred Southern prisoners. Four days later, when Confederate forces mounted a major assault against Union troops at Seven Pines, five miles east of Richmond, poorly drawn orders and lack of coordination between Confederate divisions nullified the Confederate superiority in numbers. The bloody battle which commenced on May 31 and petered out on June 1 was a stand-off. The tide of the war changed,

Burying the dead and burning horses at the Twin Houses after the second day's fight at Seven Pines. (*Battles and Leaders of the Civil War*, Grant-Lee Edition, CCHS.)

General Robert E. Lee. (*The Photographic History of the Civil War*, Francis T. Miller, 1912, CCHS.)

however, when Joe Johnston, a slow-moving, defense-minded general, was wounded and replaced by Robert E. Lee as commander of the Army of Northern Virginia.[31]

After the battle at Seven Pines, the Pennsylvania Reserves left Fredericksburg for the front at Richmond. James's company marched seven miles to the Rappahannock River on June 9, bivouacked there overnight, and boarded a steamer the next morning. Two days later the regiment disembarked at White House Landing on the Pamunkey River. James wrote Annie at length about the trip:

> There are a few handsome places along the bank of the river but very few. Only three or four villages that I saw and they miserable affairs. The white people wherever we saw them stood in grim silence. The negroes everywhere exhibit the greatest evidence of joy, waving handkerchiefs and throwing up their arms.... One man on whose farm we halted a few minutes on our march had one hundred field hands. Now he has one the rest having left. We passed a little town yesterday called Port Royal where a few days ago they shot three negroes because they were going away.
>
> One place some 20 or 30 negro girls & women went dancing & hopping along the beach a considerable distance singing.... They are poor deluded creatures.... They have a vague idea that this war is going to benefit them in some way. It may a few. But I am inclined to think it will be an injury to most of them although it may benefit their posterity & the civilization & religion of the world.[32]

Sergeant Jacob Heffelfinger of Company H, 7th Reserves, also described riverside scenes in his diary as he progressed up the Pamunkey: "The band has been on the deck all evening discoursing its best pieces, which affords infinite satisfaction to the large crowds of negro slaves. These congregate on the banks as we pass, attracted by the music; their antics are curious and laughable. Only one white person has given us any expression of welcome thus far; he waved his hat and received a hearty cheer in return. At one place, two young women advanced toward the bank to see us pass. The soldiers cheered them...but instead of returning the salutation—they turned their backs to us and giving their skirts a significant flit of disdain, advanced in another direction. They received loud, laughing shouts of derision."[33]

The effects of combat were apparent when the Pennsylvania troops disembarked at White House Landing, where rough wood coffins were piled on the wharf awaiting shipment north and buildings along the shore advertised: "Undertakers & Embalmers of the Dead. Particular Attention Paid to Deceased Soldiers."[34] That they were in the war zone soon became clear. After disembarking, the company marched twelve miles to Dispatch Station on Friday, June 13. Late that day they received hurried orders to prepare to return to White House Landing. James wrote Annie two days later:

> [T]here were reports that a large force of rebels had got round McClellan...to capture or destroy the commissary stores of which there is a large amount there. Some guerilla cavalry were along the road that we came over during the day and probably saw us. At night they burned several cars and fired on a train.[35]

On June 18 the 7th Regiment marched to a point near Mechanicsville, four miles north of Richmond, where the regiment became part of General Fitz-John Porter's command and anchored the extreme right of the Union line.

For a week James's regiment remained on the front lines facing Confederate troops defending Richmond. Both sides' pickets were visible to each other, "but neither molested the other," wrote James. When Company A came under artillery fire, their camp was moved behind some trees where Confederate spotters couldn't see them.[36] Confederate deserters came across the lines from time to time; it was thought that some came deliberately to spread misinformation, others to see what information they might gather to take back to the Confederates. Wrote James:

> Occasionally some deserters come over from the enemy. They give a doleful account of the condition of the rebels that they are living on half rations and are in a demoralized condition.... Deserters are sometimes not very reliable men, and exaggerate very much. The corporal who fired the shots at us the other day came over that night & stated that he does not aim to hurt anybody and would have been very sorry if he has done so.[37]

Food was a problem for those in the front lines. James was tired of salt meat and hard bread and wrote, "I could eat any kind of vegetables with a ravenous appetite." A few days later he wrote Annie again, "So ravenous do I feel for vegetables that I could eat a half dozzen large raw onions at a meal if I could get them."[38]

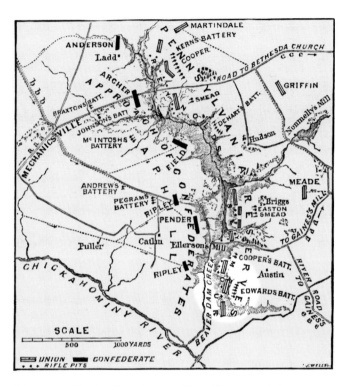

Map of the Battle of Mechanicsville. (*Battles and Leaders of the Civil War*, Grant-Lee Edition, CCHS.)

The Battle of Mechanicsville or Beaver Dam Creek saw the Federal forces defending the higher bank of the creek against Confederate assaults. Since a threat to the Federal right by Jackson's force did not materialize, the position was held with significant losses to the Confederate attackers. Once Jackson's threat was discovered, the Federals drew back to the area of Gaines' Mill and that line was cracked by Confederate attacks on the 27th of June, 1862. The position of the 7th Pa. Reserves is shown in the highlighted area.

> Leo Faller wrote the following account to his sister on June 20: "Yesterday a Rebel deserter came over to our Lines and gave himself up. He brought all his Accoutrements with him. The day we came here a little fellow came over to our lines with Richmond papers. Up to Sunday last he says he was selling them to the Rebels but as he did not sell out over there he concluded to come over to us and sell them. He was taken to Head-Quarters and the General came to the Conclusion that he was too smart a boy to let go back again and he was detained accordingly."[39]

Their letters sometimes dealt with larger issues of the war. Responding to a letter from Annie in early June, James commented:

> You seem to blame the abolitionists and the contractors with prolonging the war. The contractors no doubt would be glad to continue the war. But you do the abolitionists wrong. I am not one. And I think their cause reprehensible. But give the devil his due. It is quite fashionable to blame everything on the abolitionists.... They are for bringing the war to an end as speedily as possible, & as a general thing they are making no money out of it.

In the same letter James offered his opinion of McClellan at a time when Northern opinion regarding the general was becoming increasingly polarized:

> You seem to think that if McClellan had his way the war would be over. You often hear such sentiments.... I have nothing to say against McClellan, but I can see nothing more that he has done to entitle him to any more credit than many of our other generals. Some of them have I think exhibited more energy and military skill till this time than McClellan. If you will just take notice I think you will find that there is not a secesh sympathizer in the North that is not always praising McClellan if he praises anybody. I am willing to give him credit for anything he does. But I will wait till he does it.[40]

History would show there was good reason to be skeptical of McClellan's commitment to winning the war on the battlefield.

The bulk of enlisted men in the Union Army of the Potomac were enthusiastic supporters of McClellan. At about the same time that James expressed his opinion of McClellan in his letter, Leo Faller wrote about "our bully little General McClellen" to his family in Carlisle: "You people at home have not the least Idea of what the soldiers of this Army think of McClellen. Whenever they see him it matters nought what they are doing, wether fighting eating or doing anything else, they jump up and cheer him and cheer as long as he is in sight."[41]

Only thirty four when he was called to Washington in 1861, McClellan was an exceptional organizer and administrator, but fainthearted in battle. McClellan customarily positioned himself some distance from the actual fighting in battles and rarely took an active part in directing the movements of forces under his control. As one historian wrote, "Curiously enough, there was always something for McClellan to do more important than to fight his own battles."[42]

McClellan was quick to blame others, suspicious of conspiracies against him, and a snob. A partial explanation to his character lay in his upbringing in a wealthy, socially prominent Philadelphia family: social prejudices confirmed in his youth never left him. Always comfortable with Southerners of his own class, in 1843, while a cadet at West Point, he wrote to his brother, John: "I am sorry to say that the manners, feelings & opinions of the Southerners are far, far preferable to those of a majority of the Northerners at this place. I may be mistaken but I like them better."[43]

McClellan was contemptuous of Lincoln, considering him both socially and intellectually his inferior. "I am tired of serving fools and knaves," he wrote his wife on July 20, 1862. Three months later he wrote her again to complain of the criticism leveled at him "from men whom I know to be greatly my inferiors socially, intellectually & morally.... There never was a truer epithet applied to a certain individual [referring to Lincoln] than that of 'Gorilla.'"[44]

General George B. McClellan. (Carte de visite by D. W. Boss, Mechanicsburg, Pa., CCHS.)

Action was imminent. On June 19 James reported, "The balloon is up now examining the position of the enemy."[45] A series of bloody battles in front of Richmond began on June 25 and continued through July 1. Those battles at Oak Grove, Mechanicsville, Gaines' Mill, Savage's Station, Glendale (also known as Newmarket Road or Whiteoak Swamp), and Malvern Hill became known as The Seven Days' Battles. Although McClellan had a significant superiority in numbers, Lee's aggressive attacks unnerved the Union commander. McClellan withdrew from the front at Richmond to a new position at Harrison's Landing, eighteen miles south of Richmond on the James River, telegraphing Lincoln that his retreat was "a move to take a different base of operations."[46] The move almost became a disaster: during its retreat the Union Army was nearly cut in two at the vicious Battle of Glendale on June 30. Total Confederate casualties for all the series of battles came to 20,200; Union casualties were 15,800. Lee's will to victory was stronger than McClellan's. He had broken McClellan's spirit, forced the Union army to retreat, and changed the momentum of the war.

Professor T. S. C. Lowe's balloon, the "Intrepid," at the Battle of Seven Pines. (*Battles and Leaders of the Civil War*, Grant-Lee Edition, CCHS.)

Following Malvern Hill, the last of The Seven Days battles, at which the Confederates were driven back with heavy losses, many opposed McClellan's retreat to Harrison's Landing. General Phil Kearny, one of the Union's true fighting generals, declaimed, "I, Philip Kearny, an old soldier, enter my solemn protest against this order for retreat.... [S]uch an order can only be prompted by cowardice or treason." And General Fitz-John Porter, McClellan's friend and closest associate, advised that giving up the Union position on Malvern Hill was a terrible mistake.[47]

The Prince de Joinville, son of France's last king, Louis-Philippe, a veteran of European wars, was an admirer and unpaid member of McClellan's staff. As the Prince left the campaign to return to Europe during the army's retreat, he told General William Franklin to tell McClellan to attack "and fight a battle today; if he does, he will be in Richmond tomorrow."[48] Intent on retreating, McClellan never heeded such advice.

Battle of Malvern Hill. (*History of the Civil War in the United States*, Samuel M. Schmucker, 1865, CCHS.)

The Pennsylvania Reserves were in the thick of the murderous fight, heavily engaged at Mechanicsville, Gaines' Mill, and Glendale. They were one of the two divisions sustaining the heaviest Union losses in the battles at Richmond, suffering 3,100 casualties, approximately one-third of the division's numbers.[49] The 7th Regiment sustained 301 of those casualties.[50] On June 28, midway through the Seven Days' Battles, James wrote Annie a letter. Since she had never wanted him to go to war in the first place, he was always reticent in describing the fighting and his own participation in battle:

> We had a terrible battle on Thursday afternoon [June 26 at Mechanicsville].... The slaughter on both sides must have been great.... There were 19 in our company killed wounded & missing.... The battle may be renewed at any moment. It was fearful and terrible beyond anything you would apprehend.... The rebels fought desperately all day yesterday and at night we occupied the same ground we did when the action commenced in the morning.... Thank the Lord & his Christ that I am preserved thus far with only a slight scratch in the face.[51]

On July 6, five days after the battle at Malvern Hill, James wrote from Harrison's Landing, the site at which McClellan had established his new base after retreating from the front at Richmond:

> And oh how often & anxiously I had thought of you during those long and weary days, not knowing what moment I might be cut off from you and our dear children forever. But thanks to our Lord Jesus Christ, I am still in the land of the living.... The scenes through which I passed were terrible, but I do not feel like giving any description of them.[52]

In subsequent letters he gave a few further details of the battles. Orderly Sergeant Zimmerman had been wounded on June 30 during the battle at Glendale, and along with other wounded, he was left behind when the Union army retreated. Private David Curriden, unwounded, brother of the editor of the *Shippensburg News*, volunteered to remain behind with the wounded until Confederate medical personnel arrived to take charge of the Union wounded and transfer them to appropriate medical facilities.[53] In his July 30 letter to Annie, James provided further information regarding the role of the Reserves in the battles of The Seven Days' Battles and warned her not to believe everything she read in the local papers. "The reserves did not do all the fighting...as you suppose. You must remember that...it is Pennsylvania papers that you read." But, James wrote, the Reserves "did bravely and nobly especially in the first two battles [Mechanicsville and Gaines' Mill]." At Glendale the men "were so fatigued...that many...were scarcely able to walk." Other units, however, "did their duty nobly & bravely as the reserves."[54] Confirming the severity of the battles and the respect in which Confederate troops were held by Union soldiers, Leo Faller wrote home on July 12, "If anyone tells you that the Rebels will not fight just tell them to come down to this neck of the country and try them on."[55]

CARLISLE FENCIBLES, CAPT. HENDERSON'S COMP. A, 7TH REG'T. INFANTRY.

Wounded in Action—Present.

Capt. Henderson, left shoulder, June 30.
Sergt. W. R. Holmes, hand, June 26.
John G. Spangenberg, side, June 26.

Wounded in Action and put on Board the Boat for Fortress Monroe.

W. B. Culp, arm and thigh, June 27.
John S. Humer, left breast, " "
W. A. Ensminger, left hand, " 30.
John L. Waggoner, arm, " "
Wilson Burkholder, temple, " "

Wounded—Missing in Action.

Sergt. W. Zimmerman, left breast, (field hospital,) June 30.
W. Wyre, left leg, (field hospital,) June 30.
H. L. Hecker, arm and foot, (field hospital,) June 27.
Sergt. John E. Burkholder, wounded and left on battle-field, June 27.
Corp. Wm. B. Hubley, forehead, left on battle field, June 27.

Missing in Action.

James L. Halbert, June 30.
John T. Harris, June 27.
John H. Hendricks, "
Jesse B. Humer, "
John A. Natcher, "
Samuel E. Smith, "

Reported Killed in Action.

David Haverstick, June 27.
Jacques Noble, "
Jacob L. Meloy, June 30.

List of losses and injuries, *American Democrat*, 23 July 1862.

A PRISONER.—DAVID D CURRIDEN—a brother of the editor of this paper—belonging to Capt. Henderson's company, from this county, was taken prisoner at the recent battle before Richmond. At the close of the battle on Monday, he was left to take care of several of his wounded comrades, when they were surrounded by a body of rebels and conveyed to Richmond. Mr. Barnet Hubly, a member of the same company, whose name appears among the list of prisoners, is said to have been wounded in the head by a grape shot.—*Shippensburg News*.

Notice from the *American Volunteer*, 17 July 1862.

James wrote Annie little of his own activities during battle. A hint of those activities may be gained from a letter written him on August 4 from Shippensburg by A. H. Wolf, father of Edgar Wolf, a private in Company A. Wolf wrote to ask James's help in having Edgar promoted from private. In a fulsome letter, having no doubt heard of the battles from his son, Wolf wrote:

> Respected and Honured Sir.... I admire the heroic act of bravery in one of our own fellow citizens who picked up the standard of our country's honour whose bearer had been pierced with the enemy's bullet & bore aloft as I have been cribly informed with a strong arm & a brave heart unfurled it to the breeze in the face of a desperate foe during the remainder of the day, and in that person who was none less than your humble self for which you fully merit the admiration of your countrymen.[56]

No hint of any such heroics ever appeared in James's letters to Annie. Edgar Wolf never was promoted from private.

Wolf's entreaty on behalf of his son was not uncommon. Company officers were expected to help those at home who had family members serving in their companies. Mrs. E. M. Holmes, mother of "Dear Son William," a private in Company A who had been wounded in the hand during The Seven Days' Battles, asked James to take special care of her son, and concluded, "Excuse a Mother's fond weakness." On September 3, 1862, Annie wrote, "If you know anything of a Charley Holbert in Co A, please tell me as his mother is very anxious not having heard for more than a month." A few days later she wrote of a visit from a Mrs. Long who was "in a great state of excitement regarding her son," from whom she had not recently heard. "She wishes you to make inquiries about him & let me know whether he is well."[57]

Illustration from a Civil War letter dated 8 June 1864. (Manuscript Collection, CCHS.)

William R. Holmes, who served in Company A under James Colwell. (D. Scott Hartzell Collection, U.S. Army Military History Institute.)

Two excerpts from Mrs. E. M. Holmes's letter to James Colwell, dated 22 July 1862.

But if some bore the nightmare of battle without running, others did not. The army was by this time used to enlisted men disappearing from the front lines; men who ran from battle one day often performed valiantly the next day. The opinions of others, both fellow soldiers and civilians, played a role in curbing desertion and flight from battle. Said one soldier, "I don't want to be shot in the back. Oh my oh, I'd never tell of it at home."[58]

Enlisted men, generally understanding of their fellows who sought to avoid battle, were not so tolerant of their officers. Officers who showed fear in battle or actual cowardice permanently lost the respect of those they commanded. Thus it was with Colonel Harvey, commander of the 7th Regiment. The regiment's official history merely indicates that at Gaines' Mill, "Early in the engagement Colonel Harvey became separated from his regiment," and that "On the 4th of July Colonel Harvey resigned."[59] James, however, related the specific reason for Harvey's resignation in a letter to Annie:

> It is true that Col Harvey has resigned. I presume he did so to prevent being dismissed. He did not behave well in the battle-field.... The fact is that a great many of the officers who have resigned have done so because they received hints—sometimes very broad ones—that it would be to their credit to do so. They were not wanted.[60]

In his next letter James wrote further:

> Father Hunt [Regimental Chaplain] followed Col. Harvey. He was of no account. Nobody had any respect for him.... He was in the army for the pay. Nothing else.... [N]obody regrets it.... He was no honor to the cause he professed to serve.[61]

Colonel Elisha B. Harvey. (D. Scott Hartzell Collection, U.S. Army Military History Institute.)

Generally there was little publicity in the press about individuals, whether men or officers, who exhibited cowardice in battle. But the facts surrounding Harvey's resignation soon became known. In a lengthy article summarizing the activities of Company A since the start of the war, the *Shippensburg News* reported three months later, "On the 31st July Col. E. B. Harvey was dismissed from the service for cowardice in the battles on the Peninsula."[62]

After the battles, articles in the local papers recounted the resignations of a number of officers without immediately identifying the cause. When Annie wrote James suggesting he resign, he responded that only officers who had exhibited incompetence or cowardice in battle had resigned. "I do not know of one [officer] who had good health and was considered a meritorious officer whose resignation has been accepted."[63] When Colonel Harvey resigned on July 4, the regiment's Lieutenant Colonel, H. C. Bolinger, was promoted to colonel, and Captain R. M. Henderson of James's Company A was appointed lieutenant colonel. James was himself promoted to captain and now commanded Company A. Almost immediately, however, James was detailed to act as brigade quartermaster during the absence of the regular quartermaster who had gone home on sick leave.

Colonel Henry C. Bolinger. (D. Scott Hartzell Collection, U.S. Army Military History Institute.)

The 7th regiment has been re-organized since the engagements before Richmond, in which it bore so conspicuous a part.—Its field officers now are Col. H. G. Bolinger, of Lock Haven; Lieut. Col. Robert M. Henderson, of Carlisle; Major C. H. Lyman, of Lock Haven. Under these officers we are confident the regiment will be rapidly restored to a high state of discipline and efficiency. Our young men cannot do better than join the ranks of the 7th.

Excerpt from an article,
American Democrat,
20 Aug. 1862.

Promoted.—We are pleased to learn that Sergeant S. V. Ruby, of the Carlisle Fencibles, has been promoted to a Second Lieutenancy in that company. The officers of the company now are J. S. Colwell, Captain, and Messrs. Beatty and Ruby, Lieutenants—Capt. Henderson having been promoted to Lieutenant Colonel.

Promotion notice,
American Democrat,
27 Aug. 1862.

"Capt. Henderson has been promoted to the Lieutenant Colonelcy of his (the 7th) regiment; Lieutenant Colwell to the Captaincy, Second Lieutenant Beatty to the First Lieutenancy, and Sergt. Ruby to the Second Lieutenancy. These are all worthy promotions.... Capt. Henderson and Lieut. Colwell won unfading laurels in the battles before Richmond and proved their capacity to command and their courage to face the enemy's fire." (*Shippensburg News*, 16 August 1862.)

1st Lieutenant Samuel V. Ruby. (D. Scott Hartzell Collection, U.S. Army Military History Institute.)

This post kept James absent from his company and regiment. He described his quartermaster unit to Annie as comprising twenty-three wagon teams, two horse-drawn ambulances, thirty-three men, and blacksmith, carpenter, and saddler shops, but "the shops are only tents and the stock of tools very light."[64] When Annie wrote that she hoped that as a quartermaster James would avoid the fighting, he responded,

> You are mistaken about quartermaster's not having fighting to do. That is true to some extent.... [I]t is true that when the wagon trains are moving...the quartermaster must be with his train. But then it is also true that the enemy always shell the trains...as they contain the provisions...and other valuable stores. Still as a general thing it is not as dangerous I suppose as commanding a company in the field.[65]

James's optimism about an early end to the war was waning. On July 6 he wrote, "When this war will be ended it is difficult to say now.

It will probably be two or three months but I trust it will not be very long."[66] A month later he wrote, "I believe the war can be ended before six months expire if it is conducted energetically."[67] Two weeks later he wrote how much he wished to see her. "My sincere hope is that this boon may be vouchsafed to me before many months."[68]

Following the reverses on the Peninsula, Lincoln issued a call for three hundred thousand more troops and subsequently threatened that if any state failed to meet its assigned quota of additional troops, the deficiency would be made up by a draft. On July 8 Lincoln himself went to the Peninsula to talk with McClellan, and after discerning McClellan's weak commitment to victory, concluded that a general with more resolution would be required. When Lincoln returned to Washington three days later, he named General Henry Halleck general-in-chief of the army. Halleck arrived in Washington July 23, proceeded to the Peninsula to meet with McClellan, and ordered McClellan to withdraw his army to the Washington area a week later. Confederate success on the Peninsula, due both to McClellan's ineptitude as a military leader and to Lee's mastery of the same craft, helped to produce a conclusion neither general desired. For Northern opinion began to change: fewer voices were raised thereafter in the North to promote a negotiated, gentlemanly end to the war which would permit the continued existence of slavery in the South.

In Carlisle the magnitude of the casualty lists from the battles in front of Richmond had a powerful impact, reinforcing determination to see the war through to a victorious end. Under the headline, "Our Fallen Brave," the Carlisle *Herald* reported the casualties on the Peninsula on July 11: "It is with a heavy heart, and a trembling hand, that we sit down to record the names of those of our fellow-citizens who...have fallen." In the same issue the paper applauded Lincoln's call for more troops. "To Arms, Ye Brave," resounded an editorial:

> Our brothers call upon us to reinforce them. Shall we leave them in this, their dire extremity.... The very bones of those slain in the swamps of the Chickahominy, would rise up and rebuke us. Let us then, at once commence recruiting, and before another week we can have another company from old Cumberland on its way to the rescue.[69]

Attitudes in the North hardened: in a subsequent issue, emphasizing its opinion in capital letters, the *Herald* proclaimed in uncompromising terms:

> WE ARE FOR THE UNION AS IT IS, AND THE ENFORCEMENT OF THE LAWS AS THEY ARE, UNTIL EVERY REBEL LAYS DOWN HIS ARMS, IS KILLED IN BATTLE OR HUNG.... "NO COMPROMISE—NO DELUSIVE CRY OF PEACE; THE NATION SHALL BE PRESERVED."[70]

Even the *Volunteer* muted its criticism of the Administration. On July 17 Bratton editorialized:

THE NEW CALL FOR TROOPS.—We publish in another column the President's call for 300,000 fresh troops to put down this hellish rebellion. It will be received with acclamation everywhere. We must finish this work thoroughly and speedily, and to do it, more men are needed. The governors of the various states have come forward, urging this course, and the response of the people will prove that there is no want of the same patriotism that has already sent forward more than half a million of brave men to fight the battles of the Union. The call of Governor Curtin for Pennsylvania's quota of the new levy will probably be issued immediately. Let the answer be prompt and honorable to our old Commonwealth.

Call for troops, *American Democrat*, 9 July 1862.

Patriots ! Unionists ! lovers of Freedom ! this must not be ! You must heroicly prevent it ! Resolve now that the needed force shall be raised promptly and fully—you that are of proper age and full vigor must volunteer, while the infirm or superanuated must freely contribute of their substance to sustain the families of those who peril their lives for the country ! Resolve to do it at once !

Hours are precious. Some great disaster may befall us while we are getting ready to avert it. You who can possibly be spared and are able to fight, let not a day be lost in offering your services to your distracted, imperiled country.

Excerpt from an article, *Carlisle American*, 9 July 1862.

The present fratricidal war has been prolific in horror, suffering and death.... Our glorious Union...rent in twain; brother arrayed against brother.... The work of death still goes on.... The stern Moloch of war demands more victims; and it is likely to obtain them.... What will the end be? The belligerent resolutions passed by some of the Southerners never to surrender, are but little better than paper bullets.... [O]ur country will develop on its own traditions of human liberty, regardless of the intrigues of Southern demagogues.[71]

Like most Union soldiers, James agreed with the president's call for more troops: "I think the president ought also to draft...all the men he has power by law to do." The war would soon be over, he added, "if the government would put 500,000 or more men in the field."[72]

Second Lieutenant Ekuries Beatty, wounded during The Seven Days' Battles, and promoted to first lieutenant when James was promoted to captain, was sent home to Carlisle on combined convalescent leave and recruiting duty. Under the headline, "Cumberland County Boys—To the Rescue," all the local papers printed Beatty's notice in July and August:

> Company A. 7th Regiment, Pa. Reserve Corps. will need at least THIRTY RECRUITS.... Young men, your country calls you to arms! Let not the call be made in vain, but let every young man of spirit and patriotism respond promptly to the appeal...and the black banner of Treason and Rebellion will soon be trailing in the dust.
>
> E. BEATTY[73]

The initial response to Lincoln's call for three hundred thousand additional troops was disappointing. Several state governors, including Governor Curtin of Pennsylvania, indicated that they would utilize the draft if their state quotas were not filled by volunteers.

FILL UP THE OLD REGIMENTS!— Within the last week, Recruiting Officers have been sent off, from we presume every regiment in the Army of the Potomac, to enlist volunteers to fill up the ranks of the old regiments. Lieut. BEATTY, of Carlisle, with a detail of non-commissioned officers and privates, has been put on duty as Recruiting Officer for the 7th regiment of our noble Pa. Reserve Corps. We hope he may be successful. In case the old regiments are not filled up by volunteers prior to the 1st of September, they will be filled by draft. To drafted men no bounties or advance pay are given. But volunteers who enlist for the war will receive the $100 Government bounty and the first month's pay in advance. It will be good policy, therefore, to volunteer at once for the old regiments, thereby securing not only the bounties, but the advantages of going into the field under skillful officers who have the experience which enables them to take good care of their men.

Article from the *American Democrat*, 20 Aug. 1862.

The *Herald* reported a typical enrollment incident in St. Louis: "Considerable excitement took place at St. Louis on Friday, in consequence of the enrollment of militia. Many persons ran to the British Consul's office to claim the protection of the British flag, in order to be exempt under the recent order of the Governor." (Carlisle *Herald*, 1 August 1862.)

To prevent such activity Secretary of War Stanton ordered the arrest of any person subject to the draft who went abroad or absented himself from his county or state before the actual draft might be made and the arrest and imprisonment of any person who "by any act of speech or writing" attempted to discourage volunteer enlisting. The writ of habeas corpus was suspended "in respect to all persons arrested for disloyal practices." Orders issued August 8, 1862 by Secretary of War Edwin M. Stanton, quoted in *Carlisle American*, 13 August 1862.

Edwin M. Stanton. (*Civil War Illustrations*, reprints, Carol Grafton, 1995.)

Governor Curtin ordered that an organization be established in each county in Pennsylvania to register all those of draft age in case insufficient volunteers came forward. James's law partner, R. P. McClure of Shippensburg, who had been appointed head of Cumberland County's draft board, ordered all eligible males between the ages of eighteen and forty-five subject to military duty to enroll.

However much the armies might fight, march, and counter-march across the face of the country, Northern opinion increasingly recognized slavery itself as the crux of the war. On July 22 Lincoln presented his cabinet with a preliminary draft of the Emancipation Proclamation. Although it met with general approval, the president was temporarily dissuaded from promulgating it by Secretary of State Seward, who argued that the proclamation might be considered an act of desperation following the reverse on the Peninsula and urged Lincoln to wait for a victory.[74]

The matter was brought home strongly to Carlisle that summer as the ebb and flow of war across northern Virginia induced thousands of former slaves to flee across Union lines to free states in the North. "Contrabands are constantly pouring in," reported a soldier's letter to the *Herald*. "They all evince inexpressible delight at getting within the Federal Lines."[75] It was not only in the front lines that contrabands began to materialize. In late May and early June, when Stonewall Jackson's successes in the Shenandoah Valley drove Union forces back to the Potomac at Harper's Ferry, some five thousand blacks followed the retreating troops north. In Maryland the Shenandoah Valley becomes the Cumberland Valley and continues northeastward into Pennsylvania. Carlisle lies in the middle of the Cumberland Valley only eighty miles north of Harper's Ferry. Former slaves moving north inevitably reached Carlisle in large numbers. On May 30 the *Herald* reported of Carlisle:

> CONTRABANDS.—Large numbers of the bipeds are arriving daily from the regions of Jeffdom.... A fine young fellow...tells us that he was the slave of a man named Queen [who left] his plantation and slaves in the care of a black foreman. On the advent of the Union forces, these slaves—foreman and all, concluded to tear themselves away from the Arcadia of Dixie; and here they are. Who blames them?[76]

A few proposals to deal with this influx appeared in the Carlisle newspapers. The *American Democrat*, Carlisle's Union-supporting Democratic paper, wrote in a different vein about "The Negro Exodus," as the paper termed it, in early June:

> A small minority of them may have industry and management sufficient to enable them to make a living, but the great body of them will speedily become a burthen upon the community.... We think it is high time for the people of this state to devise some means of protecting them against this evil.—We are in favor of a law preventing any negroes from coming into this State with the design of settling.[77]

☞ R. P. M'CLURE, Esq., of Shippensburg, has been appointed Commissioner for Cumberland county, to enroll those subject to be drafted for the army. He will be assisted by numerous deputies, all of whom will enter upon their duties at once. All persons to whom application is made for information are bound, under severe penalties, to afford the officer every facility for the faithful performance of his duty.

Notice from the *American Volunteer*, 28 Aug. 1862.

On June 2 Leo Faller wrote home to his sister, "There are four Contrabands in our Company;" all were serving as cooks for different messes.[78]

James wrote Annie at the same time, "We have got a contraband as cook and he seems to get along pretty well." (JSC to AHC 4 June 1862.)

The same week the *Carlisle American*, a pro-Administration paper, editorialized in a similar vein:

> WHAT SHALL WE DO WITH THE NEGROES?—This is a question which is seriously agitating the minds of the working classes in our midst. The great influx of contrabands has only commenced, but loud are the complaints against them. While the white laborer commands but poor requite for his toil, that of the negro comes in, and, in some instances, takes his place.... It is time steps were taken to prevent this influx of negroes.[79]

More significant was the beginning of discussion regarding blacks serving in the Union armies, as Northern opinion about the ultimate goal of the war was changing from maintenance of the Union to the abolition of slavery. If blacks could serve in the army, it was clear that the pre-war society of the country was being transformed. The *Herald* reprinted a significant editorial from the New York *World*, a strongly Democratic paper:

> The study is no longer to be how to carry on this war with the least damage to slavery. The old infatuation of...measuring the force of the blow so as to hit the rebellion, if possible, and yet by all means strike clear of the peculiar institution, is to be given up. Many of us would like to see this style of doing things succeed, but unfortunately...secesh is at our throat.... [T]his sort of chivalry will hardly apply to warfare on a large scale, especially where a nation's life is concerned.... [W]e will strike from the shoulder straight out at secesh, even though it prove a finisher, not only to itself, but its beloved.[80]

It was the *World* which had ridiculed the idea the previous December, editorializing, "*The Secesh are upon us. Ho! Niggers to the Rescue.*"

The hardening of opinion in the North took concrete form on July 12 when Congress enacted legislation providing that all those who joined in the rebellion would be subject to fine, imprisonment, and the loss of their slaves. Escaped slaves or those captured would be forever free. A few weeks later Lincoln publicly replied to Horace Greeley, editor of the New York *Tribune*, who complained that Lincoln was too soft on slavery. "I would save the Union," wrote Lincoln in his famous response.

> If I could save the Union without freeing *any* slave, I would do it; and if I could save it by freeing *all* the slaves, I would do it, and if I could save it by freeing some and leaving others alone I would also do that.... I have here stated my purpose according to my view of *official* duty; and I intend no modification of my oft expressed *personal* wish that all men could be free.[81]

Lincoln was disingenuous. He had already determined to issue the preliminary Emancipation Proclamation and was only waiting for a favorable moment to do so.

Failure on the Peninsula had changed the dynamics of the war. Pessimism prevailed in the North, and the stirrings of foreign opinion

> THE PRESIDENT REFUSES TO ACCEPT NEGRO SOLDIERS.—A deputation of Western men called upon the President last Monday to tender the services of two regiments of colored soldiers. They were attentively heard, but the President positively declines to put arms in the hands of negroes. He says it would be the signal for the Border States to turn against the Union, and we cannot afford to lose them. He intends to carry out the Emancipation and Confiscation acts thoroughly; and press the war with the utmost vigor; he will employ all slaves in any available manner except as fighting men.

Article from the *American Volunteer*, 14 Aug. 1862.

were closely watched. In a lengthy editorial headed "Will England Interfere?" the *Shippensburg News* reported the announcement by a Tory member of the British Parliament that he would introduce a motion on July 12 "that the Government be called upon to put an end to the war in America by mediation or otherwise." The editorial continued by quoting the London *Post*, "the organ of Lord Palmerston," the British Prime Minister:

> Should folly still reign supreme, should three hundred thousand men be levied, and should another invasion of the Southern Confederacy be projected, it will then remain for neutral states to determine whether the South has not by its recent prowess established its claim to be independent.[82]

As the hot summer of 1862 rolled on, the South went on the offensive and the Union army was recalled from the Peninsula. While determination to pursue the war to a successful conclusion did not flag, gloom prevailed throughout the North over the Union's immediate prospects.

Endnotes

[1] The best summary of the Peninsula Campaign is Stephen W. Sears, *To the Gates of Richmond* (New York: Ticknor & Fields, 1992).

[2] JSC to AHC 21 March 1862.

[3] George Meade, *The Life and Letters of George Gordon Meade* (New York: Charles Scribner's Sons, 1913), 252.

[4] JSC to AHC 21 March 1862 and 30 May 1862. Sypher, *Pennsylvania Reserve Corps*, 169.

[5] JSC to AHC 6 April 1862.

[6] JSC to AHC 8 April 1862.

[7] JSC to AHC 19 January 1862.

[8] JSC to AHC 9 March 1862.

[9] JSC to AHC 23 March 1862.

[10] JSC to AHC 25 March 1862.

[11] JSC to AHC 13 March 1862.

[12] JSC to AHC 13 April 1862.

[13] JSC to AHC 13 May 1862.

[14] JSC to AHC 6 April 1862.

[15] Sears, *Gates of Richmond*, 89-91.

[16] Salmon P. Chase, *Inside Lincoln's Cabinet: The Civil War Diaries of Salmon P. Chase*, ed. David Donald (New York: Longmans, Green & Co., 1954), 85.

[17] JSC to AHC 7 May 1862, postscript dated 9 May.

[18] JSC to AHC 13 May 1862.

[19] *American Democrat*, 2 April 1862.

[20] *American Democrat*, 14 May 1862.

[21] *Shippensburg News*, 26 April 1862.

[22] Carlisle *Herald*, 4 April 1862.

[23] Carlisle *Herald*, 2 May 1862.

[24] *American Volunteer*, 8 May 1862.

[25] JSC to AHC 13 April 1862.

[26] JSC to AHC 17 April 1862.

[27] JSC to AHC 20 April 1862, 7 May 1862, 9 May postscript, and 22 May 1862. In the May 22 letter James also wrote, "It is pretty certain that Genl Anderson (our cousin) is in command over there. I could probably see him by an hour or two's ride, but I think I will postpone the visit till I get a larger party along." James had the wrong Anderson. The Confederate commander at Fredericksburg was Brigadier General Joseph R. Anderson, not R. H. Anderson, husband of Annie's cousin, Sallie Gibson Anderson.

[28] JSC to AHC 27 May 1862.

[29] Sears, *Gates of Richmond*, 110. For Jackson's 1862 campaign in the Shenandoah Valley see John C. Waugh, *The Class of 1846* (New York: Warner Books, 1994), 275-338.

[30] Letter from McClellan to wife, 25 May 1862. Quoted in Sears, *Gates of Richmond*, 111.

[31] Sears, *Gates of Richmond*, 138-140.

[32] JSC to AHC 11 June 1862.

[33] "Jacob Heffelfinger Diaries," U.S. Military History Institute, Carlisle Barracks, Carlisle, Pa., 61.

[34] "Robert Taggart Diary," 14 June 1862, and memoir, Pennsylvania Historical and Museum Commission. Quoted in Sears, *Gates of Richmond*, 163.

[35] JSC to AHC 15 June 1862. What James had encountered was J.E.B. Stuart's famous ride around the Union army outside Richmond. By the time James's company was put on the alert, however, Stuart had already passed to the south as his cavalry troop circled McClellan's forces. Sears, *Gates of Richmond*, 167-173.

[36] JSC to AHC 22 June 1862.

[37] JSC to AHC 24 June 1862.

[38] JSC to AHC 15 June 1862 and 24 June 1862.

[39] *Dear Folks at Home*, 78.

[40] JSC to AHC 4 June 1862.

41 *Dear Folks at Home*, 81.

42 Francis W. Palfrey, Military Historical Society of Mass., *Peninsular Campaign*, 96. Quoted in Sears, *Gates of Richmond*, 81. For other assessments of McClellan's character see Warren W. Hassler, Jr., *General George B. McClellan, Sword of the Union* (Baton Rouge: Louisiana State University Press, 1957); Catton, *Terrible Swift Sword*; Joseph P. Cullen, *The Peninsula Campaign, 1862* (Harrisburg, Pa.: Stackpole Books, 1973); Stephen W. Sears, *George B. McClellan: The Young Napoleon* (New York: Ticknor & Fields, 1988); James M. McPherson, *Battle Cry of Freedom* (New York: Oxford University Press, 1988); and Waugh, *Class of 1846*.

43 Letter dated 21 January 1843, George B. McClellan, Jr. Papers, Manuscript Division, Library of Congress, Washington, D.C., quoted in Waugh, *Class of 1846*, 41.

44 *The Civil War Papers of George B. McClellan: Selected Correspondence, 1860-1865*, ed. Stephen W. Sears (New York: Ticknor & Fields, 1989), 368, 515.

45 JSC to AHC 22 June 1862.

46 McClellan, *Civil War Papers*, ed. Sears, 339.

47 Sears, *Gates of Richmond*, 338.

48 General William B. Franklin, *Battles and Leaders of the Civil War*, 4 vols. (New York: The Century Co., 1887; repr., Secaucus, N.J., n.d.), vol. 2, 382.

49 Sears, *Gates of Richmond*, 345.

50 Samuel P. Bates, *Pennsylvania Volunteers*, vol. 1, 725.

51 JSC to AHC 28 June 1862.

52 JSC to AHC 6 July 1862.

53 JSC to AHC 21 July 1862.

54 JSC to AHC 30 July 1862.

55 *Dear Folks at Home*, 82-85.

56 A. H. Wolf to JSC 4 August 1862. The incident described in the letter may have occurred at the battle of Glendale when every man in the color guard of the 7th Regiment went down. Sears, *Gates of Richmond*, 298.

57 Mrs. E. M. Holmes to JSC 22 July 1862; AHC to JSC 3 September 1862; AHC to JSC 8 September 1862.

58 Alexander Bates, Hummelstown [Pa.] *Sun*, 19 July 1895.

59 Bates, *Pennsylvania Volunteers*, vol. 1, 724-725.

60 JSC to AHC 30 July 1862.

61 JSC to AHC 3 August 1862.

62 *Shippensburg News*, 11 October 1862.

63 JSC to AHC 30 July 1862.

64 JSC to AHC 30 July 1862.

65 JSC to AHC 3 August 1862.

66 JSC to AHC 6 July 1862.

67 JSC to AHC 8 August 1862.

68 JSC to AHC 21 August 1862.

69 Carlisle *Herald*, 11 July 1862.

70 Carlisle *Herald*, 1 August 1862.

71 *American Volunteer*, 17 July 1862.

72 JSC to AHC 25 July 1862.

73 Carlisle *Herald*, 25 July 1862.

74 Gideon Welles, *Diary of Gideon Welles* (Boston: Houghton Mifflin Company, 1909), 70-71. For a more detailed history of the Emancipation Proclamation see John Hope Franklin, *The Emancipation Proclamation* (Garden City, N.Y.: Doubleday & Co., 1963).

75 Carlisle *Herald*, 30 May 1862.

76 Carlisle *Herald*, 30 May 1862.

77 *American Democrat*, 4 June 1862.

78 *Dear Folks at Home*, 72.

79 *Carlisle American*, 4 June 1862.

80 Carlisle *Herald*, 8 August 1862, quoting the New York *World*.

81 Quoted in the Carlisle *Herald*, 29 August 1862.

82 *Shippensburg News*, 2 August 1862. Charles Francis Adams, the American Minister to Britain, thought Lord Palmerston had been "hostile all along." Charles Francis Adams [Jr.], *Charles Francis Adams* (Boston: Houghton, Mifflin & Co., 1900), 250.

Letters 4:
March 1862 – July 1862

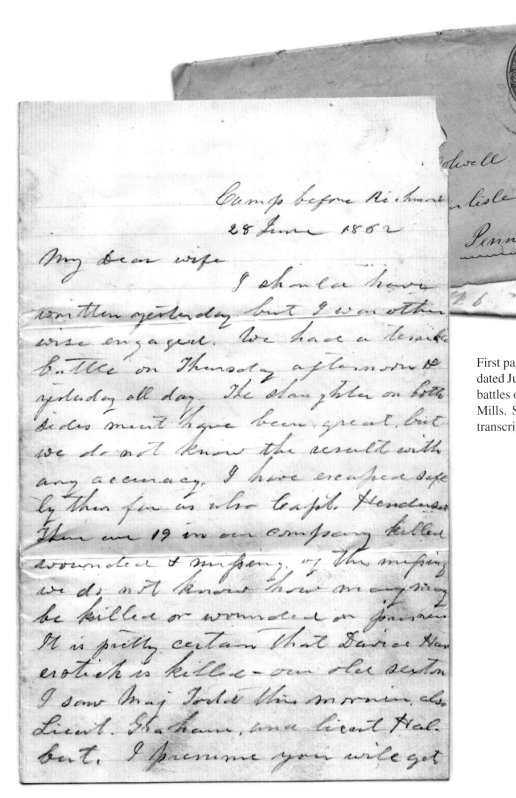

First page of James's letter to Annie, dated June 28, 1862, and written after the battles of Mechanicsville and Gaines' Mills. See page 119 for a complete transcription.

Soldiers marching in the rain on their way to Fair Oaks, Virginia. (*Battles and Leaders of the Civil War*, Grant-Lee Edition, CCHS.)

DIED.

On the 12th inst., WILLIAM M. HENDERSON Jr., Son of Major William M. Henderson, aged 25 years.

(The deceased was a member of his brother's (Capt. R. M. HENDERSON) Company, at Camp Pierpont where he contracted a cold, which settled on his lungs, and reached home only two weeks before his death. He was a most estimable young man, a kind son and brother, and a brave soldier.)

Death notice of William Henderson, Jr., *Carlisle American*, 19 March 1862.

JSC to AHC, March 17, 1862

Near Alexandria Va
17th March 1862

My Dear wife,

I was truly glad to receive your two letters of the 13th & 14th inst. yesterday evening or rather last night. I had heard nothing from you directly for more than a week. I received a letter from Sister Libby while at Hunter's Mills. I wrote to you twice from there.

On Thursday morning about 5 o'clock we received orders to pack up & in 15 minutes we were on the road to Alexandria. We marched that night to a place near Jackson's mills where we arrived about 10 or 11 o'clock at night where we lay or sat till morning a slow drizzling rain all night, but we had fires. The next morning we were in line half past six. But it having been ascertained that a couple of bridges on our direct route had been destroyed, after standing about 1 1/2 hours in the rain we turned back the way we had come for about two miles and marched to within three miles of our old Camp Pierpont then took off for the Alexandria Pike.

And such a march. The roads were almost impassable, and the rain poured down almost in torrents. We trudged on however till about 4 o'clock P.M. when we halted in a pine woods. With great difficulty we got up some fires. I held the end of a gum blanket over while others kindled the fire till my fingers were quite benumbed. After we got the fire under way we had that comfort but the rain continued to pour down till we were drenched completely. In fact we were drenched before we halted. I sat all night by the fire without a minute's sleep. At about 10 or 11 o'clock it ceased raining but every place was too wet to lie down, and I preferred sitting up although I slept none

the night before except about 10 minutes.

I got my clothes pretty well dried out by morning only one stocking. I took off one boot & wrung out the stocking & dried it, but such a labor had I to get my boot on again that I left the other one on to dry itself. At ten o'clock yesterday morning we started again and got here in the evening. I had two crackers & some coffee for breakfast yesterday was all I had till about sundown, when I got my supper at a house near camp.

I was sorry to hear of Will Henderson's death. I had not the slightest idea that he was so ill. He was very delicate as I have learned since we came into the army. He should not have come. Another month of such times as we had last week would use up a good many men.

We are here now waiting to be shipped south. We expected to go on board as soon as we would arrive here, but it is said there is not sufficient coal for the steamer and we must await its arrival. We may go tomorrow—we may not go for several days. I am in hopes you have a letter on the way that will reach me before we start. When I will have an opportunity of writing you again I cannot say. I do not know where we are going. Some say to join Burnside. Others name other points. I presume the better way for you to direct a letter would be to me Co. A, 7 Regt, P.R.V.C., McCall's Division, near Washington City. I presume letters will be sent after us. Write often. I will do so as often as I can find opportunity.

My prayer to God & heart's desire is that he may protect us all and that we may meet again in peace & happiness & so live many years.

Your truly devoted husband
James

Since commencing this letter I have seen Mr. Beatty & he says that he saw Sam Clelans & he told him he was going to send my trunk home by express. I hope he will. I will send the key if I get an opportunity. Sam's wife lives in Carlisle. If the trunk does not come see her where Sam is or write to him about it. If the key don't arrive some time soon you can get Healey to pick the lock.

Fairfax Courthouse, Virginia. (*Battles and Leaders of the Civil War,* Grant-Lee Edition, CCHS.)

JSC to AHC, April 13, 1862

Camp Near Manassas Junction Va
13 April 1862

My Dear wife,

I wrote you last on Thursday evening I believe. I have heard nothing since from you. We will probably get a mail from Washington tomorrow or next day. I write today but do not know what day it will get mailed.

We left our old camp near Alexandria on Friday morning at six o'clock A.M. We took the road to Fairfax courthouse on foot, & march to a place about six miles south of F.C. where we bivouacked for the night. Next morning we started at six o'clock for Centreville & Manassas junction, and arrived here about the middle of the afternoon yesterday. The march was not so hard as some we have had & I was not much fatigued, but my feet were quite sore the first day, & yesterday morning I could not walk without pain when I first got up in the morning. This is the first time I have had sore feet and I can hardly account for it. Yesterday they became better as we proceeded and this morning they were entirely well and I feel as if I could march all day. But I presume we will not move before to-morrow.

We came through the renowned places of Fairfax Courthouse, Centreville & Manassas, all of them insig-

nificant places of themselves. F.C. is the largest and is about the size of Newburg—I believe you have been there—but some of the homes are more elegant than any in Newburg, but most of them are no better. A majority of the houses seem to be deserted. Centreville is a miserable looking place & always has been I judge. The homes now seem nearly all abandoned & the windows broken. It occurred to me that Centreville was the place Miss McKinney & those other ladies lived who were in Carlisle some nine or ten years ago. I remember very well there were some ladies at your mother's from that place and I think they were the parties. If I had seen any citizen in the place I should have made inquiries about them.

Manassas junction I judge had not more than a half dozen houses before the secesh war began. A number of rough board houses have been put up apparently since the secesh army came here.

The country north or rather northeast of the place [Manassas] is beautiful. Far different from any idea I had of it. In fact it is a beautiful country all around here, but on the south side it seems to be poor while on the opposite side the ground seems naturally to have been good but impoverished by bad culture. At present the whole country is desolated. The fences for miles all gone, most of the houses deserted, and many of them destroyed. How the secesh have suffered here for their disunion principles. And the people are utterly & ignorant of everything. And think that the yankees or northern people are a set of abolitionists worse than the heathen.

One of our men told me that he was in the house of a secesh lady yesterday and she thought everything had gone to destruction in the north. That the yankees had utterly destroyed the capital at Washington and all the pictures etc. and when he told her she was mistaken that he had been in it himself & that it was all right, she would not believe him & he could not get her to believe him. She said it would have been a great deal better to let the Southern people have Washington & they would have taken care of it. Thus have these people been deluded & made to believe that the preservation of the country depended on the south & that the northern people are no better than barbarians. The church call has just beaten & I believe I will go to church.

> Your devoted husband
> James

JSC to AHC, April 20, 1862

> Fauquier County Va
> Near Catlet's Station
> 20th April 1862

My Dear wife,

I would have written you before this but on Thursday morning we left our camp at Manassas and I had not time & opportunity to write since. And if I had written no mail has gone since from our regiment. A mail will go to Washington tomorrow morning.

At 2 o'clock A.M. on Thursday we were aroused with the order to prepare to march. The men got up & got their breakfast and laid about till 6 o'clock. We reached this place about 3 o'clock P.M. the same day. Between 4 & 5 we started out on picket duty a couple of miles off. As the wagons had just got into camp I had to go without my supper. I had some biscuit & dry beef, & got along very well. About noon it commenced to rain and rained all afternoon. We returned to camp about dark and had a wet night. It is still raining at intervals and it is quite cold. For a few days previously the weather had been quite warm

The pear & cherry trees are out in full bloom and the fields beginning to look green. There is some beautiful country that we have passed over some of it very poor. But if it were farmed like the land of our good

PROMOTED.—We are pleased to learn that Maj. L. Todd of the 1st Regiment P. R. V. C. has been appointed Colonel of the 84th Regiment P. V. vice Col. Murray, killed in battle.

Capt. R. M. Henderson, of the Carlisle Fencibles, has been elected Lieut. Colonel of the 7th Regiment P. R. V. C., vice Lieut. Colonel Totten, resigned on account of ill health.

These are excellent selections, and we are confident that when opportunity offers, both will acquit themselves with credit.

Notice from the *American Democrat*, 16 April 1862.

farmers in Pennsylvania, it would make a splendid farming country. The Virginians, whether from slavery among them or some other cause, are "a shiftless set."

I believe a great deal has been conceded to the South just because she claimed it. I believe now that her claims are mere pretension, without foundation. The Southerners will now have to take their place as inferiors taken as a race or a nation and submit to the sentiment of the civilized world.

The paymaster is here and we expect to be paid today. I will send you some money the first opportunity. As Mr. McClure sent you some you are not bad off. The papers stated a day or two ago that the reserves had been paid off. This was true as to part of the reserves but not as to all. You cannot believe the fourth of what you see in the papers. It was stated that Major Todd is Colonel of the 84th Penna. & Capt Henderson lieut. Col. of the 7th P.V.R.C. I know nothing about whether Todd is a Colonel but I know that Totten is Lieut. Col. of the 7th. His resignation has not been accepted & if it was I think it is doubtful whether Henderson would be made Lieut. Col. as there are several other candidates for the place. This you need say nothing about as I don't wish to circulate such reports as he may be elected but there will be a strong opposition. So you perceive your chance of being a Captain is not so bright.

We are about ten miles from Manassas. I have no idea how long we will remain here.

I received yours of the 14th last night. There must be two on the way for me and another will leave tomorrow morning, making three.

It is true I never told you that Miss Culbertson was a sweetheart of mine. But is just as true that I did tell you all the sweethearts I ever had. And whoever told you she was one told you what never had any foundation in fact. I never even was attentive enough to her to start a report of that kind. I was once at a sleighing party with her and a number of couples were married in sport & she & I were among the number. And we were teazed some about such marriages being held binding. There never was any other grounds for calling her my sweetheart. She was not my style as the saying is. Perhaps you wish she had been Mrs. Colwell in as much as you sometimes wish you had never seen me. If I had married Miss Culbertson that would have answered you just as well, I being a disconsolate widower could never gained your ear and consequently could not have had the nice darling "unambitious" little wife—decidedly the best one I have any knowledge of—I now have. But she has some faults, one of the chief of which is: that she is so headstrong & self-willed I never can convince her how much I love her.

I have not read the Soldier's Talisman which you enclose with your letter but I will this afternoon if some order or duty does not turn up to prevent it.

Genl Ord's brigade has not gone to Yorktown. The whole reserve is within a few miles of where we are except some of the cavalry who are at Yorktown. One regiment, the 4th, is at Manassas Gap, the 5th is between Alexandria & Manassas. The rest of the reserves are here.

It is still raining and it is dinner time.

Your devoted husband
James

JSC to AHC, May 4, 1862

Camp Near Falmouth, Va
4th May 1862

My Dear Wife,

I have received nothing from you since I left Catlett's. I think the last letter I received was dated the 18th or 19th of April. That I received in due time about the 22nd or 23rd. The Regiment received a mail from Washington since we arrived here I think the 30th. I received no letter from you at which I was greatly disappointed and would have thought you sick, or some great calamity had befallen you. But fortu-nately Capt Henderson's wife mentioned in one of her letters that she met you purchasing garden seeds the day she wrote which was only two or three days before the letter arrived here. I am unable to account for your not writing on any other grounds than that you had forgotten me. As I have written to you several times since the date of your last received I hope some one of them will remind you of me. I wrote you on Wednesday and the mail left on Thursday the 1st May. I expect to hear from you when the return mail arrives. We looked for it yesterday evening but it has not arrived yet. We have heard that the mail carrier took sick on the road but several persons have told me that it takes four days sometimes to go to Washington & back. I had half intended not to write again till I would hear from you but Lieut. Col. Totten has been discharged at last and he intends to leave for home in an hour or two. And I could not let the opportunity pass with[out] embracing it.

I had a dream about you last night. I thought that I had returned home. The war was over and I was going to be very happy. I felt so. I dreamed that I saw you and you looked just as you did eleven or twelve years ago but you proposed that we should not live together & withdrew yourself from me. And just then I awoke to find it a dream.

I sent you $160—to the care of W. M. Beetem. I trust you have received it before this. I would like if you would acknowledge its receipt in a couple of your letters so that if one would miscarry I would still have a chance of hearing that you had received it.

We are still in the same place we encamped when we first arrived here. The weather for two days has been very warm. The apple trees here are in full bloom and the woods are getting quite green. I suppose vegetation is two or three weeks earlier here than with you. It is a poor country here but is sure to be good on the other side of the river. The place where Washington was born and where he cut down the cherry tree & threw the stone into the Rappahannock etc. is said to be only about a half mile from our camp. I have not seen it yet but have some notion of visiting the place if I can.

I have no idea how soon we will move from here but I have no doubt it will be as soon as the railroad is completed that we can get provisions & forage.

Don't forget any more to write often and direct to Washington as heretofore.

> Your devoted husband
> James

I don't know when I will write again. If we move, our mail arrangement may be broken up so that we cannot send letters every day. I hope however you will continue to write as usual—rather a little more punctual than usual. The letters will be forwarded to the regiment somehow.

I enclose a note to Sister Libby which please hand to her. I have not time to write much this evening.

> Most sincerely
> Your affte. husband
> James

JSC to AHC, June 4, 1862

> Camp opposite Fredericksburg
> 4th June 1862

My Dear wife,

It is several days since I have written you. I received your few lines written on the 29th ult. on Sunday morning. You stated in that that you would write again the next day. I have been waiting for it ever since, but it has not arrived yet.

Besides I have not been very well especially yesterday. Today I am pretty well. The heat has been oppressive for a few days with numerous showers. On Saturday & Saturday night I was on guard. It drizzled most of the day. And about 2 or 3 o'clock in the morning we had a tremendous thunderstorm. The rain poured in torrents. Monday night another thunderstorm. And yesterday evening another. A tree was struck yesterday evening about 200 yards from our camp. Last night it rained nearly all night and it has been raining all day. Now near noon. Our tent does not protect us very well, as the rain blows in and the tent leaks till our blankets are quite wet. You never mentioned whether the hailstorm you had did much damage.

We are still in the same camp we moved to last Monday week. There are no troops here but McCall's division and a few other regiments. McDowell and all the others left a week ago. I do not know where they are but presume they have gone back towards Winchester after Jackson, or wherever he is.

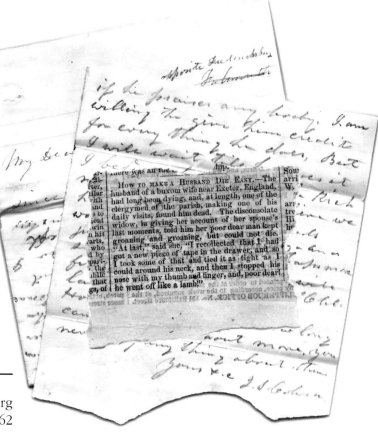

James included a newspaper clipping with his June 4 letter. (Colwell Family Collection.)

This is a famous country for snakes and bugs and insects of nearly every kind. Several have found snakes in their tents in the morning. A couple mornings ago a black snake was discovered lying between two of our men "as snug as a bug in a rug."

We have left the mess and are now at housekeeping again. We have got a contraband as cook and he seems to get along pretty well.

Day after tomorrow it will be one year since I left home. At that time I believed the war would be over and I at home in one year. Of course I have given that up. The war now might come to an end suddenly any day and it might be protracted a considerable time although I am inclined to think it cannot last much longer.

You seem to blame the abolitionists & contractors with prolonging the war. The contractors no doubt would be glad to continue the war. But you do the abolitionists wrong. I am not one. And I think their cause reprehensible. But give the devil his due. It is quite fashionable to blame everything on the abolitionists. They used to be blamed for hurrying things too much to bring the war to an end and not giving the generals time to mature their plans. And that is the truth. They are for bring[ing] the war to an end as speedily as possible, & as a general thing they are making no money out of it. You seem to think that if McClellan had had his way the war would have been over. You often hear such sentiments. But who knows what McClellan's plan was. It is generally believed that he wanted to take the whole army of the Potomac to Richmond. If the president had permitted him to do so I have no doubt that the secesh would have been in Washington before today. I have nothing to say against McClellan, but I can see nothing that he has done to entitle him to any more credit than many of our other generals. Some of them have I think exhibited more energy & military skill till this time than McClellan. If you will just take notice I think you will find that there is not a secesh sympathizer in the North that is not always praising McClellan if he praises anybody. I am willing to give him credit for everything he does. But I will wait till he does it. I believe he will take Richmond. But I also believe we have many other generals [who] would do the same thing—and just as speedily and perhaps more so. The contractors you will find are nearly all for McClellan.

How are your friends. How long can you do without more. You never say anything about them.

Yours etc

J.S. Colwell

JSC to AHC, June 11, 1862

Chesapeake Bay Va. 11th June /62
On board the Rockland

My Dear Wife,

We are not quite in the bay yet but are at the mouth of the Rappahannock and expect to be in the bay in a few minutes.

I received your letters of the 2nd & 4th June in due time, and presume I would have had one of later date had we remained in our former camp. I wrote to you last on Sunday the 8th. I trust you have received the letter before this. When you will get this it is impossible to say.

We left our camp on Monday about 12 o'clock M. and marched seven miles down the river to the place we were to embark and bivouacked for the night. We

Dis Chile's Contraban'

Illustration representing a child contraband from a Civil War era envelope. (Manuscript Collection, CCHS.)

had a pleasant day to march having a cool breeze although we had the heat of the day to march. We arrived at the point about 3 o'clock P.M. I retired about 10 with a clear bright sky without the slightest idea that we would have rain. I arose about 4 A.M. raining pretty fast. Had breakfast at 5 and laid around till about 8 when we received orders to go on board. It had been raining all morning and continued to rain very heavily till we were all on board which occupied us some two hours. Some were completely soaked but I fortunately having a good gum coat was comparatively dry excepting my feet & legs. We left the landing about 1 o'clock P.M. & steamed down the river till dark when we cast anchor and remained till daylight.

The first brigade and half of the second had gone before us. We have two boats together with the 7th Regt all but two companies. We have 4 1/2 companies and the other boat 3 1/2 companies on board. There are a few handsome places along the bank of the river but very few. Only three or four villages that I saw and they miserable affairs. The white people wherever we saw them stood in grim silence. The negroes everywhere exhibit the greatest evidence of joy, waving handkerchiefs and throwing up their arms. We see but few men either white or black. The former I suppose having gone to the army or hiding themselves and the latter having run away. One man on whose farm we halted a few minutes on our march had had one hundred field hands. Now he has one the rest having left. We passed a little town yesterday called

Port Royal where a few days ago they shot three negroes because they were going away.

One place some 20 or 30 negro girls & women went dancing & hopping along the beach a considerable distance singing and uttering some exclamations which I could not distinguish. They are poor deluded creatures, that do not know what they are rejoiced about. They have a vague idea that this war is going to benefit them in some way. It may a few. But I am inclined to think it will be an injury to most of them although it may benefit their posterity & the civilization & religion of the world in general.

There is one thing I think you have learned by this war of which I used to endeavor to convince you but always without success. And that is, that you can live and live just as well & happy without me as with me if you have the means to live on. I judge that you enjoy yourself quite as highly as you ever did.

There is one remark in your letter before the last that needs explanation. You state that John thinks that you are too out setting and follow it with the remark that John reminds you <u>very</u> much of Ban when he was young and you used to receive beaux under difficulties. How is that? Do you receive beaux under difficulties now? If not how does John remind you of Ban. I trust you will have no beaux nor the reputation of having them. You have several times mentioned about being a grass widow. A term I hate applied to any friend of mine and I conceive a very vulgar term although sometimes used in polite society, but never ought to be. This much I will say that they as a class have to be very careful as they lose their Reputation easier than any other class. They are in more danger than any others and more of them fall than any others. You remember what the gypsy told you although you never told me. Enjoy yourself but do as you always did when I was with you. You exclaim lecturing. No indeed. But I know how artless and unsuspecting you are & how very much the reverse the world is.

I do not know when I will be able to mail this letter. We are on our way to McClellan's army & expect to get there tomorrow or next day & I will forward this as soon as I can. In the meantime I will keep

White House, McClellan's base of supplies on the Pamunkey. (*Battles and Leaders of the Civil War*, Grant-Lee Edition, CCHS.)

it open as long as possible. Write often and direct as heretofore till further instructed.

12th June. We laid all night last night on the Pamunkey River 10 or 12 miles below White House where we will land and are now nearly there. I may have an opportunity to mail this there. We had a most delightful day yesterday. I was not well and felt uncomfortable. I slept scarcely any last night but feel better this morning. I hope to be well in a day or two.

I have heard no news since Mondays papers. I expect the mail will soon be sent after us, when I hope to obtain a budget from you & Sister Libby. I will forward this the first opportunity and hope you will write often to

> Your ever faithful husband
> James

JSC to AHC, June 15, 1862

P.V.R.C.
Camp of the 2nd Brigade
15th June 1862

My Dear wife,

I do not know the name of our present camp. But it is near Dispatch Station on the railroad from White House landing to Richmond about 12 miles from the latter place. We arrived here on Friday evening a little before sundown expecting to remain all night but McClellan sent word to Genl McCall to hasten on as fast as possible. Our orders were to get some coffee as quickly as we could and move on. By the time we got coffee the orders were countermanded and new

Postage stamp used to mail Colwell letter. (Colwell Family Collection.)

orders to hold ourselves in readiness to march at any time during the night back towards White House landing as there were reports that a large force of rebels had got round McClellan & were making their way to that point to capture or destroy the commissary stores of which there is a large amount there. Some guerilla cavalry were along the road that we came over during the day and probably they saw us. At night they burned several cars and fired on a train of cars and shot several, They also burned a number of wagons report says. They did burn the cars & fire on the trains. The 1st Brigade started back yesterday morning after them. We are still in the same place waiting.

I would have written you yesterday but was busy acting as brigade commissary. And in the evening was very much fatigucd. Don't know that I was ever nearer giving out. The weather has been excessively warm here the last two days. This morning is comparatively pleasant though still warm.

I wrote you on board the boat & mailed my letter on landing Thursday morning. It is probable you received it yesterday. I have received nothing from you since yours of the 4th inst. which was received last Sunday. No mail has arrived in camp since except the one we would have received on Monday at our old camp had we remained. It was brought on after us. The third brigade has not arrived yet. The mails will all come together I presume as soon as we get to our destination. Direct to Co A. 7th Regt P.R.V.C. Or 2nd Brigade McCall's Division Washington City D.C. And don't forget to write.

I feel better this morning than I have for several days. I am getting the fat off very rapidly. One trouble we have is to get something good to eat. I am tired of salt meat & hard bread. This morning I had a piece of onion for breakfast. I hardly ever eat anything that tasted better. I could eat any kind of vegetables with a ravenous appetite. But it almost impossible to get any.

We can hear the cannonading very distinctly yesterday morning and this morning a while. All is quiet now. I presume there will be a tremendous battle near Richmond some day before a great while unless the rebels retreat which I believe they will do if McClellan gives them time. I think it would be better to capture them if possible before retreating and that would end the war. If they retreat it will be to make a stand someplace else. I see Genl Ord is to go to genl Halleck's army. I suppose in that case Sharpe will go along.

Truly your devoted husband
James

JSC to AHC, June 22, 1862

Camp Near New Bridge Va
22 June 1862

My Dear wife,

Yesterday I had the great joy of receiving your letters of the 12th & 16th and Libby's of the 11th altogether. I presume now the mails have all been forwarded and hereafter we will get the letters regularly. I cannot say whether I have received all yours or not. If you would mention in each succeeding letter when you wrote last, I would always know if any miscarry. From the 12th to the 16th is a long time between letters. You used to write every other day and I would be glad if you would continue the practice. I write three times a week except sometimes when not practicable or I have not heard from you. I wrote you last on Thursday morning, which you probably received yesterday or will tomorrow.

I was on picket yesterday when your letters were forwarded. We had a very pleasant day. The rebel pickets were in sight but neither molested the other. Several deserters came over on Friday night but none of them to line our company occupied. There has been more or less firing every day since we have been here. We can see the enemies batteries, and where their camps are behind the hills and woods. Day before yesterday they shelled our camp so that we were obliged to move it a little back. One shell burst just over us and a piece of shell went through the tent of one of our men about ten or twelve feet from where I was standing, no harm was done. I presume they do not know where our camp is now.

There was a short fight yesterday afternoon a little below us. But I have heard no particulars. I heard firing during the night. We were called out this morning about three o'clock and stood under arms till about sun up, when we were dismissed to hold ourselves in readiness to fall in at a moment's notice. So I write this not knowing what moment I may have to close. It is evident that our side are apprehensive of an attack. I think however there will be none today. I saw Capt John Smead on Friday or Thursday and also Jim Piper. Their battery is only a few hundred yards from us

I feel much better for the last five days than I have for two or three weeks previously, although I have a slight cold. I have lost all my fat & am getting quite thin. Suppose you are still growing fat. Was sorry to hear of the childrens sickness, hope they are nearly recovered by this time. It will require some of your careful nursing to prevent any subsequent ill effects.

I did not say that I supposed you were becoming reconciled to my absence. That I suppose would be impossible as long as you retained any regard for me. You misunderstood. I think I said that you had discovered you could live without me, and be happy and content. That is all. Is it not so? I have no doubt you would have your lonely maybe sad moments. Everyone has no matter in what station or condition they may be. When I was home you had them. You always will have them. All I meant was that you have learned that you will not always be miserable without me.

The balloon is up now examining the position of the enemy.

I presume Libby talks of leaving you soon. Would you just as soon be without her. She does not say whether she intends to return. Does Minnie intend to go to New York. Did she get tired living at Cousin Margaretta's.

Truly your devoted husband

James

I wrote in my last to send me a half dozen stamps for postage.

Battle scene. (*Civil War Illustrations*, reprints, Carol Grafton, 1995.)

JSC to AHC, June 28, 1862

Camp before Richmond

My Dear wife,

I should have written yesterday but I was otherwise engaged. We had a terrible battle on Thursday afternoon & yesterday all day. [James is referring to the battles of Mechanicsville and Gaines' Mills.] The slaughter on both sides must have been great. But we do not know the result with any accuracy. I have escaped safely thus far as has Capt Henderson. There were 19 in our company killed wounded & missing. Of the missing we do not know how many may be killed or wounded or prisoners. It is pretty certain that David Haverstick is killed—our old sexton.

Article about death of David Haverstick, *American Volunteer*, 10 July 1862.

Article listing killed and wounded, *American Democrat*, 9 July 1862.

I saw Maj Todd this morning also Lieut. Graham and Lieut. Halbert. I presume you will get the particulars more accurately and earlier than I can. Capt. Sergeant of Harrisburg is present & well while I write. He desires me to say so. I did not know him & I suppose you did not. He married Miss Espy, and cannot write.

The battle may be renewed at any moment. It was fearful and terrible beyond anything you would apprehend. The rebels fought desperately all day yesterday and at night we occupied the same ground we did when the action commenced in the morning but we left it during the night & crossed the chickahominy. What is going on today I have no information of. It is now 11 o'clock A.M. and we are awaiting orders.

I would & will telegraph to you if I can get a message to the telegraph office which is doubtful. Our fate & that of Richmond will be decided I think in a day or two. Thank the Lord & his Christ that I am preserved thus far with only a slight scratch in the face. I hear cannonading now in the distance.

Give my love to the children and all the friends. No mail has been received since Wednesday. I hope to receive something from you when we get a mail. Will write at first opportunity again.

Genl Anderson was in the fight on the other side and is reported killed, with what truth I cannot say. Probably without any foundation.

I remain your devoted husband
James

JSC to AHC, undated by probably July 21, 1862

Camp Near Harrison's Landing Va

My Dear wife,

After writing my last letter the 18th I had the gratification of receiving yours of the fourteenth—mailed 15th. Four days from the mailing of your previous letter of the 11th. I was glad to hear that you had received mine of the 8th on Saturday only four days after it was written. But then after that you did not write till Monday night! There were two other letters if not three, previously written there on the way which I trust you have received ere this.

I cannot say that it is warmer here than it was on the Chickahominy. Some days it is exceptionally hot here and some days not so warm as it was there. Friday night and Saturday morning was quite cold, and yesterday was very pleasant. Today very warm.

You can tell Mrs Holmes that her son was wounded in the finger, not seriously in the first battle on the 26th. It is nearly well now. He has been not very well but is now nearly well. I presume she will have heard from him before you receive this. Perhaps the reason he did not write earlier was that it was his middle finger was wounded.

Zimmerman was wounded in the fight of Monday the 30th. I saw him or rather conversed with him on Monday night after dark at the hospital. He told me he was wounded and pointed to the place in his breast or between that & the shoulder or perhaps a little lower.

We left that night and were obliged to leave the wounded who couldn't walk, behind and he was with them and I have no doubt he is a prisoner now. Some prisoners who were in other regiments and have returned say that the prisoners were well treated as far as they knew. E.[D.] Curriden a member of our company from Shippensburg and who was perfectly well remained with the wounded. The wounded had not been examined by the Surgeons when we left but I do not think any of our company at that hospital were mortally wounded.

It is reported now it is said on the authority of an officer returned from Richmond that Capt. Biddle was not killed but was seriously—but not mortally wounded and is a prisoner at Richmond. I hope it is true. He was a brave & deserving officer.

The paymaster is here & the regiment is paid off at last. All but the officers. They will be paid today or tomorrow I presume. I will send some money at the earliest opportunity.

As you don't appear to be delighted with miss S I hope she has left you. If she is so violent you can imagine how violent the ladies are in Virginia as I have written you. If a Northern lady expresses her opinion in favor of the union in the South she is imprisoned or offered indignities. Yet they are the chivalry.

I can say amen to Daisy's wish all but putting up the stove this kind of weather. I should dearly love to be nursing her.

Write a little oftener to your sincerely attached husband

    James

Soldier receiving hand wound. (*Civil War Illustrations*, reprints, Carol Grafton, 1995.)

CHAPTER 5

"The Bitter, Bitter Fruits of this War"

A Good Suggestion.--At the war meeting yesterday the ladies of Carlisle handed in a communication which was read by the President, calling upon the young men who are in the habit of congregating on the corners, greatly to the annoyance of all good citizens, to volunteer their services in the cause of the Union, and they (the ladies) would pledge themselves to take their places and fill them with equal grace. We wonder whether the hint will take? If they don't go to war we hope they will try and please the ladies, by abandoning the mean habit of which our fair sex accuse them. We will see.

Article from the *Carlisle American*,
30 July 1862.

The draft. (*Civil War Illustrations*,
reprints, Carol Grafton, 1995.)

In the summer of 1862, as the North rushed to enlist new troops after the Peninsula campaign, anyone who expressed less than whole-hearted support for the Union became the object of suspicion. In Carlisle, Annie's friend, Mary Seavers, probably from Baltimore, came to visit and remained until August. Miss Seavers was outspoken in her support for secession; Annie wrote James frequently of the trouble she caused. James answered one of her letters on July 21, "As you don't appear to be too delighted with Miss S I hope she has left you. If she is so violent you can imagine how violent the ladies are in Virginia."[1] Three weeks later he wrote, "You speak in your last [letter] of Mary Severs being in such continual troubles.... Has she been guilty of improper conduct?"[2] George and Minnie, Annie's brother and sister, had already caused difficulties for Annie in Carlisle by expressing sympathies for the South at the outbreak of the war. A related concern now arose for Annie: if Maryland did not fill its quota of volunteers in Lincoln's call for three hundred thousand new troops, Ban, her brother in Baltimore, was likely to be drafted to serve in the Union army. James wrote, "How is Ban coming on? Is he in Baltimore yet? I presume he will be very much afraid of being drafted as he would have to fight against his beloved secesh."[3]

The need for additional troops was widely recognized in the North. On August 1 the *Herald* printed a new poem by Oliver Wendell Holmes. Addressed to the young men of the North and entitled, "A Call for Volunteers," the first and last verses read:

Listen, Young heroes! Your country is calling!
Time strikes the hour for the brave and the true!
Now, while the foremost are fighting and falling,
Fill up the ranks that have opened for you.

From the hot plains where they perish outnumbered,
Furrowed and ridged by the battlefield's plough,
Comes the loud summons: too long have you slumbered,
Hear the last Angel Trump—Never or Now.

(Carlisle *Herald*, 1 August 1862)

The war came close to home in Carlisle. In mid-August the ladies of the town joined together to raise money for sick and wounded soldiers by presenting a program of vocal and instrumental music and tableaux. The army band from the Carlisle Barracks participated. Ticket sales for the event realized a profit of $120. The affair was so successful that a repeat performance was staged a few weeks later.[4] The draft also affected the town. Under the direction of R. P. McClure, Cumberland County's director of registration, lists were compiled of all able-bodied men up to the age of forty-five. Under the headline "WEAK KNEED PATRIOTS" the *Herald* wrote of those who sought to dodge the draft:

> Again we have those who stand in bodily fear of the draft. They bolt in all directions or go *skipping* around like maggots in an old cheese, trying to find some way to get clear of serving their country like honest men.[5]

Annie wrote James that one of McClure's agents had been to the house to obtain details regarding James's service:

> Today Mr. Holbert called here to get your name & age as the business of drafting has commenced. I gave your age about 40. Mr. Croft [Annie's next door neighbor] can't be taken because he is 45. Now if you had not gone already we might have added a few years to your age & kept you at home.[6]

Annie seems not to have known James's true age. His forty-ninth birthday was in April of 1862. Perhaps he had never told her that he was twenty years older than she.

The casualty lists printed in the paper took on real meaning. Wrote Annie:

> I felt very sad this afternoon in seeing the lady of poor young Zimmerman.... I had no idea his wound would prove fatal.... [T]o be cut off so early is sad. How many useful lives have been lost by this war & how many broken hearts it has made.

Exhibitions for the Sick and Wounded Soldiers.

According to announcement, the grand exhibitions for the benefit of the sick and wounded soldiers, were given at Rheems Hall, on Friday and Saturday evenings of last week. The programme consisted of vocal and instrumental music and tableaux. The Barracks Band was in attendance and furnished the audience with some of their choice music. The hall on both nights, was crowded, and we have no doubt that quite a large sum of money was realized, which will be immediatly forwarded to some of the hospitals. The credit for these exhibitions belongs chiefly to the ladies, who have spent much time and labor in getting up the material for the occasion, and as they cannot themselves go to fight the battles of the country, they can do a great deal to relieve the sufferings of our sick and wounded countrymen, May God bless them, and may they never grow weary in the good work which they have so cheerfully entered into. We understand that they intend to resume these exhibitions in a few weeks, due notice of which will be given.

Article from the *Carlisle American*, 20 Aug. 1862.

The Draft is Coming.

Marshall MILWARD, of Philadelphia, who has been appointed by Governor CURTIN to conduct the draft in the State, has appointed R. P. McCLURE, Esq., of Shippensburg, as the proper person to make the draft in Cumberland County. He has already entered upon the work of enrolling the militia. We have no doubt that the doctors will have many "patients" just now.

Draft notice, *Carlisle American*, 27 Aug. 1862.

DIED,

In this borough, on the 14th inst., Mrs. CAROLINE VANASDLEN, in the 18th year of her age.

At McKim's Hospital, Baltimore, Md., on the morning of the 22d inst., Sergt. WM. ZIMMERMAN, of Company A, 7th Regiment P. V R. C.

The deceased was a member of Capt. Henderson's company, and participated in the battles before Richmond, where he was severely wounded in the arm.— After being wounded he was taken prisoner by the rebels and sent to Richmond, where he remained but a short time, when he was exchanged. He was then taken to the hospital at Baltimore, where proper medical attention was given to his wound, but in consequence of the non-attention of the rebels, his arm had to be amputated. Mortification then ensused, which caused his death a few hours after the amputation. His body was brought home on last Friday afternoon, and followed to the grave on Saturday by a large number of mourning relatives and friends. Thus has another of the brave volunteers of Carlisle fallen in the defense of his country.

James had written on July 21 that "Zimmerman was wounded in the fight of Monday the 30th [Glendale]. I saw him or rather conversed with him on Monday night after dark at the hospital. He told me he was wounded and pointed to the place in his chest or between that & the shoulder or perhaps a little lower. We left that night and were obliged to leave the wounded who couldn't walk, behind." (JSC to AHC 21 July 1862.) Zimmerman was exchanged and subsequently died of his wounds.

Death notice for William Zimmerman from the *Carlisle American*, 27 Aug. 1862.

Supplying the hungry at Harrison's Landing on the James River, Virginia. (*Battles and Leaders of the Civil War*, Grant-Lee Edition, CCHS.)

In the same letter she described Lieutenant Beatty, home in Carlisle on recruiting duty after being wounded during The Seven Days' Battles, "I am surprised to notice Mr. Beatty growing so gray."[7] A report of Southern reaction to the Peninsula campaign came from Annie's cousin, Sallie Anderson:

> Cousin Margaret had a letter recently from Sallie Anderson [who was in Richmond with her husband, Gen. R. H. Anderson]. She says she is gayer, receives more kindness & goes out more than in all her life & sends for handsome clothing. That don't look much like the South suffering.[8]

As acting brigade quartermaster, James was detached from his regiment and was occupied supervising the hauling of supplies from the James River landing to the brigade. Confederate artillery on the other side of the river sporadically shelled the Union positions. James described such a cannonade to Annie:

> On Thursday my slumbers were disturbed by the sound of a cannon down towards the river.... I heard the shell whistle. I knew what that meant. I jumped up & put on my clothes.... The rebels...rained the shells & solid shot all around. Dangerous as it was it was a grand sight. We could follow the course of the shells which passed off a distance from us by their fuses which were lighted, but those which come directly toward us we cannot see however we could hear them, and could easily step out of the way if we knew exactly the place they would pass; but we would be just as likely to pass right into the path of the ball as out of it so it is just about as safe to stand still.[9]

At forty-nine James was more than twice the age of most Union soldiers. He related that in the course of his duties as quartermaster he had stopped at a spring on the Peninsula "down at the river where no one knew me." There was a single drinking cup and men waited their turn to use it.

> When one was satisfied and was about handing the cup to his neighbor, the latter told him to "give it to that old fellow first." "That old fellow" was your humble servant—your husband.[10]

Despite the war and the miles between them there were exchanges of warmth and tenderness. Indignant at the portrayal of James as being old, Annie replied,

> Oh! You will fare so well for I am making so many nice things in anticipation of your return. You will have to show your gratitude by growing fat & driving all care away from your brow, so that no one would think of offering "that old man" a drink again.[11]

James, too, would occasionally express his affection and deep feeling for her. Remembering the past, he wrote her at about the same time:

> And then I thought of a little light haired, bright eyed girl that used to be moving noiselessly around in those days who was of far more interest to me than aught else, and who although a girl no longer, still occupies my thoughts by day & by night. Her hair is not so light nor her eyes so black as in those days. But the same bright-ness sparkles in her face.... What would I not give now for one long look into the deep depths of those dancing eyes and to remain in their light for long years to come.[12]

Annie wrote back, "Your letter of the 21st was so sweet that I gave your picture a huge kiss."[13]

James often described his military duties and the activities of the army. When Annie raised the subject of a possible furlough, James wrote:

> It does seem as you say that a great many officers get leaves of absence, but you see the complaints about it. And it should not be allowed in the extent that it is. The officers who ask for it ought to be ashamed of themselves.[14]

On August 10 he reported receiving orders to load the troops' knapsacks on board transports. "This means I suppose that we are going to move," he wrote. "Where I have no idea."[15] Two days later the brigade left by water for Fort Monroe. James did not go:

> I am obliged to remain here till I get rid of my teams. I have over fifty of them now and quartermaster's stores. I expect to get off in a day or two but may have to remain here several days.[16]

Annie Colwell. Copy of a carte de visite from a Colwell Family album, c.1870. (Charles L. Lochman, Colwell Family Collection.)

Two days later he wrote again, "We are all packed up and loaded.... I write this sitting in a wagon."[17] On August 15 he finally moved:

> I left camp near Harrison's Landing on Friday about noon and arrived here [Fort Monroe] on Sunday morning. I mounted my horse at nine o'clock [to] take some teams to the landing to have provisions unloaded and then we started, and traveled all day and all night without food stopped next morning about 20 minutes to feed the horses and went on again till after dark when we halted till the moon rose about 11 o'clock P.M. when we started again and arrived here as stated above.... I was pretty considerably fatigued on arrival here having been in the saddle about fifty-six hours with very little rest. The troops all came down on boats.... The 7th Regiment is out on the bay.... Our brigade all except the 7th Regiment left several days before us.[18]

James and his teams camped two miles from Fort Monroe at Hampton, a small town which Confederate troops had burned to the ground the previous August when it was rumored that it would become a settlement for runaway slaves. "It appears as if it might have been a pretty village," James wrote, but now it was "an utter desolation. A fit place for owls and bats."[19]

Fort Monroe on the Chesapeake Bay on the Lower Peninsula. (*Battles and Leaders of the Civil War*, Grant-Lee Edition, CCHS.)

Ruins of Hampton, Virginia, from a sketch made in April 1862. (*Battles and Leaders of the Civil War*, Grant-Lee Edition, CCHS.)

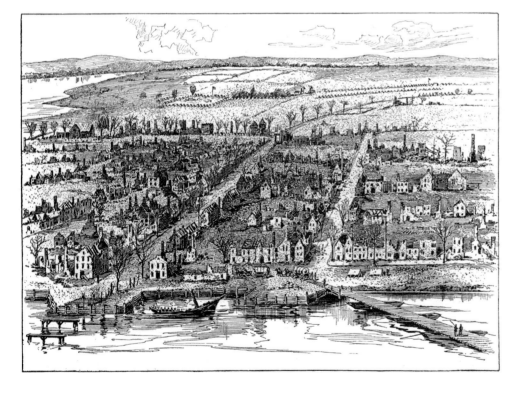

James wrote too of the contrabands:

> I don't remember whether I wrote you about the contrabands we have in the Army. At Harrison's Landing there was quite a city of them, dwelling in tents. We were here but an hour or two till they were beside us putting up their tents. I believe there was not one left behind. What is to be done with them I do not know.[20]

Movement of the armies in the summer of 1862 also caused a flood of former slaves to course north up the Cumberland Valley. Reported Annie of Carlisle, "The town is full of contrabands."[21]

Like Lincoln's, James's opinion of McClellan was worsening:

> Genl McClellan seems to be fading away.... His plan has turned out a failure. He ought to have been in Richmond long ago. The army could have taken there months ago.... I never could see what such a clamor was got up in McClellan's favor for. He never had done anything to justify it.[22]

And in the same letter he wrote of casualties in the war:

> The men that have died in battle are few compared with those who have died of disease. Therefore the quicker the war can be ended the fewer lives it will cost.... My health remains good thus far. I pray God it may continue so for the Army is a terrible place for a sick man. I have no doubt that hundreds die for want of proper attention who might live with proper care.[23]

Union casualties for the Civil War showed 110,000 soldiers killed in action or dying subsequently from battle wounds, and 249,000 dead from illness and disease.[24] Similar detailed figures were not maintained for Confederate losses. William F. Fox estimates that 94,000 Confederate soldiers were killed or mortally wounded in action; no doubt the relationship of deaths from disease to deaths in action was similar to that for Union soldiers.

Battle casualties. (*Battles and Leaders of the Civil War*, Grant-Lee Edition, CCHS.)

An engagement prior to the Second Battle of Bull Run. (*Battles and Leaders of the Civil War*, Grant-Lee Edition, CCHS.)

John Pope. (*The Soldier in the Civil War*, John Leslie, 1893, CCHS.)

Lincoln commented in private that he thought McClellan really wanted Pope to fail.[26] McClellan clearly hoped that Pope would fail. Lincoln's doubts regarding McClellan were underscored by a message he received from the general on August 29. McClellan was then at Alexandria under orders to march his troops to Pope's assistance as soon as possible. His message laid out two alternatives: to move his troops forward to help Pope, or "To leave him to get out of his scrape & at once use all our means to make the Capital perfectly safe."[27] Lincoln believed that McClellan deliberately chose to withhold help from Pope and "to leave him get out of his scrape" by himself.

As usual McClellan moved slowly in transferring his troops from the Peninsula to General John Pope's command in the vicinity of Washington. The first troops boarded transports only on August 19. In contrast Lee, who had the measure of McClellan, moved troops rapidly north, gained a victory at Cedar Mountain fifty miles northwest of Richmond on August 9, and two weeks later sent Stonewall Jackson and his corps on a long, looping march to the northwest, hoping to catch Pope by surprise in the rear. At the Second Battle of Bull Run on August 29-30 he did exactly that, routing the Union troops, many of whom fled in panic back to Washington. Poor generalship on Pope's part was the immediate cause. Equally responsible was the lethargy with which the forces formerly under McClellan's command moved to Pope's aid.

Union casualties at the Second Battle of Bull Run were heavy, Carlisle troops among them. Lieutenant Colonel R. M. Henderson, formerly captain of Company A, who commanded the 7th Regiment at the battle, was severely wounded. Captain John Smead, who commanded a battery of artillery at Second Bull Run, was killed in action. He was a West Point graduate and husband of Annie Ege, a cousin and Carlisle friend of Annie. Lengthening Union casualty lists and news of Confederate successes at the battles on the Peninsula, at Cedar Mountain, and at Second Bull Run brought dejection to the North. The spring hopes for an early end to the war were over. Annie wrote:

> My own Husband how much I hope & pray & trust that you are safe. God only knows! That your life may be saved & that you may be returned to us is my daily & most ardent prayer & all things else sink into nothing in comparison.... What will be the end of all this? We seem to be gaining and losing all the time.[25]

KILLED AND WOUNDED SOLDIERS.—We have endeavored to procure a list of the killed and wounded soldiers, belonging to this county, in the recent battles near Washington, but have only partially succeeded.— No doubt others than those mentioned below, have been more or less injured. The following have been reported :

Killed.—Capt. John Smead, U. S. Artillery.

Wounded.—Lieut. Col. R. M. Henderson, 7th Pa., Reserves ; A. Walton, Co. A, 11th Pa., hand ; Augustus Sites, do., head ; T. Conway, do., leg ; J. Vansant, do., side ; Charles Wonderlich, A, 7th Reserves, shoulder ; Patrick Branson, do ; Conrad Kuntz A, 11th Pa ; Lieut. James Noble, A, 11th Pa ; W. H. Harkness, A. 7th Reserves, slightly.

KILLED IN BATTLE.—Capt. John Smead, of the U. S. Artillery, and a citizen of Carlisle, was killed in action last week, near Washington. Captain S. was a meritorious officer, and leaves a wife and child to mourn his loss.

Death notice of John Smead from the *American Democrat*, 3 Sept. 1862.

Announcement of killed and wounded from the *American Democrat*, 10 Sept. 1862.

John Smead, from a daguerreotype. Inside the case is an inscription "My Beloved Brother," written by John's sister, Elizabeth Smead. This image may have been taken when John was at West Point, c.1852. (Courtesy of Raphael S. Hays II.)

The day she attended John Smead's funeral she wrote James:

> Oh, the bitter, bitter fruits of this war are seen & felt everywhere.... Oh I would give nearly all my life if I could feel assured that you are out of danger this night.... Everything anything to have you again home. May Heaven answer this my constant prayer.[28]

James remained at Hampton for two weeks before transport for his teams could be arranged. His optimism as to an early end to the war fading, James wrote Annie when he learned the outcome of Second Bull Run, "What a terrible war this is, and the end don't appear to be visible yet."[29]

After the Union defeat at Second Bull Run, Lee resolved on a bold gamble: to cross the Potomac, invade Maryland, and carry the war home to the North for the first time. Lee also believed that many pro-Southern Marylanders would join his army once it appeared on that state's soil.[30] On September 5 the first of Lee's troops crossed the Potomac in the vicinity of Leesburg, Virginia, thirty miles up the Potomac from Washington, and entered the city of Frederick, Maryland, the next day. To meet the emergency following the defeat at Second Bull Run, Lincoln sent an embittered Pope, his reputation damaged beyond repair, west to deal with a Sioux uprising in Minnesota. Against the advice of a majority of his cabinet he requested that McClellan reorganize the Army of the Potomac and pursue Lee.

McClellan considered Lincoln's move a vindication of his previous leadership of the army. It was not. Lincoln was well aware of McClellan's reluctance to come to battle; but more than anything else at that moment the army needed to be reorganized and Lincoln recognized McClellan's skill in organization and administration. Secretary of the Navy Gideon Welles quoted Lincoln: "I must have McClellan to reorganize the army and bring it out of chaos, but there has been a design, a purpose in breaking down Pope, without regard of consequences to the country. It is shocking to see and know this; but there is no remedy at present. McClellan has the army with him."[31]

Lee's ultimate aim was to destroy the railroad bridge at Harrisburg on the Susquehanna River and thus cut the chief supply link between the Union east and west. Confederate Major General John Walker quoted Lee as saying on September 8, "McClellan['s]...army is in a very demoralized and chaotic condition, and will not be prepared for offensive operations—or he will not think it so—for three or four weeks. Before that time I hope to be on the Susquehanna."[32] It was the same goal Lee sought the following summer when his invasion strategies were thwarted for a second time at Gettysburg.

The Harris Ferry House and Railroad and Wagon Bridge over the Susquehanna River at Harrisburg, c.1880. (H. Frank Beidel stereograph card, courtesy of Bob Rowe.)

James's long delay on the Peninsula finally came to an end. On August 31 he embarked on the tug *Kingston* with a few of his horses while the wagons and most of the horses were loaded on another vessel. "What I am to do when I get to Alexandria I have no idea. Whether remain there or go on to the regiment," he wrote Annie from the *Kingston* as he steamed up the Potomac to Alexandria, where he arrived on September 2.[33] When he wrote Annie two days later, still in Alexandria awaiting the horses and wagons, disorganization among the Union forces following the defeat at Second Bull Run was evident:

> This city is so crowded that I can find no place to stay except to lie on the floor. I stay down on the wharf where I have some horses, and have my blankets. I am tired of living the way I have been for the last year but more especially for the last six months.[34]

The teams finally arrived at Alexandria on Friday night, September 5, the day the first of Lee's troops crossed the Potomac upstream. By midnight the following day James had off-loaded the horses and wagons and set up the teams. He spent the rest of the night loading. Leaving Alexandria before 10 o'clock Sunday morning, he wrote Annie:

> Alarm and gloom were prevalent in Washington. After Second Bull Run skepticism regarding the Union's chances of winning the war spread to foreign observers. On September 7 the French minister told Secretary of State Seward that he considered it time for his country to recognize the Confederacy.[36]

> We passed through Washington as the people were going to church on Sunday evening. I could not stop to write you a line, nor even to get something to eat. I got up with the brigade about midnight that night about 10 miles out from Washington. On Monday morning I was sent back to the company. So I am now footing it in the old way.[35]

In Carlisle the news of the Confederate invasion of Maryland caused immediate concern. Pennsylvania Governor Andrew Curtin ordered the formation of volunteer companies of armed militia and directed businesses to close in mid-afternoon.[37] Annie wrote James on September 6:

> Our normally quiet valley is in quite a commotion anticipating a visit from Stonewall Jackson. All the stores are closed and businesses suspended after 3 o'clock every day by order from the Governor so that the men can drill & provide themselves with arms in case of an attack.[38]

Two days later she wrote again, "We have four companies formed in town for the defense of the state," and asked James, "Don't you think you could come home now that you are near us again?"[39] The *Herald* bragged:

> Should Stonewall Jackson, with his traitorous legions, be so fool hardy, as to attempt an invasion of our quiet and beautiful valley, he will meet with an affection quite as warm as the most affectionate could desire.[40]

The general public was less confident than the *Herald*. Annie wrote of the general reaction in Carlisle to the Confederate advance:

> We are constantly in receipt of wild rumors about Jackson's approaching us but I do not feel afraid yet many are very uneasy & are packing up their valuables lest they may be destroyed. I cannot think the Rebels would burn our town or interfere with the women & children.... I think if we do have to leave town Perry County would be the most out-of-the-way place.

As Lee pushed north, a new wave of former slaves moved ahead of the Confederate advance. In the same letter Annie wrote, "Yesterday quite a colony of contrabands arrived here."[41]

After Lee reached Frederick, he divided his forces, sending the larger part of his troops west under Stonewall Jackson to capture Martinsburg and Harper's Ferry, while he led the remainder of his army across South Mountain to the west; Jackson's forces would rejoin Lee after the capture of Harper's Ferry. Lee intended to move up the Cumberland Valley, screened by South Mountain, and reach Harrisburg before Union troops could overtake him. He advanced as far as Hagerstown, Maryland, only fifty miles from Carlisle, leaving a sparse line of Confederate troops to block any Union advance through the passes across South Mountain.

> Stonewall Jackson astonished townspeople in Frederick when he publicly requested a map of Chambersburg, Pa. It may have been an inadvertent slip thus to reveal future plans of the Confederate army, or it may have been intended deliberately to throw a scare into the North.[42] That request may have been responsible for the concern regarding a "Jackson" invasion of Pennsylvania mentioned in the press and in Annie's letters to James.

The press applauded the formation of civilian militia units. "To Work! To Work! To Work!" headlined an editorial in the *American Democrat*, which continued, "It becomes our imperative duty to make every preparation in our power for self-defence.... Cumberland County must shake off the lethargy which has too long bound her, and arouse to the work now before her." (*American Democrat*, 10 September 1862.)

CLOSING PLACES OF BUSINESS.—It has been urged by many, that our business places and work shops be closed from 4 to 6 o'clock, daily, to enable all our citizens to drill. Some have done so for several days past, but a large majority have refused.— Would it not be well to have a town meeting and agree upon some uniform plan?

News note from the *American Democrat*, 10 Sept. 1862.

THE DARING REBEL RAID INTO PENNSYLVANIA.

OCCUPATION OF CHAMBERSBURG.

DESTRUCTION OF GOVERNMENT PROPERTY.

IMMENSE QUANTITIES OF CLOTHING AND HORSES CAPTURED.

Gen. Wool at Carlisle.

TROOPS FORWARDED FROM HARRISBURG.

The Rebels Make a Circuit of Our Lines.

Gen. Pleasanton After Them.

THEY ARRIVE AT MONROVIA AND TEAR UP THE RAILROAD TRACK.

THE REBELS LOADED WITH BOOTS AND SHOES.

Their Escape into Virginia with the Loss of Thirty of their Number.

Headlines from the *American Volunteer*, 16 Oct. 1862.

View of the ruins of Chambersburg looking north, 1864. Stuart's cavalry raid of Chambersburg in October 1862 was just a foretaste of the 30 July 1864 invasion and burning of the town by General McCausland. This view was taken shortly after the 1864 event by Carlisle photographer, Charles L. Lochman, and sold as a stereoscopic view. (Robin Stanford Collection, CCHS.)

Lee's good fortune ran out in September 1862. The anticipated Maryland recruits for his army never materialized. A further piece of extraordinary bad luck befell Lee. As his army marched west from Frederick, a copy of his orders directing the division of his forces, part to Harper's Ferry and part to continue further northwest to Hagerstown, fell into the hands of Union troops on September 13 and was delivered to McClellan, who saw an opportunity to attack Lee's divided army, and for once moved with some alacrity to take advantage of the situation. Union forces moved rapidly west that day; by nightfall thousands of Union troops were camped at the eastern edge of South Mountain. Jeb Stuart, commanding the Confederate rear guard, realized the danger and sent word to Hagerstown, fifteen miles away, where Lee decided to defend the passes across South Mountain with his outnumbered forces until Jackson's forces could rejoin him. The Battle of South Mountain took place the next day.

Marylanders who might have considered joining Lee's army were deterred by the shocking physical condition of his troops. They were famished, eating apples and green corn taken from fields through which they passed; their uniforms were tattered; they marched barefoot or with feet bound up with rags.[43]

The New York *Times* reported that few joined Lee's army in Frederick, although some five hundred men came in from Baltimore and Maryland's eastern counties: "After seeing the character of the army and the life which the men lead, many of them refused to join and were getting home again.... I have never seen such a mass of filthy, strong-smelling men.... Their sympathizers at Frederick have been greatly disappointed...and most of them are now as anxious for them to disappear as they were for them to come. [Lee's soldiers'] features, hair, and clothing [were] matted with dirt and filth and the scratching they kept up gave warrant of vermin in abundance." (New York *Times*, 14 September 1862.)

James, who caught up with his company on September 8, marched west with it and on September 13 wrote Annie from "about 4 miles from Frederick":

> We remained in camp till Tuesday [September 9] and have been marching every day since. We arrived here a few minutes ago, 12 o'clock M. [Meridian] How long we will remain I have no idea. We can hear firing all forenoon on the other side of Frederick from us.[44]

On September 14 greatly outnumbered Confederate troops attempted to hold the three main passes across South Mountain, Turner's Gap, Fox's Gap, and Crampton's Gap, against superior Union forces. The Confederates held the high ground: the Federals had to work their way uphill against them. Under General George Meade at the extreme right of the Union line the Pennsylvania Reserves fought hard and well, moving uphill during the latter part of the afternoon through groves of trees and across open fields, finally forcing the Confederate units back to Turner's Gap. Union troops took all three of the passes late in the day.

Pursuit of a fleeing enemy and hard night marches were not McClellan's style. His troops encamped after the battle, failed to follow Confederate troops retreating down the west side of the mountain, and lost the chance to relieve the siege of Harper's Ferry.[45] Exhibiting no urgency, McClellan's troops moved slowly down the west side of South Mountain through the little town of Boonsboro on September 15, a day when McClellan commanded seventy-five thousand troops, while Lee, his forces still divided, had only eighteen thousand men with him. The next day, September 16, the Union army took up positions near the little town of Sharpsburg, which lay between Antietam Creek and the Potomac.

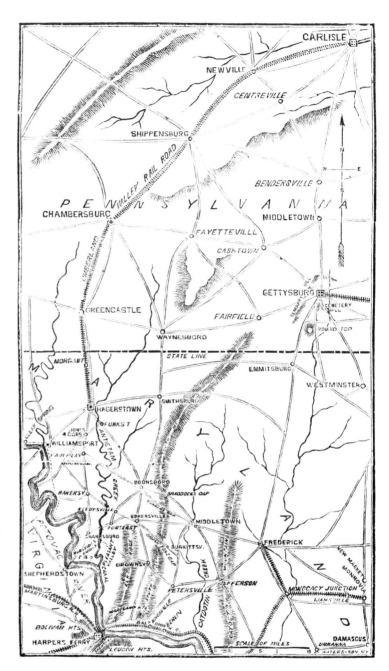

Map showing the area between Harpers Ferry and Carlisle. (*History of the Civil War in the United States*, Samuel M. Schmucker, 1865, CCHS.)

When troops under Union General William Franklin broke through Crampton's Gap, toward the southern end of South Mountain, late in the afternoon of September 14, they were only eight miles from Harper's Ferry. Had they marched that night, or even at first light the next day, they could have relieved the twelve thousand Union troops at Harper's Ferry whose commander surrendered to Stonewall Jackson at 8 a.m. the morning of September 15.

After the battle of South Mountain, James found himself out of writing paper. He took an envelope which had enclosed one of Annie's letters to him, tore it open, and wrote a brief letter on the inside of the envelope:

> We have been on the march since yesterday we had a fight. We drove the Rebs clear over the mountain. We are now about 4 miles south of Boonsborough towards the Potomac. There is fighting three or four miles in advance. The Rebs are in full retreat I think towards Va. Never to return. The end of this war has commenced. I escaped unhurt again through the favor of the Lord & his Christ.[46]

In Carlisle Annie, worried, wrote on September 13:

> Again writing to my own dear husband & have heard nothing from him for so very long a time consequently I am in very bad spirits.... Now my own dear husband do please try to find out some way of communicating.... [T]o know that you are well is the only comfort that I have these times.

In the same letter she wrote of the effect the Confederate movements had in town:

> Since I wrote you on Thursday our town has been in a great commotion owing to Jackson's anticipated visit to this valley. Many families have left town.... Numbers who remain are packed up for a start.... I think I won't leave till the Rebels get to Chambersburg [thirty-five miles down the valley from Carlisle]. Then of course the track will be torn up & it will take them a day or two to march here so in that time we can hide some place.[47]

Scene from the Battle of Antietam. (*History of the Civil War in the United States*, Samuel M. Schmucker, 1865, CCHS.)

After lying in position most of September 16, McClellan ordered his troops forward a mile or two across Antietam Creek late that afternoon, to positions from which they opened the Battle of Antietam the next morning. The delay was just long enough to permit Lee to reassemble his forces, some arriving the afternoon of September 16 from Harper's Ferry, the remainder reaching the battlefield late on September 17, barely in time to thwart the last Union attack on Sharpsburg and prevent what would have been a Union victory.

There were greater casualties at the daylong battle of Antietam than on any other single day during the Civil War.[48] Vicious fighting commenced at daybreak at the north end of the battlefield and moved south along the battle lines during the day. The Pennsylvania Reserves, a part of Hooker's First Corps, took part in savage early-morning battles swirling around The Cornfield at the north end of the battlefield. Casualties were heavy as attack and counter-attack moved back and forth across the field. As regiments were shattered on both sides, reserve units were thrown into action, decimated in turn, and replaced by others. Bullets and shells mowed down nearly ripe corn as well as men.

After Union troops under General Ambrose Burnside finally carried the bridge over Antietam Creek at the south end of the battlefield, their drive on the town of Sharpsburg itself was frustrated by Confederate General A. P. Hill's troops who arrived in the nick of time after a seventeen-mile forced march from Harper's Ferry. Hill's successful counter-attack against Burnside's troops not long after four in the afternoon brought the battle to an end.

Fighting was intense throughout the day. "The Cornfield," "Bloody Lane," and "Burnside's Bridge" are names familiar to all interested in the Civil War. Casualties were extraordinarily high as Union and Confederate regiments marched across open fields, pressing home attacks at point-blank range. At the end of the day the armies stood not far from their starting points that morning. Yet McClellan had two army corps, those of Franklin and Porter, which he never ordered into battle that day or the next when Lee's forces lay exhausted in their lines. On September 19 Lee retreated back across the Potomac.

McClellan wrote his wife of his "complete victory" and reported to her, "Those in whose judgment I rely told me that I fought the battle splendidly and that it was a masterpiece of art," probably a comment of McClellan's sycophantic associate, Fitz-John Porter.[49]

Burnside's Bridge over the Antietam Creek. (*Battles and Leaders of the Civil War*, Grant-Lee Edition, CCHS.)

In his official battle report Hooker wrote of The Cornfield:

> In the time I am writing every stalk of corn in the northern and greater part of the field was cut as closely as could have been done with a knife, and the slain lay in rows precisely as they had stood in their ranks a few moments before.[50]

James's 7th Regiment, a part of the 2nd Brigade, was heavily engaged in The Cornfield and then moved to the left to reinforce another Union unit. Colonel A. L. Magilton, 2nd Brigade Commander, reported that the brigade came "under a dreadful fire" as it moved left, started to give way, "but rallying immediately, afterward advanced to the front, and drove the enemy after an obstinate resistance."[51] By 10 a.m. the fighting died down at the north end of the battlefield. After heavy casualties, the Reserves withdrew and fell to the rear.

In Carlisle, Annie, aware of the fighting sixty miles south in Maryland, had not heard from James since his letter of September 4, written in Alexandria while he was awaiting the arrival of his horses and wagons from the Peninsula. She grew desperate:

> I am so much dispirited in not having heard from you for so long a time. Two weeks! that I cannot write neither can I do anything till I hear from you.... If the road between Hagerstown & Frederick was fixed I could go to see you.... Won't you give me some encouragement to go?.... Oh! this terrible war how much bitterness & misery it is creating.[52]

A Union charge through the Cornfield, north of the Dunker Church. (*Battles and Leaders of the Civil War*, Grant-Lee Edition, CCHS.)

Annie had reason to be desperate. Early in the morning of September 17, as the fighting reached its peak in The Cornfield, a single Confederate shell burst on the lines of Company A, 7th Pennsylvania Reserves. The shell killed Captain James Colwell and killed or mortally wounded privates Leo Faller (whose letters home have been quoted earlier), John Callio, David Spahr, and William Culp.[53] Annie did not know she was already a widow when she wrote her last letter.

She knew soon enough. Chaplain William Earnshaw of the 49th Pennsylvania, who came from Shippensburg and was acquainted with both James and Annie, wrote her on September 17 after the battle (among the many letters he doubtless wrote that evening):

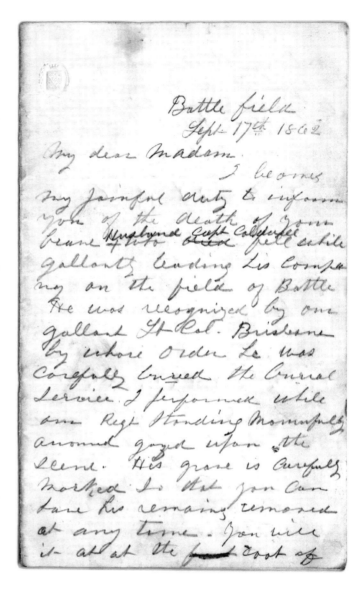

First page of Chaplain Earnshaw's letter to Annie Colwell, informing her of James's death. (Colwell Family Collection.)

> Battle field
> Sept 17th 1862
>
> My dear Madam,
>
> It becomes my painful duty to inform you of the death of your brave husband Capt Colwell who fell while gallantly leading his Company on the field of battle. He was recognized by our gallant Lt. Col. Brisbane by whose order he was carefully buried. The burial service I performed while our Regt standing mournfully around gazed upon the scene. His grave is carefully marked so that you can have his remains removed at any time. You will [find] it at the foot of a large tree on the edge of a grove near a pond on the Diffenbaugh farm near Funkstown Md.[54] His name is marked on the tree. I will render any assistance if in this place when you send for the body—and will furnish any other information you may desire—His effects are in the hands of his Lieutenant. Let me say that we deeply sympathize with you in this sad affliction and pray that God may comfort & sustain you and your dear children. You have much to be proud of—in such a husband & father. He was heroic generous & brave—and so he fell—while defending his flag. May Gods blessing rest upon you and your beloved family.
>
> Yours very truly
> Wm Earnshaw
> Chaplain 49th
> Rgt Pa Vols
>
> P.S. By the side of the Capt we buried one of his men, John Callio
>
> W.E.

Bad news travels fast: Annie already knew of James's death when that letter arrived in Carlisle. Her young cousin, Charley McClure, although in the Quartermaster Corps, had fought with the infantry at South Mountain. His duties then brought him back to Carlisle; thus he escaped the bloodshed at Antietam. It was to him that Chaplain Earnshaw's letter was delivered, the mailman perhaps knowing of James Colwell's death and aware of Charley McClure's relationship to the widow. A pencil note on the back of the chaplain's letter reads:

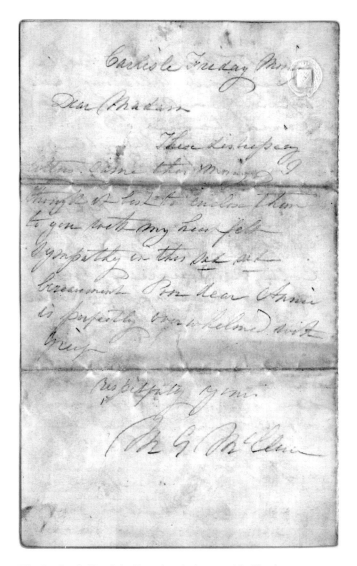

Carlisle Friday morning
[September 19, 1862]

Dear Madam,

These distressing letters came this morning. I thought it best to enclose them to you with my heartfelt sympathy in this <u>sad</u>, <u>sad</u> bereavement. Poor dear Annie is perfectly overwhelmed with grief.

Respectfully yours,
Ch G McClure

Annie's sister, Minnie, or a neighbor may have been with her at the time.

James's body was disinterred from its temporary grave at Antietam, brought home to Carlisle September 25, and buried in the Carlisle graveyard on September 26. "The remains were followed to the grave by the surviving members of his company, and the members of the Carlisle Bar." John Callio, killed by the same shell as James, was buried in Carlisle three days later on September 29.[55]

The back of Chaplain Earnshaw's letter with Charles McClure's note. (Colwell Family Collection.)

Union burial party at Antietam. (*Battles and Leaders of the Civil War*, Grant-Lee Edition, CCHS.)

OUR KILLED AND WOUNDED.—We give below a list, as full as we can procure it, of the killed and wounded from this County in the engagements of the past week:

Killed—Captain James S. Colwell, Capt. Thomas P. Dwen, John Callio, Leo Faller, Joseph U. Steel, David Spahr, Curt. Griffith, A. F. Brownawell, Joseph Weaver.

Wounded—Corporal Charles A. Smith, Michael Smith, William Ingenberger, Wm. Corbet, Alfred Harder, E. C. Kutz, P. F. Eitlebaugh, John R, Stoey, Wm. Fenicle, Wm. Sterner, Wm. Humerich, Leander C. Cornman, William Neely, George W Lyne, D. K. Huyett, Daniel Keeney, W. E. Greason, Samuel McBeth, William Culp, John Cuddy, Capt. T. Kauffman, Samuel McNaughten, David Bailey, D. Baxter, Oiler, Napoleon Sowers, and Lieut. McManus.

Thus have our brave men fallen in their efforts to crush out a most unholy rebellion May their graves be green above them.

Notice of killed and wounded from the *American Democrat*, 24 Sept. 1862.

COLWELL AND DWEN.—It is with pain and sorrow that we have to chronicle the death of Capt. James S. Colwell and Capt. Thomas P. Dwen. They died on the field fighting for the Constitution and the Union.— They were true and loyal men who had gone forth, from no mercenary motives, but with a firm determination to sustain the Union as erected and created by our forefathers. Peace to their ashes.

Editor's note, *American Democrat*, 24 Sept. 1862.

Killed and Wounded from this Town.

The following is a list of the killed and wounded in the several companies from this town in the late bloody battles in Western Maryland.

Killed.

Capt. Jas S. Colwell,
Capt. Thos. P. Dwin,
Privates John Callio,
" Joseph Steel,
" Joseph Weaver,
" Leo. Fowler,
" David Spahr,
" Curtis Griffin,
" A. F. Brownawell,

Wounded.

Capt. T. Kauffman,	Wm. Humerfefr,
Corp. Chas. A. Smith,	Leonard Cornman,
Michael Smith,	William Nealy,
Wm. Ingenberger,	Geo. W. Line,
Wm. Corbit,	D. K. Huyett,
Saml. McNattan,	W. E. Greason,
E. C. Kurtz,	David Baily,
P. F. Eightlebaugh,	Samuel McBeth,
John R. Soey,	William Culp,
Wm. Finicle,	John Cuddy,
W. Steiner,	Dainel Keeny,
Thaddeus McKeehan,	
—— Baxter,	—— Oiler,
—— Sowers,	—— McMannis.

Casualty list from the battles in Western Maryland, *Carlisle American*, 24 Sept. 1862.

At Antietam, Van B. Eby removed personal effects from the body of James Colwell and sent them to his family in Carlisle. His father, Jason W. Eby, a prominent Carlisle merchant, placed the items in an envelope and forwarded them to Annie Colwell. Among other items which may have been in the envelope were very likely all of Annie's letters to him since August 22, 1862, which he had been carrying with him, as well as those which arrived after his death. (Colwell Family Collection.)

Enclosed is a few articles taken from the dead body of Capt. Colwell—by Van B. Eby to be Kept untill Van Returns home if Spared. Should he never Return or direct otherwise then we are to give it to the Family—They were Sent to us by Van through Mr. Early[?]

22 Sept'br   J. W. Eby

Sergeant Van Buren Eby, a member of Company A. (D. Scott Hartzell Collection, U.S. Army Military History Institute.)

Killed in Batttle at Sharpsburg on Wednesday last.—Capt. James S. Colwell, Co. A, 7th, P. R. C.

Thus has fallen in the cause of his country a brave soldier, a true patriot, and a Christian gentleman. The breaking out of this unhallowed rebellion found him a lawyer in practice at the Carlisle bar, and though retiring and modest in his disposition, his highly-cultivated and acute mind, and his marked talents were fully appreciated by his fellow-citizens; his rank promised to be among the first jurists of the country. His kind and amiable disposition had endeared him to all who knew him. His high moral character and exemplary life had made him a bright example in our midst. A wife and children clustered around him, and added the charms of domestic life to the advantages of his position. His wife and children were to him as dear as life.

The war broke out, and from a stern sense of duty alone, he sacrificed the comforts of home and his professional hopes to take up arms for his country. There was no ambition in this ; he desired no place ; he sought no renown ; he saw, amid the sulphurous clouds of war, no future official honors ; he sought none, but moved by pure patriotism alone ; he became a soldier ; that kind and amiable gentleman soon became the stern soldier of real war. On many battle-fields he proved his courage and military skill, beloved by his men, where he led they followed, and he was always willing to lead. He has fallen and left a vacancy which it will be hard to fill with his equal. His wife and children mourn not alone, the whole community mingle their tears over his untimely death. He has died the death of the patriot, as he lived the life of the Christian. Let the lofty marble mark his last resting-place and thereon inscribe a fitting record of his virtues.

DULCE ET DECORUM—PRO PATRI MORI.

Eulogy for James Colwell from the *Carlisle American*, 24 Sept. 1862.

Captain Colwell accepted his commission as first lieutenant in the company on the 19th of April, 1861. He entered the service, as he said, to a friend, "from a sense of duty to his country." The same lofty patriotism which led him to enter the service sustained him under its every privation, and made him a hero in every battle. He died as the true soldier prefers to die, amid the tumult of battle, facing his country's foes. He passed safely through the battles on the Peninsula, and was made Captain by appointment of Gen. McClellan on the 1st of August. At Harrison's Landing he was made Assistant Commissary of Subsistence for the Second Brigade, and filled that position until the battle of South Mountain, when he resumed command of the company. He passed through that battle safely and fell at the head of his company on the battle-field of the Antietam. His body was recognized late in the day, by Lieut.-Col. Brisbane, formerly of Carlisle, as the 49th regiment passed over the ground. Just then his company returned from the charge in which he fell. The burial service was performed by Chaplain Earnshaw, while the men stood around in sorrow, as

—" Slowly and sadly they laid him down," mourning for him as for a father, for as such he was beloved by every member of his company. His ashes have since been removed, and now sleep peacefully in the native valley he died in defending. *Farewell*, NOBLE FRIEND !

Excerpt from an article by David Curriden in the *American Democrat*, 22 Oct. 1862.

Annie Colwell dressed in widow's garb. Copy of a carte de visite in a Colwell Family album, c.1875. (Mrs. R. A. Smith, Colwell Family Collection.)

Burial of Capt. Colwell.

The body of Capt. COLWELL, who was killed in the battle of Antietam Creek, was brought home on Thursday, last and on Friday morning interred in the public grave-yard. His remains were followed to the grave by the surviving members of his company, and the members of the Carlisle Bar.

Notice of James Colwell's burial, *Carlisle American*, 1 Oct. 1862.

Colwell Family plot in the Old Carlisle Graveyard, 1997. (Jim Bradley, Mother Cumberland Collection.)

Base of the Colwell Family monument in the Old Carlisle Grave-yard showing inscriptions for Anne Hall and James S. Colwell. (Jim Bradley, Mother Cumberland Collection.)

A bill directed variously to "Mrs. Capt. Caldwell," "J.S. Colwell dec," and "Mrs. Annie H. Colwell" from the store of A.W. Bentz in Carlisle indicates the purchase of 3 1/4 yards of crape, pins, 17 pairs of men's silk gloves, 8 3/8 yards of black scarfing silk, and 5 yards of ribbon on September 25, all no doubt in preparation for the funeral. (Colwell Family Collection.)

At a formal meeting of the Cumberland County Bar on September 25, James was memorialized by a resolution noting his "stern integrity...firm and inflexible persever-ance...the disinterested sacrifice which he made in hazarding his life for his country."[56] The *Carlisle American* printed a glowing eulogy. Editor George Zinn, Carlisle Postmaster since 1861, and an associate of James since they together attended the first ever Union County Convention in 1856 in support of Fremont, called James "a brave soldier, a true patriot, and a Christian gentleman."[57] In a laudatory letter dated September 29, D. D. Curriden, brother of the editor of the *Shippensburg News*, wrote of James from the camp of Company A at Antietam, "*Farewell*, NOBLE FRIEND."[58]

James and the thousands of others who fell at Antietam did not die in vain. Technically a draw since both armies remained in their lines at the end of the day, the battle was a major reverse for the South. Antietam marked the end of the beginning; it was a turning point in the Civil War, a hinge on which the history of the Republic turned. The carnage served a purpose: casualties sustained there made clear across the North that persistence, determination and more casualties would be required to defeat the Confederacy. Those casualties reinforced Northern determination to fight the war to a finish. The war had hardened those in the ranks of the Northern armies as it hardened their families at home. Union soldiers left their innocence behind. So did the country.[59]

Abraham Lincoln. (*The Soldier in the Civil War*, John Leslie, 1893, CCHS.)

Even more important, the battle gave Lincoln the opportunity to issue the Preliminary Emancipation Proclamation, which he had refrained from doing previously for fear it would seem an act of desperation by those losing the war. Once the war was cast in the moral terms of abolishing slavery, there was little possibility that the nations of Europe would assist the Confederacy. What the country was to do with freed slaves was a matter to which there were as yet no answers, a matter which events would determine at a later date. But after Antietam it became clear to the North what the war was all about: it was a war to end slavery. And so it did.

Endnotes

1 JSC to AHC 21 July 1862.

2 JSC to AHC 14 August 1862.

3 JSC to AHC 21 August 1862.

4 Carlisle *Herald*, 20 August 1862; AHC to JSC 22 August 1862. This is the first letter from Annie since the previous winter that has survived.

5 Carlisle *Herald*, 15 August 1862. The *Herald* reported early in September that the total number of men eligible for the draft in Carlisle was 893 and that 293, one-third of those eligible, were already serving. Carlisle *Herald*, 3 September 1862.

6 AHC to JSC 28 August 1862.

7 AHC to JSC 22 August 1862.

8 AHC to JSC 26 August 1862.

9 JSC to AHC 3 August 1662.

10 JSC to AHC 8 August 1862.

11 AHC to JSC 22 August 1862.

12 JSC to AHC 21 August 1862.

13 AHC to JSC 26 August 1862.

14 JSC to AHC 10 August 1862.

15 JSC to AHC 10 August 1862.

16 JSC to AHC 12 August 1862.

17 JSC to AHC 14 August 1862.

18 JSC to AHC 19 August 1862.

19 JSC to AHC 21 August 1862.

20 JSC to AHC 23 August 1862.

21 AHC to JSC 28 August 1862.

22 Others shared the same view. For example, George Meade, himself subsequently commander of the Army of the Potomac, wrote his wife of McClellan's performance on the Peninsula, "McClellan...has lost the greatest chance any man ever had on this continent." Meade, *Life and Letters*, 303.

23 JSC to AHC 23 August 1862.

24 The sources for most published casualty figures are Fox, *Regimental Losses in the American Civil War* and Thomas L. Livermore, *Numbers and Losses in the Civil War in America 1861-65* (Boston: Houghton Mifflin & Co., 1900).

25 AHC to JSC 1 September 1862.

26 John Hay, *Lincoln and the Civil War in the Diaries and Letters of John Hay*, ed. Tyler Dennett (New York: Dodd, Mead & Co., 1939), 45.

27 McClellan, *Civil War Papers*, ed. Sears, 416.

28 AHC to JSC 3 September 1862.

29 JSC to AHC 4 September 1862.

30 J. Thomas Scharf, *History of Maryland*, 3 vols. (repr., Hatboro, Pa.: Tradition Press, 1967), vol. III, 498.

31 Welles, *Diary of Gideon Welles*, 113.

32 Edward J. Stackpole, *From Cedar Mountain to Antietam* (Harrisburg, Pa.: The Stackpole Company, 1959) 300-301.

33 JSC to AHC 2 September 1862.

34 JSC to AHC 4 September 1862.

35 JSC to AHC 13 September 1862.

36 Morison et al., *Growth of the American Republic*, vol. 1, 667.

37 "Proclamation of Governor Andrew G. Curtin, September 4th, 1 P.M.," *Shippensburg News*, 6 September 1862.

38 AHC to JSC 6 September 1862.

39 AHC to JSC 8 September 1862.

40 Carlisle *Herald*, 12 September 1862.

41 AHC to JSC 12 September 1862. Perry County lay over the mountain immediately to the north of Carlisle. Passes over that mountain to Perry County were few and difficult.

42 John Michael Priest, *Before Antietam: The Battle for South Mountain* (Shippensburg, Pa.: White Mane Publishing Company, Inc., 1992), 60.

43 Catton, *Terrible Swift Sword*, 449-450.

44 JSC to AHC 13 September 1862. This letter was postmarked September 18, never entering the mail system until five days later.

45 The best description of the battle of South Mountain is Priest, *Before Antietam: The Battle for South Mountain*.

46 JSC to AHC 15 September 1862. The letter is actually dated "14th Sept 5 O'clock P.M.;" but James's company was still clawing its way uphill against Confederate fire on South Mountain on the afternoon of September 14. The content of the letter makes clear that he has misdated it.

47 AHC to JSC 13 September 1862.

48 Two of the best accounts of the Battle of Antietam are John Michael Priest, *Antietam: The Soldier's Battle* (Shippensburg, Pa.: White Mane Publishing Co., 1989) and Stephen W. Sears, *Landscape Turned Red: The Battle of Antietam* (New York: Ticknor & Fields, 1983).

49 McClellan, *Civil War Papers*, ed. Sears, 469. Another view of McClellan's performance at Antietam is contained in Waugh, *The Class of 1846*, 383-392.

50 *The War of the Rebellion: A Compilation of the Official Records of the Union and Confederate Armies*, 128 vols. (Washington: Government Printing Office, 1887), vol. 19, 218.

51 Ibid, 274.

52 AHC to JSC 18 September 1862. For the full text of this letter, written after James's death but before Annie knew of it, see pages 163-164.

53 Letter from soldier correspondent Typo, *Shippensburg News*, 11 October 1862.

54 The reference to "Funkstown, Md." is puzzling, since other sources indicate that the burial took place on or near the Antietam battlefield. Funkstown is approximately ten miles north of Antietam.

55 *Carlisle American*, 1 October 1862.

56 *American Democrat*, 1 October 1862.

57 *Carlisle American*, 24 September 1862.

58 *Shippensburg News*, 11 October 1862. A long letter appearing in this issue gave the history of Company A from its induction in June, 1861 to the Battle of Antietam.

59 Thoughtful discussions of the change in the character of the war and in the attitude of the North after Antietam may be found in Catton, *Terrible Swift Sword*, 461-463 and Sears, *Landscape Turned Red*, 317-319.

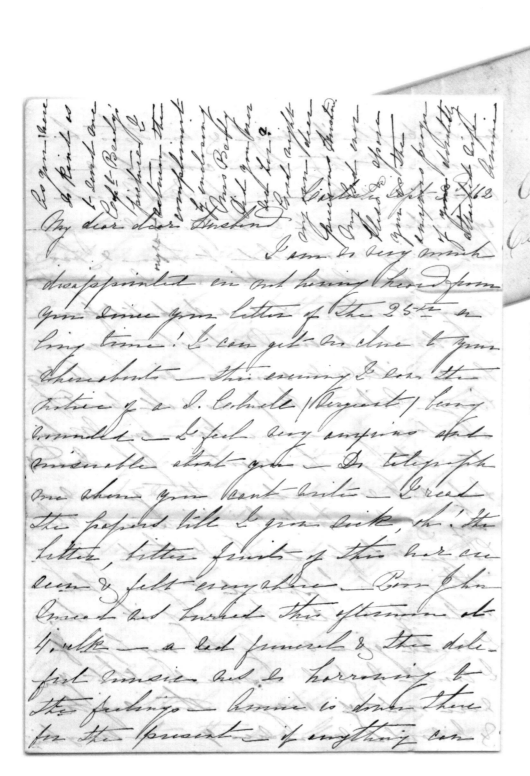

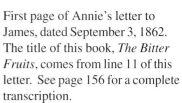

First page of Annie's letter to James, dated September 3, 1862. The title of this book, *The Bitter Fruits*, comes from line 11 of this letter. See page 156 for a complete transcription.

Transporting supplies by wagon. (*The Photographic History of the Civil War*, Francis T. Miller, 1912, CCHS.)

JSC to AHC, July 25, 1862

2nd Brigade Quartermaster Dept
Near Harrison's Landing
25th July 1862

My Dear wife,

After writing to you day before yesterday I received your letter of the 19th inst. I do not think with you that things look darker for the union. I think I can see the beginning of a brighter day. But I think the president ought also to draft or require the governors to do so of all the men he has power by law to do. If government would put 500,000 or more men in the field at once the war would be soon ended. I fear the number demanded cannot be raised by volunteers.

I sent you some money $340 on Tuesday, to go by express. You ought to receive it today if not yesterday. I wrote you also day before yesterday by a German barber from Carlisle named Ninnecool. I dont know whether I spell his name right.

I am detailed to act as brigade Quartermaster during the absence of the brig quartermaster—gone home on sick leave for twenty days.

Capt Henderson is acting Lieut Colonel and most probably will get a commission. How long I may be in my present position I cannot say. It is doubtful whether the quartermaster will ever return. I have an opportunity to send this by him part of the way and he is about starting.

Write me as soon as you get the money. Also if you don't get it.

Capt Henderson is well, although he has been complaining some for a few days.

Truly your devoted husband
James

JSC to AHC, July 27, 1862

Camp Near Harrison's
Landing Va. 27th July 1862

My Dear wife,

I had the pleasure of receiving yours of the 22nd mailed the 23rd this morning. But I see you will extend the time between letters. Your former letter was mailed the 19th the last the 23rd. Four days. I wrote you five letters last week three of which I sent part of the way by private means thinking you would receive them earlier. One on Sunday one on Monday one on Tuesday one on Wednesday and one on Friday. I hope you have or will receive them all. But I am more concerned that you receive $340 that I sent on Tuesday to be expressed from Baltimore. I hope you have received it. If you have not write to me immediately on receipt of this.

As I stated in my last I am acting as assistant quartermaster of the brigade. This keeps me away from the regiment about a half mile. I expect to move my quarters nearer the regiment tomorrow. The assistant quartermaster has gone home sick and I am put here till he recovers. His leave of absence is twenty days.

You say Molly Baird has started for Fortress Monroe. Poor Molly. It is a pity she ever heard that her husband was living. She will arrive at the fortress to hear that she will never see him alive if she does not learn it before she gets there. I heard here two or three days ago that he had died, and I see it is confirmed by the newspapers. I fear it is too true.

You speak in one of your letters about my resigning. I presume it would not be accepted if I did. Maj Todd it is said has tendered his twice since we have been here and it has not been accepted. And also many others. But it would hardly be proper for me to resign at the present time when the government is calling for more troops and can scarcely get them. Do you think it would?

My eyes seem to be failing very much. I can hardly see to write. This is old age coming on. We had a heavy rain last evening which was very acceptable, as the roads had become very dusty. Everything was quite fresh this morning but today has been quite warm.

What is the name of the servant you have now. I have always drawn my pay in Vienna's name. The capt H. drawing in the name of the one we have had together. We are entitled to pay for a servant but we have to give the name etc.

Send me postage stamps. I can't get them here. Send me till I have two or three dozzen. Endeavour to write every other day. I think the war will be over in six months perhaps less. I hope it will and that I may be safely at home.

Your devoted husband
James

JSC to AHC, July 30, 1862

Camp at Harrison's Landing Va
30th July 1862

My Dear wife,

I was highly delighted at the receipt of your two letters of the 24th & 25th respectively yesterday morning. I was delighted because the former was a good long letter written in good spirits and the latter acknowledged the safe arrival of the money of which I was a little fearful.

I should have answered your letters yesterday but I was so busy I was unable to do so. We had to move our quarters on Monday & had scarcely got fixed rightly till I received another order to move again which we did today. I have twenty three wagon-teams one four horse & one two horse ambulance and thirty-three men, one blacksmith shop—one carpenter shop & a saddler shop. The shops are only tents and the stock of tools very light. Sometimes I have a great deal to attend to and sometimes very little. On the whole the labor is lighter than in the company and I can have more conveniences, but the responsibility is much greater.

I think you will not have much difficulty in getting change in a few weeks. The postage stamp will be out, and the government one & two dollar notes. The

Postage stamps used to mail Colwell letters. (Colwell Family Collection.)

POSTAGE STAMPS.—The United States postage stamps, which are coming so freely into circulation, besides having the amount of their value in figures upon the upper corners, may be readily recognized by their colors and vignettes, which are as follows:—

Amount.	Vignette	Color
I cent	Franklin	Blue.
3 cent	Washington	Pink,
5 cent	Jefferson	Chockolate.
10 cent	Washington	Green.
20 cent	Washington	Black·
24 cent	Washington	Lilac.
30 cent	Franklin	Yellow.
90 cent	Washington	Blue.

Note from the *Carlisle American*, 30 July 1862.

postage stamps intended for change will not answer for letters but will be for change altogether. However they will answer every purpose as you can get other stamps for them. You recollect I cautioned you to be careful of your change & gold. I was expecting the scarcity of specie that has come. How much have you now.

I hope George will make out well in his speculation in gold but I see the premium has come down to $17 per cent. It was as high as $20 & $21.

You say I never say anything about resigning. I think it is hardly worth while. But I did write you something in my last written on the 27th which I hope you will receive in due time. My letters now will hardly arrive so promptly as they did last week as I then had opportunities of send them part of the way by private hands. I wrote you by Capt. Ringwalt on Friday morning. He lives in Chester County and went home on sick leave for twenty days. I hope you have received the letter before this. I am acting assistant quartermaster of the 2nd Brigade in his place, till he recovers. I believe that is the position Charley Penrose had in Bank's army.

On the 31st of July, Col. E. B. Harvey, was dismissed from the service for coward-ice in the battles on the Peninsula. Lieut.-Col. Bollinger, was appointed Colonel in Harvey's stead, and Captain Henderson made Lieutenant-Colonel of the regiment, and First Lieutenant Colwell appointed Captain, Second Lieutenant Beatty, First Lieutenant, and Sergeant Ruby, Second Lieutenant of the company.

Excerpt from a correspondent's article, *American Democrat*, 22 Oct. 1862.

By the way I see that W. M. Penrose was partici-pating in the war meeting at Carlisle the other evening. Has he a notion to gird on his armor again and take the field?

It is true that Col Harvey has resigned. I presume he did so to prevent being dismissed. He did not be-have well on the battlefields. But I have never written to anybody about it. The fact is that a great many of the officers who have resigned have done so because they have received hints—sometimes very broad ones—that it would be to their credit to do so. They were not wanted. Others were sick & their health would not permit their remaining in the service. A great many officers have resigned but I do not know of one who had good health and was considered a meritorious of-ficer whose resignation has been accepted.

The reserves have done considerable fighting but it is a mistake to suppose that they have done more or as much as some others. They were in the battles of Mechanicsville, Gaines' Mill & New Market Road—three. That is all. Some divisions have been in a num-ber more battles and severe ones too and in some of those same ones. The reserves did not do all the fight-ing on that memorable retreat as you suppose. Nor the half of it. You must remember that they are all Penn-sylvanians and that it is Pennsylvania papers that you read. And I have discovered that a great deal that you see in the papers is not true. But I do not desire to detract from the reserves. They did bravely and nobly especially in the first two battles. In the third they were so fatigued and worn out from marching and watching and loss of sleep that many of the men were scarcely able to walk. It is quite probable that if the reserves had not been there the army could not have escaped. But others did their duty nobly & bravely as the reserves.

There is nothing new here. Everything is quiet. It is rumored that a movement may be made from here soon, but I think that very uncertain, and will depend altogether on future contingencies.

I have received a letter from Mrs Holmes inquiring about her son. She says she received one from Capt. Henderson. I will write her tomorrow if I can get time.

Don't forget to write every other day. Your letters generally come very regularly, although yours of the 24th & 25th came together.

Your most devoted husband

James

JSC to AHC, August 3, 1862

Camp Near Harrison's Landing Va

3rd August 1862

My Dear wife,

Since I last wrote I have had the gratification of receiving three letters from you—two yesterday of the 26th & 28th and one this morning of the 30th ult. No I mistake I received yours of the 26th before, but I received one from Sister Libby with yours yesterday morning. My last letter to you was written on Wednes-day morning. I hope you will excuse me. I have been very busy this week. On Tuesday, and Friday & Satur-day especially. That I could not find time to write you. I was drawing quartermasters stores and camp & garri-son equipage and issuing them to the regiments. I think I am through the heaviest part of that for a while at least.

It has been pretty warm here some days, but I have not felt the heat so oppressive any time some of the first few days after we arrived at James river still I sometimes feel very uncomfortable from the heat.

I presume it was too warm for you to enjoy your-self to the full extent at Mr. Hamilton's "pic a nic a."

Neither Capt Henderson, Beatty or myself have received any commissions other than we had but have all been named for promotion as I understand and act in that capacity except Mr. Beatty. The people gener-ally get ahead on these things. Capt Biddle was al-ways called Col. in Carlisle. I mean Harry Biddle. I believe he was a Lieut. Col. in the state service but was only a captain in the U.S. service.

You are mistaken about quartermaster's not having fighting to do. That is true to some extent. You think they are not field officers. Captains of companies & Lieuts are not field officers. Only Genls & Colonels Lieut Cols & Majors are. The others are officers of the line or company officers. A brigade quartermaster belongs to the brigadier generals staff. But it is true that when the wagon trains are moving as during the battles before Richmond the quartermaster must be with his train. But then it is also true that the enemy always shell the trains and attack them at every opportunity, as they contain the provisions of the soldiers and other valuable stores. Still as a general thing it is not as dangerous I suppose as commanding a company in the field although that depends on circumstances. Sometimes the trains are shelled when the soldiers are not molested. Parties go out to attack trains & cut them off.

On Thursday night my slumbers were disturbed by the report of a cannon down towards the river but I paid no attention to it as it is no unusual thing to hear two or three shots during the night, but at the 2nd or third shot I heard the shell whistle. I knew what that meant. I jumped up & put on my clothes & by the time I got out the shells were flying pretty fast. The rebels had planted batteries up the river & down it and along it and when they all got started they rained the shells & solid shot all around. Dangerous as it was it was a grand sight. We could follow the course of the shells which passed off a distance from us by their fuses which were lighted, but those which come directly toward us we cannot see however we could hear them, and could easily step out of the way if we knew exactly the place they would pass; but we would be just as likely to pass right into the track of the ball as out of it so it is just about as safe to stand still.

I do not think there is much danger of the rebels cutting off our supplies while we remain here. I have no doubt they would do so if they could, but I think they cannot succeed.

It is rather strange that an officer in the union army would be so very intimate with a lady who would speak of his government & army as May Sever's does of the U.S. Government.

I am glad you have plenty of berries. I would like much to eat some. I never see a berry. I have been where there are quantities of all sorts of berries & peaches but always green when I saw them. I do not suppose I will taste a berry this summer. The season will soon be over.

I am afraid you will not have much money left when you get all your bills paid. I thought that you would have none but Steel's and the shoemakers, un-

Attack upon a Union baggage train by Stuart's cavalry. (*Battles and Leaders of the Civil War*, Grant-Lee Edition, CCHS.)

less you have paid Steel in which case I thought you would have contracted others. Be careful about running up bills. They grow unaware like tares in the night.

Father Hunt followed Col. Harvey. He was of no account. Nobody had any respect for him and I believe he was requested to resign which he did very reluctantly. He was in the army for the pay. Nothing else. I believe he has gone & nobody regrets it. He was no honor to the cause he professed to serve. Write often.

    Your loving husband
      James

Last fall & winter you often desired me to send you a photograph likeness of myself, but I never had an opportunity of getting one. You have not asked for one for some time. But having succeeded at last in getting a photograph I send you one hoping it will not be unacceptable now. Please let me know whether you think I am changed in appearance.

    Your devoted husband
      James

JSC to AHC, August 8, 1862

        Camp Near Harrison's Landing
           Va. 8th August 1862
Since writing last on Tuesday I have received yours of the 2nd inst. I had not time to write yesterday. This forenoon I went into my tent to write you and it was so hot I was obliged to beat a retreat. It has been very warm all this week and the nights are almost as warm

as the days. I have a Sibley tent and it is so warm I can not remain in it during the heat of the day. I write this in the tent of my clerk which is not so warm as mine. I dont know whether I told you before that I have a clerk, or not. I have and as he is a pretty good looking young man and writes a good hand perhaps you would like if he would write you sometimes instead of me.

You seem to think that it is the glare of the sun that has affected my eyes. Doubtless that had something to do with the failure of my sight. I find my eyes are recovering somewhat since I came into my present position where I am not so much in the sun as formerly.

With regard to the question of age I will relate to you what occurred yesterday. I stopped at a spring to get a drink down at the river where no one knew me. There was but a single drinking cup and the spring was surrounded by men waiting for their turn. When one was satisfied and was about handing the cup to his neighbor, the latter told him to "give it to that old fellow first." "That old fellow" was your humble servant—your husband.

I think it was a good deal of a risk for you to undertake to drive to the mountains with the children. You could drive a quiet horse well enough but if any thing had gone wrong—"and accidents will happen in the best regulated families"—I do not know what you would have done. I think you would have been frightened and almost powerless to get out of the difficulty. I am glad however that you got back safely and that you all enjoyed yourselves.

I am glad to know that the government has waked up at last and are going to draft 300,000 men in addition to the 300,000 new volunteers making 600,000 additional troops. They should have done it long ago. If we had had half that many additional last spring the war would have been over and we at home. I believe the war can be ended before six months expire if it is conducted energetically. And I sincerely hope it will be and I safe at home with you all, where I would dearly love to be.

I received the two stamps with your last and the ten—not a dozzen—you sent sometime since. I received your letter acknowledging the receipt of the money I sent. I presume you have received the letter before this.

Oh but it is warm! The perspiration is rolling off me. Clerky complains of it being the warmest day we have had. He has fallen asleep however and does not feel the heat I presume.

> Your truly devoted husband
> James

JSC to AHC, August 19, 1862

> Near Fortress Monroe Va
> Hampton 19th Aug. 1862

My Dear wife,

I left camp near Harrison's Landing on Friday about noon and arrived here on Sunday morning. I mounted my horse at nine o'clock to take some teams to the landing to have provisions unloaded and then we started, and traveled all day and all night without feed. Stopped next morning about 20 minutes to feed the horses and went on again till after dark when we halted till the moon rose about 11 1/2 o'clock P.M. when we started again and arrived here as stated above.

We have been awaiting orders ever since. It is the impression that we are to go on board here for transportation to Acquia creek. I was pretty considerably fatigued on arrival here having been in the saddle about fifty-six hours with very little rest. The troops all came down on boats. I mean McCall's division. The 7th Regiment is out on the bay here on board as I am informed. We are about two miles from Fortress Monroe. I went over yesterday evening but could not ascertain the position of the boat till dark when it was too late to go out.

So you see that those who were not quartermasters had the easiest position that time. We saw no enemy on our road nor did we hear a gun fired. It is said that the guerilla's seventy-five in number made a dash at one of the trains and instead of capturing the wagons were themselves captured.

Our brigade all except the 7th Regt left several days before us and are said to be at Fredericksburg, where I presume we are going. The 1st & 3rd brigades are out in the bay near the fort as is said.

I have received no letter from you since my last nor do I expect to receive any till we get into camp again somewhere. But I hope to receive them all some day soon and desire you to write as usual.

> Your affte husband
> James

Baggage-wagons on their way to Richmond. (*Battles and Leaders of the Civil War*, Grant-Lee Edition, CCHS.)

JSC to AHC, August 21, 1862

Hampton Near Ft. Monroe Va
21st August 1862

My Dear Wife.

I wrote you day before yesterday, not having the least idea at that time that I would remain here so long. But you perceive I am still here and still more I do not know when we will get away.

The water here is very bad and the dust is sometimes almost choking. The fact is dust has been more abundant than anything else for the last two weeks. Before we left Harrison's Landing it had become very annoying. So many wagons & horses moving about kept the dust in continual motion. And on the way here we were surrounded & covered with dust. And since our arrival here there is no improvement.

Since we left Harrison's landing we have had comparatively cool weather, especially at nights, so that we have been spared the discomforts of the very scorching weather we had previously during the march. If it had been as warm as formerly I hardly know how we could have got through without water or food for the horses. While speaking of the weather I may say that it is very warm this morning, and gives token of a very hot day.

This is the town the rebels burned when they left it. You perhaps saw the account of it in the papers at the time. There are but one or two houses left standing in the suburbs. Nothing is left standing but the chimneys and parts of broken walls. And the whole place seems an utter desolation. A fit abode for owls & bats. Here and there the negroes have erected a board shanty, but that adds nothing to the improvement of the place. It appears as if it might have been a pretty village in its prosperous days. Many of the houses were of brick. We are in the gardens or rather what was once gardens or yards. Now overgrown with weeds, and a great abundance of fig trees laden with figs but green. They say they are figs I dont know. They must have been very plenty here in other days.

Yesterday I rode over to and through the fort. It is quite a pretty place. And I thought of Mrs. Brent who was wont to talk so much about "old point" comfort. And then I thought of a little light haired, bright eyed girl that used to be moving noiselessly around in those days who was of far more interest to me than aught else, and who although a girl no longer, still occupies my thoughts by day & by night. Her hair is not so light nor her eyes so black as in those days. But the same brightness sparkles in her eyes and spreads sunshine all over her face. I am not going to tell you who it is lest you might become jealous and you know jealousy is "a green eyed monster" which when aroused can scarcely be appeased. What would I not give now for one long look into the deep depths of those dancing eyes and to remain in their light for long years to come. My sincere hope is that this boon may be vouchsafed to me before many months.

I have heard nothing from you since yours of the 9th inst. I do not expect to receive any of your letters till I get where the company is. The reserves have all gone to Acquia creek as I am informed. From there I presume they will go to Fredericksburg and then "on to Richmond" I suppose.

How is Ban coming on. Is he in Baltimore yet. I presume he will be very much afraid of being drafted as he would have to fight against his beloved secesh.

Watermelons are quite abundant here but they are dear. There are also some peaches but pretty hard to get hold of. I got a saucer of ice cream yesterday, the first I have tasted since I was at home. That is nearly eight months ago. It seems a long time since I have seen you—too long. How much longer it will be till I can see you & be with you I have no conception. But I pray the time may come at last. I think it cannot be eight months more. The rebellion ought to be suppressed before the end of this year and by the blessing of God I think it will be.

I remain your sincerely attached husband
James

View of Carlisle from the road leading into S. Hanover St., c.1865. (A. A. Line, CCHS.)

AHC to JSC, August 22, 1862

Carlisle Aug 22nd 1862

My own dear husband,

I have had the great joy of receiving your letter of the 19th which came in an incredibly short time. You have had a very fatiguing journey. I suppose you are now at the end of it. I am so thankful that you continue in good health. So many suffer during this season with diarrhea. You have never spoken of it so I conclude you have escaped. A very good & simple remedy for that disease is clove tea—hot water poured over a few cloves & let steam & drink at intervals—during fruit & corn season I find it very useful among the children. Our tomatoes are at perfection now though the drought is injuring them, I still put up a goodly quantity for you. Oh! you will fare so well for I am making so many nice things in anticipation of your return. You will have to show your gratitude by growing fat & driving all care away from your brow, so that no one would think of offering that "old man a drink" again.

I am surprised to notice Mr. Beatty growing so gray. He has a mammoth flag out of his window & notices posted all round the town recruiting for the 7th Regt. I suppose Mrs. Holmes is happy in having her son home with her.

I felt very sad this afternoon in seeing the body of poor young Zimmerman carried by here. I had no idea his wound would prove fatal. When I saw him last winter he appeared so robust with a promise of long life, to be cut off so early is sad. How many useful lives have been lost by this war & how many broken

RECRUITS FOR COMPANY A.—It will be seen that Lieut. BEATTY is enlisting recruits for Capt. Henderson's company, now stationed on the banks of the James river. He is prepared to pay the sum of ten dollars to all who may respond, independent of the bounties offered by the Government, State and County. Already some have left, and we hear of others who intend following their example. The "Fencibles" did the fighting of the 7th while in the engagements, and only wait for orders to enter into the work with renewed energy.

News note from the *Carlisle American,* 30 July 1862.

hearts it has made! I pray that God in his infinite mercy will spare us.

I am told that Charley Penrose is released on his parole. Mr. Penrose is keeping bachelor's hall & entertaining his sisters & their families whilst his wife is in New York. Miss Martha Duncan has recently heard of the death of Mrs. Bannesille who formerly lived here. The tableaux passed off so well that there is to be a repetition of them in a few weeks. $120.00 were cleared after paying all expenses.

I think I told you of the treasure of a servant I thought I had secured. Just before I made the final arrangement with her I received a note from Miss Virginia Lyon telling me that her figure was not such as an unmarried person's ought to be so I'd better be wary of her. On investigation I think I have made a narrow escape by declining taking her. I now have my eye on another treasure in the country. I hope that she will suit so that I shall never have to change again.

We had a promise of a rainy night but it has passed

off with a light shower. We have real August weather now delightfully cool nights & oppressively hot at mid-day.

George is still here, quite an invalid. Charley & Lizzie return to Chicago next month. I am expecting any day to see Ban's name in the papers for refusing to support the government. He feels the loss of his Beauregard keenly.

Nan & John are having a conversation in my hearing on the subject of ghosts. Today after the marvellous had been dwelt on for some time John remarked that he had never heard of any before excepting the Holy Ghost, and he wondered if they were all holy. Daisy is getting very companionable & grows fast. James is as sweet as ever & I think is remarkably intelligent. Of his age though his speech must be like Paul's rather stammering as yet.

I believe I always wind up my letters with a domestic recital which is only very dear to you & I. I think people who have no children must necessarily grow egotistical. Nan & John wont be transferred till Monday week because they were sick at the time of the regular examination.

Genl. Elliott has been here on a visit to his family. Mrs Elliott says he will soon be a Major Genl. Report says that John Lee is making every exertion to advance himself. I have seen nothing more of Edgar Hayes since he left us for Harrisburg. Neither have I heard anything from Shippensburg.

Anderson's body-guard is being recruited here now. Martin's hotel is very much of a rendezvous for them. So of course St. James' Square is very popular with the young ladies.

Write soon often & good long letters telling me all about yourself. Good night.

> truly your devotedly attached wife
> Annie

JSC to AHC, August 23, 1862

> Hampton Near Fortress
> Monroe Va. 23rd August 1862

My Dear wife,

Here we are still without the least sign of our moving still I think we will go within two or three days or perhaps today. I wish we could get to the brigade as I do not expect to hear anything from you till I get with it. I hope you are still writing. If you discontinue I will get nothing but old letters when I do get there, and then none for a long time. If I had known we would have been here so long and had written you before we left Harrison's Landing to write here, I might have received several letters while here.

We had a fine rain here yesterday morning which laid the dust and it has been quite cool and pleasant since. It is delightful this morning—cool & cloudy. I hope it will not get at raining again.

I don't remember whether I wrote you about the contrabands we have in the Army. At Harrisons Landing there was quite a city of them, dwelling in tents. We were here but an hour or two till they were beside us putting up their tents. I believe there was not one left behind. What is to be done with them I do not know. I suppose they are more uncomfortable than they were with their masters.

It is said that this army is to be put under Genl Burnside. Genl McClellan seems to be fading away. His friends are not nearly so numerous as they were formerly. His plan has turned out a failure. He ought to have been in Richmond long ago. The army could have been taken there months ago I believe with far less loss of life than has been sustained by it. Notwithstanding the great loss of life we are no nearer Richmond than we were last April. And it will be more difficult to go there now than it would have been then. Still I believe we will go there before many more weeks or give it up.

I never could see what such a clamor was got up in McClellan's favor for. He never had done anything to justify it. I did not desire to condemn him but always wished to wait till he would do something to hurrah about before commencing it. I believe I wrote you as much a long time ago as you appeared to be infected with the McClellan mania at that time. I dont know how you feel now. He has not fulfilled the expectations of his friends. There will probably be some hard fighting the coming fall, but not harder than we have had but I think we will go to Richmond with the blessing of God.

The men that have died in battle are few compared with those who have died of disease. Therefore the quicker the war can be ended the fewer lives it will cost.

I see David Nevin who formerly belonged to our company and was made a lieutenant last winter in the 109th Pennsylvania vols has been taken prisoner and I suppose is in a cell now as Jeff Davis threatened to scare thus any of Pope's officers he would take prisoner.

My health remains good thus far. I pray God it may continue so for the Army is a terrible place for a sick man. I have no doubt that hundreds die for want of proper attention who might live with care. It seems impossible to give the sick the attention they ought to have. They are so many and the accommodations so inferior.

The children have not written me a letter since last winter and now vacation is over and they will plead want of time. Will they be transferred to a higher school or did their sickness prevent it.

It is beginning to look very much like rain and I have to go two miles to the post office so I must close soon.

I wish you would make me a couple flannel shirts. Cassimere is the best. It is barred or striped dark & light grey. Make them long, long as my white shirts and wide in the sleeves etc. but I will write you again before you get the stuff. I will want drawers too. The flannel you made my drawers of last winter did not wear at all.

Very truly your affte husband
James

AHC to JSC, August 28, 1862

Carlisle Aug 28th /62

My Darling Husband,

I have heard nothing from you since I last wrote.

I had the childrens' likenesses taken this week. They promise to be very good. I have not seen them since they were finished. The four were taken together without any trouble & with the first sitting. We will love to look at them when we get old.

Aunt Miller is failing very rapidly. Cousin Catherine Smyzer is there now. Some of the Coopers & Jane Smyzer are to be here this week. Galbraith Miller is here again. I do think he is getting quite imbecile. I think he is a pretty hard drinker. This morning he showed me some of his wife's letters, wanted to know what I call you, & altogether behaved in a most non-

The Anderson Cavalry.

Recruits for this new regiment have been arriving at Carlisle Barracks all last week from Philadelphia and other parts of the State There are now about five hundred encamped in the field outside of the Barracks. The men belonging to this regiment are all picked and hail from nearly every county in the State of Pennsylvania. Lieut. SPENCER is now here and will attend to the drilling of the men, and we have no doubt will be one of the highest officers, (if not commander) in the regiment. When they are drilled and equipped they will proceed to Tennessee where they will act as a body guard to Gen. Buell. We understand that, when full, the regiment will number 800 strong.

Article about the Anderson Cavalry,
Carlisle American, 27 Aug. 1862.

sensical style. Even our John remarked to me how badly he managed his little boy, teaching him to fight, lie & reproved & praised him in the same breath. He says his wife cant manage him, but I think he is getting the worst kind of management now.

This afternoon I was interrupted in my writing, but since then I have had the great joy of receiving yours of the 25th. You were not very well, have you entirely recovered? Do be prudent—about your eating.

If you left Hampton as you anticipated doing on that day, you will have received quite a budget of letters ere this reaches you. I have no idea where the Brigade are. Have not seen any of the Anderson's lately.

You must feel so lonely in the evening with none but strangers about you, but you will probably find some of them pleasant acquaintances.

Today Mr. Halbert called here to get your age & name as the business of drafting has commenced. I gave your age about 40. Mr Croft cant be taken because he is 45. Now if you had not gone already we might have added a few years to your age & kept you at home. Judge Heplen's sons stand a poor chance of staying at home any longer without buying an exemption because the poorer classes are very violent against him. Galbraith Miller has thrown up his Colonelcy in the 2nd Maryland Regt. & is applying for a Generalship. Will Watts left yesterday for Ft Leavenworth. His habits are very bad. The Anderson troop numbers nearly 300 & are camped near the Garrison. I believe there is to be a repetition of the tableaux whilst they are here at a good time to collect some spare quarters.

The old college bell sounded this morning for the first time in two months. I was real glad to hear it. Sounded like an old friend.

Last Sunday morning Minnie & I were startled by great hollering & shouting in Mrs Croft's yard & we thought we would apply our eyes to the fence holes to know the cause of the commotion. There we saw Mr. Rhoads & Mrs Croft issuing from the convenient little outhouse with a mouse in their hands & Mrs Rhoads the other side of the building with a hoe trying to extricate Mrs Croft's hen which had gotten down. Mrs Croft retired in disgust, but Mrs Rhoads made her Man whom she calls her husband persevere in the task of emancipation until his patience was exhausted. So the poor chicken remained in her new home till the next day when she was released & the poor thing expressed her joy by laying an egg.

I think I am now fixed with a servant. Yesterday afternoon I went out to the forge to see a girl who is highly recommended. She is stout & accustomed to hard work. The town is full of contrabands but so worthless, they think if they can do one thing they are accomplished. The girl we have now is delicate & I find the most of my time is spent in the kitchen which dont suit me who has so much sewing to do. Whenever you write me fully about your shirts & drawers I will be very happy to make them. Tell me particularly about the shoulders whether you prefer yokes or bands. I have seen such flannel as you describe on persons but not in the stores but Bentz could send for it.

My dear, dear husband I am so anxious to have you home. In three days it will be eight months since I was perfectly happy.

Mr. McClure has been in quite a commotion about the key of the office. I suppose Mr. Goodyear mislaid it in the hurry of going away though he writes that he left it with Gilldin.

I intend making Nan & John write you soon. I have been busy preserving & attending to the household. Daisy & James are well. Good bye write often to your dear little wife

Annie

Anna Briggs Ege, wife of Lieutenant John Smead who was killed at the second battle of Bull Run, Va. Anna was a daughter of Michael Galbraith Ege, and a first cousin once removed of Annie Colwell. (*History and Genealogy of the Ege Family*, Rev. Thompson P. Ege, 1911.)

AHC to JSC, September 1, 1862

Carlisle Sept 1st /62

My Darling Husband,

Today we have been startled by the word of the death of John Smead & of Robt Henderson being wounded. My own Husband how much I hope & pray & trust that you are safe. God only knows! That your life may be saved & that you may be returned to us is my daily & most ardent prayer & all things else sink into nothing in comparison.

I am persuaded that you are well because you have been acting as Quartermaster & I hope you are still at Fortress Monroe, & then I can neither see in the papers or hear anything of you & as bad news always comes fast I console myself. I hoped very much to hear from you today but was disappointed. Tomorrow I think will surely bring me something. This afternoon after I heard the bad news from Virginia. I waited almost breathless till I sent to the office & thought I would sink if no letters came but 'tis wonderful how we are supported under such circumstances for now I think if anything had befallen you I surely should have heard. I know you write regularly but at such times I wish it was in your power to telegraph me.

I feel so very sorry for poor Annie Smead. Hers has been a hard lot & now the future is very dark. 'Tis fortunate she had only one child. At this very trying time when the consolations of religion would be so sweet to her soul she rejects them & calls her Maker's justice into question in a most rebellious manner; but God tries us weak mortals, as it were by fire sometimes to answer his all wise ends & we can only look to him for submission & faith & say "Thy will be done." John Smead's body is to be brought up tomorrow. Old Mr. Henderson went down this afternoon.

Last night five of our physicians & a number of our Townsmen went to the hospital in a special train. We made up several boxes of jellies, farina & such things as would be grateful to the sick. The ladies have been very energetic, today they were collecting money for the wounded & succeeded very well.

What will be the end of all this? We seem to be gaining & losing all the time & this battle has been fought on the same ground of the one a year ago. Capt Churchill predicted last night that the war would be over in three days.

This morning I got Mr. Hamilton to examine Nan & John & after going through the ordeal very creditably they were transferred into Miss Julia Beetim's & Mr Masonheimer's schools. Mr. Hamilton tried to dissuade me from putting John into a boys school, but as he is prepared & has the ambition I think it right to gratify him. I shall have to study a good deal with them. The higher schools are much more prepossessing than the primary departments because not so crowded & then too they are removed from our troublesome opposite neighbors.

Aunt Miller has had quite a bevy of her relations lately. They all left today excepting Galbraith Miller. Mr Wills, Jane Smyzer's husband, gave me a pressing invitation to visit them, which of course they were very safe in doing. Galbraith Miller is past reformation I'm afraid & from his wife's letters I expect they have an unhappy time. His little boy is almost constantly at our house even all night sometimes & his father knows nothing of him. He is a sad example for the child. I do wish he would send him to Milwaukee. His Mother is the proper person under such circumstances even if

James Hamilton, who attended James and Annie Colwell's wedding in 1853, was the founder of the Carlisle Public Schools and the Cumberland County Historical Society, originally named the Hamilton Library, c.1850. (A. A. Line copy, CCHS.)

he is unmanageable.

We had a heavy rain this afternoon. Tonight is quite cold. Yesterday was our communion Sabbath. Mr Murray officiated. We had pleasant services no additions. The congregation are by no means unanimous in calling Mr. Bliss or indeed anyone.

There are about 800 of the Anderson troops here. I have never seen the encampment. They say 'tis very pretty sight.

Daisy has regained her old good looks & is very hearty. James will soon be able to say everything. I think you will be delighted with their photograph & so natural, very reasonable too only $1.50 & 75 cts for frame.

I had a letter from Ban few days ago. Quite inconsolable about his boy. Louise is in bad health. Good bye my precious husband.

Affectionately & devotedly your attached wife
    Annie

Your letter of the 25th inst. is the last I have had from you.

JSC to AHC, September 2, 1862

On board steam tug Kingston
Potomac river below Alexandria
2nd Sept. 1862

My Dear wife,

It is one week today I believe since I wrote you & nearly three weeks since I heard from you. I might have written to you last week, but we were loading vessels & waiting continually for others to come so that I could not get off to take a letter into the post office at the fort, and besides I expected to get started towards Alexandria every day, and thought I would write from there. Just as we were about leaving Hampton I discovered that a post office had been established there, but I did not know it before although I had made frequent inquiries before.

Our destination is Alexandria & we are within ten miles of the place. I have no idea where the regiment is. I saw by Saturday's paper that Pope was expecting Porter's corps at Manassas on Saturday morning. I suppose the regiment is in that direction if the army has not been driven back by the Rebs. I feel great anxiety to hear something of the result of the fight on Friday and Saturday also if there was one. I presume you have seen it in the papers of yesterday.

We left Hampton on Sunday about 11 o'clock. Lay at Fortress Monroe till after two when we started for Alexandria. It blew quite a gale out on the bay and the sea was very rough, but we have got along safely this far.

What I am to do when I get to Alexandria I have no idea. Whether remain there or go on to the regiment. Neither the wagons nor horses have arrived here, although they were all loaded & started before I did, except eight that I have along. Perhaps the old quartermaster will be waiting to take charge or perhaps a new one. I hope soon to get where the company is that I may get your letters which I know you have written and are waiting for me, unless they have got lost in the marching & moving about.

It is nearly breakfast time and I must close. I expect to be at Alexandria in an hour or hour & a half.
Truly your devoted husband
James

I have arrived in Alexandria. The news is not favorable from the army as far as I can get any. But

Burial of Capt. Smead.

This brave officer was killed on Saturday last while bravely leading his battery in thickest of the engagement at Manassas. His death was caused by a ten pound cannon ball, which came *richocheting* over the field, and struck him on the head, tearing away half of it and killing him instantly. His remains were embalmed at Washington, and arrived here on Wednesday. The funeral took place on the same day at 4 o'clock P M. The entire permament company af Carlisle Barracks, formed the escort and firing party, and a large concourse of citizens paid their last tribute to the honored dead by following the remains to their final resting place. Captain Smead was an officer of much talent, and gave promis of soon attaining a position in the front rank of the service. His untimely death is a great loss to the nation and a source of profound sorrow to his many friends.—*Herald*

Article about John Smead's death and burial, *Carlisle American*, 17 Sept. 1862.

nobody seems to know anything. I don't know where I will go tomorrow. Lieut Col Henderson was wounded on Saturday. He is in Washington. I presume he will soon be at home. His wound is not considered dangerous.

J.S.C.

AHC to JSC, September 3, 1862

Carlisle Sept. 3rd /62

My dear dear husband,

I am so very much disappointed in not having heard from you since your letter of the 25th a long time! I can get no clue to your whereabouts. This evening I saw the notice of a J. Colwell /Sergeant/ being wounded. I feel very anxious and miserable about you. Do telegraph me when you can't write. I read the papers till I grow sick.

Oh! the bitter, bitter fruits of this war are seen & felt everywhere. Poor John Smead was buried this afternoon at 4 o/clock. A sad funeral & the doleful music was so harrowing to the feelings. Annie is down there for the present. If anything can unite people 'tis grief, & in this bereavement they have certainly a common sorrow. Old Mrs Smead reproaches herself & the girls now for not being reconciled to him & his marriage before this.

Last night Mary Chambers had a dispatch from her

husband in Washington saying he was ill & come on immediately. George Gibson keeps us well posted about everyone we know in Washington. Through his exertions John Smead's body was recovered as the grave was dug & he about being interred when George interfered. I think if anything had happened to you he certainly would know of it.

Oh! I would give nearly all my life if I could feel assured that you were out of danger this night & I could soon see you. Everything anything to have you again home. May Heaven answer this my constant prayer.

If you know anything of a Charley Halbert in Co A. please tell me as his Mother is very anxious not having heard for more than a month. She is very bitter in her complaints against Robert Henderson whom she considers a most passionate hard-hearted man—& says he had only 6 votes for the colonelcy so great was his unpopularity. I am told that his wound is not dangerous but painful.—is still in Washington.

The report regarding Charley McClure's imprisonment is contradicted. Mr. McClure was here for a while last night. He is still busily engaged at the enrolling business. I will write a short letter tonight directing it to you Fortress Monroe hoping that one of these may reach you. I am so anxious if I do not hear in the course of a day or two I'm afraid I'll be perfectly good for nothing.

Nan and John are getting along nicely with their studies. They are promoted into higher books & Nan actually studies geography. I intend making them write you soon. John forms many plans for entertaining you when you return. Daisy is now old enough & sufficiently trust-worthy to go errands for me down st. She is a very dear child & retains her old fancy for being nursed. James is my little comfort till you return. He cannot bear me out of his sight & calls himself "Mama & Papa's Kitty."

As you were so kind as to send one Capt Brady's pictures I return the compliment by enclosing Mrs Brady. Did you ever see her?

Good night my own dear precious husband. May

God ever bless & spare you is the anxious prayer of your devotedly attached wife

Annie

JSC to AHC, September 4, 1862

Alexandria Va
4th Sept. 1862

My Dear wife,

I mailed you a letter here on Tuesday the day I arrived. I did not expect to be here so long at that time. The horses & wagons have not arrived yet. And cannot say when they will. I have heard nothing from them since I left them.

I have no news about the army except what I get in the papers which I suppose you see. I hear a great many rumors most of which turn out to be untrue.

It seems that the whole army is back around Washington pretty much in the same position they were last winter. The reserves are somewhere in the vicinity of Arlington heights or were yesterday.

I forgot to mention in the post-script to my last that I had received five of your letters viz. of the 12th 14th 16th 18th & 20th ult, so you have written very promptly that far for which please accept my hearty thanks. Dick Henderson had got a letter of a later date from you for me before I saw him & had given it to one of the soldiers of the regiment to give to me as he knew I had come & he was going to Washington to see his brother. He did not know the name of the soldier & I have not received the letter. The other letters are I suppose with the regimental mail. The ones I received had been sent down from Fredericksburg.

I am expecting the vesels with the horses & wagons every minute, or I would ask of you to write to me here. As soon as they arrive & are unloaded and put together, I presume I will be off.

This city is so crowded that I can find no place to stay except to lie on the floor. I stay down on the wharf where I have some horses, and have my blankets. I am tired of living the way I have been for the last year but more especially for the last six months.

John Smead was killed in the late battles as I sup-

Two of Carlisle's Civil War era businesses, c.1870. Miller & Buttorff was a hardware store. Charles Lochman's photography gallery was located on the third floor. Notice the large double window to provide natural light. Annie Colwell had some of her photos taken by Lochman. (A. A. Line, CCHS.)

pose you know. Poor Annie Ege. She will be left very desolate. Her near relatives not able to do much for her. How many children has she? She will have her pension from the government to rely on I suppose. What a terrible war this is, and the end dont appear to be visible yet. Still it may be nearer than we suppose. "The darkest hour is just before daybreak." Write often.

Your devoted husband

James

AHC to JSC, September 6, 1862

Carlisle Sept. 6th /62

Since I last wrote I have had the great pleasure of receiving two letters of the 2nd & 4th from my own very dear Husband. So long a time had intervened between the letters that I had wrought myself up to a very miserable pitch thinking you were sick, or imprisoned or something terrible had befallen you. Now I am very much relieved but I would like to know your destination if you go to Washington I want to go to see you for I don't believe this war is going to end in a long time & I am so anxious to see you & talk with you.

Our normally quiet valley is in quite a commotion anticipating a visit from Stonewall Jackson. All the stores are closed & all business suspended after 3 o'clock every day by order from the Governor so that the men can drill & provide themselves with arms in case of an attack. It seems to be regarded in a more serious light even than the anticipated attack of last year in which you figured with a club & I with four children and a basket of valuables making our way to the scene of action.

Lyle Lyon is now a prisoner on Governor's Island & Wm died recently in Richmond leaving his family extremely poor.

The Anderson troops are still here numbering 800. Everyone will be glad when they go, for ladies cant walk in the evenings without being insulted. Mr. Eales told me he was pretty near giving one of them the weight of his cane for looking impudently at Anna.

Poor Annie Smead is very much distressed of course about the death of her husband. Fortunately she has but one child. She is making her home for the present at her mother-in-law's. This mutual sorrow may make their future relations more friendly. Annie has been in delicate health for a long time. 'Tis a great pity of her.

Mary Chambers writes that her husband is much better & has captured a secesh horse with which she is much delighted & is going to bring it back to Carlisle with her.

I wrote yesterday to Sister Libby telling her that you had not been in the recent battles & were well. Edgar is still at home. John is in Capt Kelso's company. Robert Henderson is now in Baltimore. I saw a devoted friend of yours young Robinson a few evenings ago. He told me he would see you sometime soon as his leave had nearly expired. George McClure borrowed your books on military tactics as his Mother is

COL. R. M. HENDERSON.—We are glad to learn that the above named gallant officer has so far recovered from his wound as to be able to reach his home in this town.— We hope his health may be speedily restored to him. Such brave men as Col. H. cannot well be spared from among those who are now defending our " good old flag."

News note about Colonel Henderson, *American Democrat*, 24 Sept. 1862.

"Crinoline days," two Carlisle women in dresses of the Civil War era, c.1865. (A. A. Line, CCHS.)

obliged to let them learn the art—if war comes—to defend the valley.

Do you ever get any peaches? They seem to be very abundant & reasonable in this section of country. Last night Mr & Mrs Eells paid us a visit of an hour & a half long. Nan & John get along with their new teachers very well. I study with them every day. Daisy & James are laying in a fine stock of health by playing outdoors all the time.

We are enjoying delightful weather now, the nights are too beautiful to sleep.

Take good care of yourself & write often to

Your affectionately & devotedly attached wife
Annie

AHC to JSC, September 12, 1862

Carlisle Sept. 12th /62

My precious Husband,

Last night I did not write to you because I had a serious attack of blues owing to having received nothing from you for a whole week. Oh! I am so uneasy & miserable, what can be the reason that your letters dont come? Mr Haverstick has had very late advices from his sons. I retired at an early hour last night thinking I could write you more agreeably this morning— but my wanderings in search of you through dreamland were vain. I thought I was in Emmittsburg searching for you through the rooms & cells of the monastery & among the sisters & monks but no one answered to you. At last I was directed to a little chapel which

stood on the border of a dense wood where I was told you would be, but just as I got to the little ivy covered Inn & expected in the next moment to be clasped in your arms—I awoke.

Now it is quite early not clear light & to add to the gloom rain has been falling nearly all night, but I still write you regularly hoping some of my letters will reach you & I do sincerely trust some of yours will soon get here.

I have no news. We are constantly in the receipt of wild rumors about Jackson's approaching us but I do not feel afraid yet many are very uneasy & are packing up their valuables lest they may be destroyed. I cannot think that the Rebels would burn our town or interfere with the women & children. Our Army never committed any outrages in Virginia.

Yesterday quite a colony of contrabands arrived here telling of course extravagant stories & finding plenty of hearers. I think if we do have to leave town Perry County would be the most out-of-the way place.

I have just finished a nice purple calico dress which fits me very nicely. I am going to make Nan & Daisy Garibaldi's out of my old white wrapper which will look very nicely with dark skirts. The children are all well. I have no trouble with them. Providence has been very good to us in preserving their health for I know I am not an experienced nurse which is taught alone by sad experience, & I have never been thrown much with sickness. I have not seen Major Todd yet. From all I can hear he must be confined to his bed.

The shelling of Carlisle, 1 July 1863, as depicted in a drawing by Thomas Nast. The anticipated Confederate invasion of Carlisle, described by Annie in September 1862, did not become a reality until nearly a year later. Nast's scene shows the Rebels shelling the New York Militia in the first block of E. High St. The market house and Bixler building are shown on the right. (A. A. Line, CCHS.)

I sincerely trust that you are still well. I do hope you can find some means of visiting me. I have heard nothing from Shippensburg for several days. I dont know whether Mr. McClure is down this week or not. Mr Croft & Dr Mahon are in the country in the enrolling business.

Our markets are now stocked with all the good things belonging to this season of year. The children enjoy the sweet potatoes which are very fine. Yesterday I canned some tomatoes our vines did not bear so luxuriantly as they promised owing to the drought.

Good-bye my very dear husband. May God preserve & bless you is the earnest prayer of your devoted wife

Annie

AHC to JSC, September 13, 1862

Saturday night 13th

Again writing to my own dear husband & have heard nothing from him for so very long a time consequently I am in very bad spirits. Last evening I was so miserable about you that I went down to Major Todd's to ask him whether he had seen or heard of you lately but he had retired so I heard nothing there. I heard afterwards that he had been sick in a hospital before coming here so I suppose he could not enlighten me.

Some letters do come to town so I think it is strange that I get none. I have sent word to George Gibson to interest himself in finding out where you are for this uncertainty is wearing. I do think I will die if I dont hear something of you soon. I never was so long a time without letters before.

Last night there was a report that the Reserves were to pass through town. I passed a watchful night, still I think if you had been coming you would have telegraphed me. Again there is such a report but the time is not definite. If you are stationed near here I am going to see you if only for a half day.

Since I wrote you on Thursday our town has been in a great commotion owing to Jackson's anticipated visit to this valley. Many families have left town: Bairds Blaneys old Mrs Watts' family—Loomis family & many others. Numbers who still remain are packed up for a start. It seems that Genl Elliott got up this scare by getting his family off & Mr Edwrd. Biddle keeps it up by persuading others to go. I think I wont leave till the Rebels get to Chambersburg. Then of course the track will be torn up & it will take them a day or two to march here so in that time we can hide some place. George Gibson sent for Fanny Hunt & meets her tomorrow morning in Harrisburg. Egolf's boarding house is closed.

Today two companies left town for Chambersburg—two Hepburn boys George McClure our neighbor Callis & many others whom we know. Mr Fry resigned because his wife said he should not go. 'Tis well that we are away from the excitement for the people downtown say they cant sleep for the rumors & fuss while we live in blissful ignorance till it is nearly over. Some people think the end of the war is at hand though these are our dark days. I earnestly pray that it is.

Now my own dear darling husband do please try to find out some way of communicating with me, for to hear often from you & to know that you are well is the only comfort that I have these times. Our sweet children are all well & often talk of "Papa." Tomorrow will be Sunday so of course I cant hear but Oh! I pray that Monday will bring me some news from my dear dear husband.

> Ever your devoted wife
> Annie

JSC to AHC, September 13, 1862
[This letter is dated September 13, but the postmark indicates it only got into the mail system at McKeedysville on September 18.]

> about 4 miles from
> Frederick Md
> 13th Sept 1862

My Dear wife,

It is more than a week since I have had an opportunity of mailing a letter to you. I write now with the hope that I may be able to send it to you in a day or two. I think I have received all of your letters up to & including yours of the 8th inst. I had recd up to the 20th ult when I last wrote. Since that I have received yours of the 23rd, 25th 29th ult. and 2nd 4th 6th & 8th inst. The one you sent to Fortress Monroe I suppose I will never receive. I also received the one enclosing Mrs Brady's photograph, for which I am much obliged. Mrs. B. seems to be much younger than he. I have seen her often. And I must say the picture does not do her justice. I think her much handsomer and her expression much sweeter and more animated. I always thought that she was just the lady I should like to have for my wife. I do not know her equal anywhere, excepting always your dear self. There now I hope you will not be jealous of my dear Mrs. B.

The wagons & horses arrived at Alexandria on Friday night. I got them off & set up about midnight on Saturday night, got them loaded and out of Alexandria by 10 o'clock Sunday. On Saturday the Division crossed the long bridge into Washington city. We passed through Washington as the people were going to church on Sunday evening. I could not stop to write you a line, nor even to get something to eat. I got up with the brigade about midnight that night 10 miles out from Washington.

On Monday morning I was sent back to the company. So I am now footing it in the old way. We remained in camp till Tuesday and have been marching every day since. We arrived here a few minutes ago, 12 o'clock M. How long we will remain I have no idea. We can hear firing all forenoon on the other side of Frederick from us.

You wrote in one of your letters about flour. Of course get it always from McLeaf if you can.

Also you had better lay in your winter's coal at once, if it has not risen too much. If it is not over five dollars per ton lay it in. You had better get 6 or 8 tons at any rate whatever price it is.

How much money have you left. Have you paid Dr. Harman.

I dont think the Rebels will go into Pennsylvania. They will probably get back to Virginia if they can. I suppose we will follow them so I presume I will not get much nearer to you than I am now. I would love dearly to see you & have a talk with you. But I could name no place where I would be at a given time. Nor would it suit for you to be there if I could.

The reason I mention about the coal is that I think it will rise very high if it has not already.

> Your devoted husband
> James

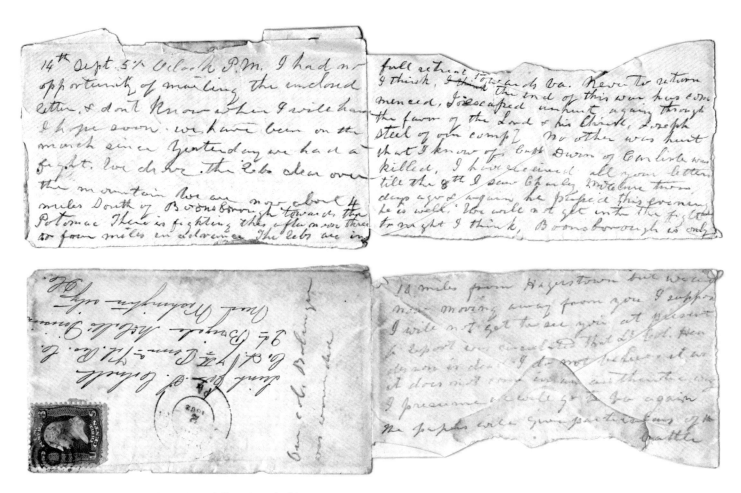

James's last letter of 14 September 1862, written inside a torn
envelope. (Colwell Family Collection.)

JSC to AHC, September 14, 1862

[This was inserted in the same envelope as JSC's 9/13/
62 letter. Apparently he had no paper: this is written
on the inside of a torn open envelope from one of
AHC's earlier letters to him. James misdated this letter.
The Battle of South Mountain was fought on September 14. It was the next day, September 15, that the
troops marched down the west side of South Mountain
and passed south of Boonsboro.]

14th Sept 5 O'clock P.M.
I had no opportunity of mailing the enclosed letter, & I
don't know when I will have. I hope soon. We have
been on the march since yesterday. We had a fight.
We drove the Rebs clear over the mountain. We are
now about 4 miles south of Boonsborough towards the
Potomac. There is fighting this afternoon three or four
miles in advance. The Rebs are in full retreat I think
towards Va. Never to return. The end of this war has
commenced. I escaped unhurt again through the favor
of the Lord & his Christ. Joseph Steel of our comp......No
other was hurt that I know of. Capt Dwin of Carlisle
was killed. I have received all your letters till the 8th.
I saw Charley McClure two days ago & again he passed
this evening. He is well. We will not get into the fight
tonight I think. Boonsborough is only 10 miles from
Hagerstown but we are now moving away from you. I
suppose I will not get to see you at present. A report
was circulated that Lt Col. Henderson is dead. I do not
believe it as it as it does not come in an authentic way.
I presume we will go to Va again. The papers will
give particulars of the battle.

Annie's last letter of 18 September 1862, written prior to her knowledge of James's death on the 17th. (Colwell Family Collection.)

AHC to JSC, September 18, 1862

Carlisle Sept. 18th /62

My Husband my own dear Husband,

This will prove but a poor apology for a letter because I am so much dispirited in not having heard from you for so long a time. Two weeks! that I cannot write neither can I do anything till I hear from you. I have written you regularly. I hope you receive some letters. I would give worlds, had I them, for one letter from you this night. Indeed I am so utterly miserable. I never felt so helpless before.

Last night I tried to telegraph you through Jim Cooper, but the telegraphic communication being broken I wrote to him begging him to find out where & how you are.

I expect you will think me foolish my dear Husband but indeed I cant help it. I do want so much to hear about you. If the road between Hagerstown & Frederick was fixed I could go to see you. As it is if there is anything the matter with you dont hesitate a moment about letting me know for I could go anyhow. Some way would be found. Young Harkness leaves in a few days I could go with him.

I do wish I was with you. Wont you give me some encouragement to go? I could find a home some place near you so that I could see you sometimes. Then my mind would be at rest.

We hear glowing accounts of McClellan's victories but the sad after part, the list of killed & wounded, is very much of a mystery. No mail or papers have come

Headstones of James Smith Colwell and Annie Hall Colwell in the Old Carlisle Graveyard, 1997. (Jim Bradley, Mother Cumberland Collection.)

today. They will be here during the night. I felt quite stunned at seeing the death of Capt Brady in yesterday's paper. His connexion with you in my mind by means of his photograph which you enclosed makes me feel singularly sad regarding an entire stranger. Oh! this terrible war how much bitterness & misery it is creating.

My husband may Heaven spare your life through all these struggles. Oh! how fervently I pray for your return.

This afternoon it rained quite heavily but a bright sunset promises a pleasant tomorrow. This is a sad letter but is the index of my feelings. When some of your good, dear letters come I will furnish you a more cheerful correspondent.

The children are all very well. Both of their schools are closed for a few days owing to the great excite-ment here. There were no passenger trains here today all being used for soldiers. There was a report this evening that Stonewall Jackson & 46,000 men had been captured which if true must surely be the beginning of the end.

Good night my darling husband.

Ever your affectionately & devotedly attached wife
    Annie H. Colwell

[This short note was inserted in this letter.]
                        Monday morning

My mind was greatly relieved regarding you. I heard last night through young Harkness that you were well and with the 7th Regt. so I presume you have received all of my letters. We are all well.

    Ever your
        Annie

CHAPTER 6

Epilogue: "Farewell, Noble Friend." "Farewell, Dear Teacher."

PRESIDENT'S PROCLAMATION.

THE SLAVES OF REBELS PROCLAIMED FREE.

By the President of the United States of America:
A PROCLAMATION.

That on the 1st of January, in the year of our Lord one thousand eight hundred and sixty three, all persons held as slaves within any State, or designated part of a State, the people whereof shall then be in rebellion against the United States, shall be then, thenceforward and forever free; and the Executive Government of the United States, including the military and naval authorities thereof, will recognize and maintain the freedom of such persons; and will do no act or acts to repress such persons, or any of them, in any efforts they may make for their actual freedom.

Excerpt from Lincoln's Proclamation,
Carlisle American, 1 Oct. 1862.

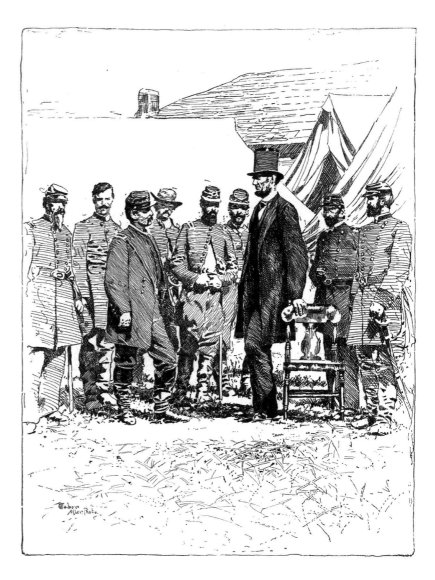

General McClellan and President Lincoln at Antietam. (*Battles and Leaders of the Civil War*, Grant-Lee Edition, CCHS.)

Lincoln issued the Preliminary Emancipation Proclamation September 22 to general approval in the North, and the country marched nobly into the future on wafer-thin constitutional grounds. The proclamation turned what many saw as a war for self-determination against a central government into a war for freedom against slavery.[1]

In Carlisle, while the Proclamation was commonly accepted as a necessary act, it was not without its critics. The pro-Administration papers supported it. The *Herald*, the conservative establishment voice of Carlisle, which had trumpeted "Sink the Nigger Question" in an editorial on October 16, 1860, only two years previously, now called the arguments supporting the proclamation "irresistible and irrefutable" and quoted extensively from supporting editorials in leading Northern newspapers.[2] The *Carlisle American* quoted the *New York Times* approvingly, "The wisdom of the step taken...is unquestionable; its necessity, indisputable."[3]

The *Shippensburg News* most clearly described the significance of the step:

> The twenty-second of September in this year will hereafter be a day to be commemorated with peculiar honor, a day illustrious in the annals not only of our country but of the world.... On that day it will be recorded, the chains of bondage were struck from the limbs of three millions of human beings.[4]

The Union-supporting *American Democrat*, however, was dismayed. Recalling the revolution of "the brutal negroes of St. Domingo," the paper termed the proclamation "unwise and uncalled for."[5] Predictably, the *American Volunteer* vehemently opposed the proclamation in a number of editorials, charging that "President Lincoln has violated that Constitution which he is sworn to uphold, defend and protect." Wrote Bratton:

> The fanatics in the late Congress acted upon the abused idea, that slavery must be destroyed before the rebellion can be crushed and the Union restored; and we regret to see, *by the acts of the President*, that he too has imbibed that ridiculous and nonsensical notion. A greater delusion no man ever labored under.... All the Proclamations that may be issued for that purpose, will most assuredly fail, and be as little heeded as the idle babblings of a madman.[6]

Editor Bratton was correct in discerning Lincoln's intentions. His predictive ability was less accurate. The *Volunteer* always retained the capacity to anger Union supporters. Later that month Union recruits training at Carlisle Barracks were so angered by the paper's editorials that they ransacked the *Volunteer's* offices. The recruits, variously reported to be ten or forty in number, were particularly angered by a *Volunteer* editorial calling on Lincoln to resign following Democratic gains in the fall 1862 local elections. "Come out of that chair, Abraham Lincoln," demanded Bratton.[7]

In 1871 a monument was erected in Carlisle in memory of those from Cumberland County who had died during the Civil War. The monument listed 344 names, including that of James S. Colwell. The monument's limestone weathered over the years and the names became increasingly indecipherable; a large bronze tablet containing all the names was added to the monument and ceremoniously dedicated in September 1993.

When Grand Army of the Republic Post #201 for Civil War veterans was established in Carlisle in 1881, it was named the Captain James S. Colwell Post.[8] John Faller, whose brother, Leo, had been killed by the same shell that killed James, long served as captain of that post.[9]

AN ARMED RAID UPON OUR OFFICE.

An armed mob of soldiers—ten in number, and members of the Anderson Troop, stationed near this place—entered our office on Friday evening, the 24th ult., at about 7½ o'clock, in the absence of ourself and hands, and destroyed some of our materials, knocked into "pi" several forms of type, hacked the bed of the press with an axe, tore up a thousand sheets of damp white paper (which had been prepared for our regular edition,) broke a pitcher, carried off an eagle cut, and committed various other very uncivil depredations. They effected an entrance by forcing the outside door, breaking the lock. They also forced open the door of our private room, but finding nothing but our books and private papers, these were not molested. They were not in the office over five minutes, and were frightened off by two boys, who threatened to arrest the whole party.

We did not refer to this outrage in our last, hoping that by another week we would be

AMERICAN VOLUNTEER,

JOHN B. BRATTON, Editor & Proprietor

CARLISLE, PA., NOVEMBER 6, 1862.

$290 REWARD.

I WILL pay the above reward to any person giving me information that will lead to the detection and conviction of the burglars, their aiders and abettors, who entered the Volunteer Printing office on the night of the 24th ult.

Nov. 6, '62.   J. B. BRATTON.

Article and notice concerning the attack on the *Volunteer's* office, *American Volunteer*, 6 Nov. 1862.

Detail of the Soldiers Monument on the Carlisle Public Square, showing the names of James S. Colwell and other officers killed in the Civil War, 1997. (Jim Bradley, Mother Cumberland Collection.)

Soldiers Monument on W. High St., shown shortly after its erection in 1871. (Charles L. Lochman, Robin Stanford Collection, CCHS.)

Civil War veterans at the G.A.R. Hall on W. Louther St., preparing for a Memorial Day parade, c.1910. (A. A. Line, CCHS.)

As for Annie Colwell, life went on, but in a different fashion. Married for only nine years, Annie grew in strength and self-reliance to meet the responsibilities thrust upon her. She remained a widow for forty-five years until her death in 1907, in straitened circumstance. With the help of the modest pension afforded widows of Civil War veterans, she successfully raised the four children. For the two boys she sought, and because of the manner of their father's death received, appointments to the Naval Academy.

Commander John Charles Colwell, c.1900. (Colwell Family Collection.)

Among the extant letters of recommendation for the appointments of John and James Colwell to the Naval Academy is a personal letter to the Secretary of the Navy from George Meade, who had commanded the Pennsylvania Reserves at Antietam. The letter of 22 January 1870 is addressed to George M. Robeson, Secretary of the Navy, and signed by Major General George G. Meade. (The Colwell Family Papers.)

James Hall Colwell as a midshipman at the Naval
Academy, c.1880. (Colwell Family Collection.)

Ann Hall Colwell with her daughter Mary Hall
(Daisy), c.1874. (Carte de visite by Mrs. R. A. Smith,
Colwell Family Collection.)

John Charles spent thirty-five years
in the navy, serving, among other
duties, as naval attache in London during
the Spanish American War. James
graduated from Annapolis in 1881, a
year when the navy was down-sizing;
his class was never commissioned. He
passed his career as a technical examiner for the U.S. Patent Office. John
Charles and James regularly sent money
to their mother to help with the expenses of the home in Carlisle as long
as she lived. The two girls, Nan and
Daisy, never married, remaining in the
family home with their mother until her
death in 1907 and thereafter until their
own deaths.

Ann Hall Colwell, her sister Mary (Mrs. Steven Cowdrey), an unknown driver,
and Mary Hall (Daisy) Colwell, on a sleigh ride, c.1905. (J. H. Andrews, Colwell
Family Collection.)

Annie died on May 29, 1907. Perhaps in her own way she was as much a hero as James had been. She had never seen any need for the war; nor had she approved of his volunteering for active duty. But James had died a hero; and Annie kept to herself whatever bitter thoughts she might have held. She passed no hint to the children that she felt that their father had died unnecessarily in a pointless war. In a death notice the Carlisle *Evening Sentinel* wrote, "A woman of great strength of character, hospitable, gracious, sympathetic and sincere, she held a prominent place in the social life of the community."[10] At the funeral her coffin was carried by six men from Carlisle who wrote a joint letter to the *Herald*:

Ann Hall Colwell, c.1895-1900. (Colwell Family Collection.)

Tribute to Ann Colwell printed in the *Carlisle Daily Herald*, 6 June 1907.

> Twenty-two years ago, in 1885, a Bible class was organized at the Biddle Mission, composed of eighteen members, all of whom were rough and ready sons of honest toil. Mrs. Anna H. Colwell was the teacher.... By her steady devotion to the cause of Christ, her kind and gentle manner and kind attentions, she drew us by the subtle chord of love, until to miss the class was to miss a treat....
>
> In the language of the immortal Lincoln, let us here highly resolve, "that the dead shall not have died in vain," that we will emulate her example, follow her teaching and so deport ourselves that each may be a bright and separate star in her crown of eternal rejoicing.
>
> Farewell, dear teacher, till we meet in that land where parting, pain and sorrow are unknown.[11]

For Annie, for the families of all 344 men whose names are recorded on Carlisle's Civil War monument, and for all the families of those listed on thousands of similar monuments across the land, the monuments were a reminder of irreplaceable loss. Those names and those monuments also mark the price the country paid to come of age.

A TOKEN OF RESPECT.

BY JOHN H. HEUSTON.

I stood beside the new made grave
Of a loved and honored Friend;
How she strove our souls to save,
And how peaceful was the end.
We stood beside her casket,
With almost bated breath,
To think the voice we loved to hear,
Was forever stilled in death.

Then came the silent cortege,
And through the gates she passed,
Borne to her Home Eternal,
By her whilom "Bible Class"
Gone to live in Heaven,
Oh blessed happy thought!
Robed in white her sins forgiven,
The reward, for which she wrought.

Dear teacher, thou wert ever
Faithful, loving, true and kind,
And we feel the deep impression
Which thou hast left behind.
And when we go to Mission,
To our old accustomed place,
And look around, Oh how we miss
Our teacher's smiling face!

We know thou art in Heaven,
Yet our hearts are filled with pain;
For while we're doomed to mourn thy loss,
'Tis thy eternal gain.
Dear Lord, we leave it all to thee,
Thou doest all things well;
Oh may we live from sin, set free,
As Anua H. Colwell!

Surviving Members of Class,
J. H. Heuston,
Charles Duey,
Joseph Lyter,
William Gibb,
Harry Albert,
John Steen
Charles Beverson

A memorial poem printed on a card, written by surviving members of Annie Colwell's bible study class at the Biddle Mission. (Colwell Family Collection.)

MRS. ANNIE HALL COLWELL.

Life Long Resident of Carlisle.

This morning between six and seven o'clock, Mrs. Annie Hall Colwell passed peacefully away at her home on North Hanover street. Death was due to general decline, she being aged 74 years and 3 months. On Monday night a specialist was called from Philadelphia, and he gave encouragement, but her decline continued until she breathed her last this morning during her sleep. Yesterday she seemed particularly cheerful.

Brief Sketch of Her Life.

Mrs. Annie Hall Colwell was born in Carlisle in February, 1833, and has since been a resident of this place. She was the widow of James S. Colwell, a well known lawyer of this place, who was killed in the battle of Antietam. He was Captain of Co. A., 7th Penn. Reserve Corps. She was the granddaughter of Major Andrew Galbraith, well known during the Revolution, having served on the staff of Gen. Washington. Her immediate relations are the only descendants of that family in this part of the country.

She is survived by one sister, Mrs. Mary Hall Cowdrey, of North Hanover street, widow of a sergeon in the U. S. Army, and by the following children: John, a commander in the United States Army; James H., legal patent examiner in Washington; Miss Annie and Miss Mary, at home. The Captain Colwell Post, of this place, was named in honor of her husband. She was a life long member of the Second Presbyterian church, a kind and upright Christian.

The funeral of the late Mrs. Annie H. Colwell will be held on Saturday afternoon at 3 o'clock.

Death notice of Annie Colwell, *Carlisle Daily Herald*, 29 May 1907.

THE DEATH RECORD.

COLWELL.

Mrs. Annie Hall Colwell, widow of the late Captain James S. Colwell, who was a prominent member of the Carlisle bar and a distinguished officer of the Civil War, entered peacefully into rest this morning at 7 o'clock at her residence on North Hanover street extended. Although ill for some months past her condition was not without encouragement, and the announcement of her death came as a shock to her friends. A woman of great strength of character, hospitable, gracious, sympathetic and sincere, she held a prominent place in the social life of the community. As a Christian she was devout and untiring in ever seeking and doing her Master's will.

Mrs Colwell was a daughter of the late Charles Hall and Ann Galbraith Hall, daughter of Major Galbraith, of the Revolution; a member of one of the prominent pioneer families of the Cumberland Valley.

She is survived by two daughters and two sons—the Misses Anna M, and Mary H. Colwell, Commander John C. Colwell, U. S. N., and James S. Colwell, Esq., of Washington, D. C. Funeral services will be held at the residence, Saturday, June 1st, at three o'clock p. m. Interment in the Old graveyard, Carlisle.

Death record of Annie Colwell, *The Evening Sentinel*, 29 May 1907.

Endnotes

[1] Lincoln well knew the transformation he was effecting in the war. In his Annual Message to Congress the following December he described the conflict on the highest moral plane, "We shall nobly save, or meanly lose, the last best, hope of the earth." Abraham Lincoln, *The Collected Works of Abraham Lincoln*, ed. Roy P. Basler, 9 vols. (New Brunswick, N.J.: Rutgers University Press, 1953), vol. 5, 537. For other assessments of the effect of the Proclamation see Davis, *Slavery and Human Progress*; Franklin, *The Emancipation Proclamation*; McPherson, *The Negro's Civil War*; and Quarles, *The Negro in the Civil War*.

[2] Carlisle *Herald*, 17 October 1862.

[3] *Carlisle American*, 1 October 1862.

[4] *Shippensburg News*, 27 September 1862.

[5] *American Democrat*, 1 October 1862.

[6] *American Volunteer*, 9 October 1862.

[7] *American Volunteer*, 23 October 1862.

[8] *History of Cumberland and Adams Counties, Pennsylvania*, 129.

[9] Faller, *Dear Folks at Home*, 142.

[10] Carlisle *Evening Sentinel*, 29 May 1907.

[11] Carlisle *Herald*, 6 June 1907.

History of the 7th Pennsylvania Reserves, Company A

by Richard L. Tritt

Company A, of the 7th Pennsylvania Reserves, was organized at Carlisle on the 19th of April 1861. It took the name of the "Carlisle Fencibles" from the fact that it was composed principally of members of a gymnastic club, and from the higher significance of the word "fencible," a defender of one's country.

The company left Carlisle on June 6, 1861, for Camp Wayne at West Chester, where it was incorporated with other companies from different parts of the state, into the Seventh Reserves. On July 21, the day of the Battle of Bull Run, the regiment received orders to be ready to march at a moment's notice, and the next morning it left West Chester. Via Harrisburg and Baltimore it reached Washington on the 25th. It encamped out on 7th Street, from the 25th until the 29th, where it was sworn into the service of the United States "for three years or during the war." On June 29 the company marched to Tenallytown, where it was encamped until October 9. On that day, with the entire Division, it crossed the Potomac, and encamped at Camp Pierpont, where it spent the winter, training for the campaigns ahead.

On March 19 the whole army advanced to Manassas Plains, the Reserves marching to Hunter's Mills. On the 15th they were ordered to Alexandria, where they remained until the Army of the Potomac, which went with General McClellan to the Peninsula, had embarked. The 7th Reserves was attached to McDowell's Army of the Rappahannock, and marched by way of Manassas Junction to Fredericksburg.

Illustration from a printed announcement for the 1899 annual reunion of the survivors of Company A, 7th Penna. Reserves. (Courtesy of Bob Rowe.)

On June 9 the Reserves embarked on transports and passed down the Rappahannock River on their way to the Peninsula, to assist McClellan in the siege of Richmond. On June 26 they fought in the Battle of Mechanicsville, on the following day the Battle of Gaines' Mill, and on the 30th the Battle of White Oak Swamp. In these three battles, the 7th Reserves lost 301 men, killed, wounded or missing. Soon afterward the Reserves were transferred from the Peninsula to the newly created Army of Virginia, under the command of Major General John Pope. The 7th fought in two battles at Second Manassas or Bull Run, on August 29 and 30, and participated in the Battles of South Mountain on the 14th, and at Antietam, on September 17.

The whole Reserves suffered terribly, and the Seventh Reserves more than any other one. This regiment, which numbered, when organized, upwards of nine hundred and fifty men, mustered less than two hundred men effective for duty after Antietam. In Company A the changes were so numerous that it could hardly be recognized as the same company. Brave to the highest degree, they suffered severely in every battle; and, though hardy and robust in constitution, disease made sad inroads upon them. The company which originally numbered 77 men, and at different times received recruits to the number of 40 (in all 117), had only 28 men effective for duty on the field after Antietam.

The Company fought with the regiment in the battle of Fredericksburg on December 13, 1862. The regiment engaged the enemy driving them from their defenses and capturing over one hundred prisoners. After encountering the enemy's reinforcements, they were in turn driven back with a loss of six men killed, seventy-two wounded and twenty-two missing. Members of Company A distinguished themselves at this battle. Jacob Cart was awarded a medal for his gallantry in seizing the battle flag of the Nineteenth Georgia from the rebel color bearer.

The 7th Reserves had become so reduced by hard fighting that the regiment was withdrawn from active operations and sent to Washington to rest and recuperate. In April of 1863 Lieutenant Colonel Robert M. Henderson resigned his Commission to accept the office of Provost Marshal of the Fifteenth District of Pennsylvania, under the general enrollment law.

Stationary illustration from Benjamin Hoffert's Civil War letter, dated 22 Oct. 1861. (Manuscript Collection, CCHS.)

After their duty in Washington, orders were received in late April 1864, directing the regiment to prepare again for active service in the field. On the second of May the regiment advanced along the Rapidan River. Crossing on the following day, and encamped at night in the Wilderness, near the Chancellorsville battleground. On the following day the Reserves were advanced in line of battle, the enemy were routed, retreating into the woods in their rear. In moving forward through the dense forest, in pursuit, the right and left flanks became detached from the body of the regiment, when suddenly they found the enemy closing in on them, with every avenue of retreat cut off. Rather than risk annihilation of his isolated command, Colonel Henry C. Bolinger surrendered his entire regiment. Two hundred and seventy-two officers and men were captured. The enlisted men were speedily conveyed to the rebel prison at Andersonville, and the officers were sent to Macon, Georgia.

Those who escaped capture, and some recruits, in all numbered one hundred and ten. This miniature battalion, the representative of the regiment had its place in the brigade, and participated in the fighting which ensued, up to the expiration of its term of service, when it was mustered out on June 16, 1864.

Muster Roll Of Company A
When Organized

Captain – Robert M. Henderson
    Wounded at Charles City Cross Roads June 30, 1862, and Second Bull Run Aug. 30, 1862. Promoted to Lieutenant Colonel July 4, 1862, and brevet Brigadier General March 13, 1865. Resigned Apr. 30, 1865.

First Lieutenant – James S. Colwell
    Promoted to Captain July 4, 1862. Killed at Antietam Sept. 17, 1862.

Second Lieutenant – Erkuries Beatty
    Wounded at Charles City Cross Roads June 30, 1862. Promoted to brevet Major and brevet Lieutenant Colonel Mar. 13, 1865.

First Sergeant – John D. Adair
    Promoted to 2nd Lieutenant Company G, Dec. 18, 1861.

Second Sergeant – William M. Henderson, Jr.
    Appointed 1st Sergeant Jan. 12, 1862. Died at Carlisle Mar. 12, 1862 while on furlough.

Third Sergeant – Samuel V. Ruby
    Promoted to 1st Sergeant March 13, 1862, 2nd Lieutenant Aug. 1, 1862, 1st Lieutenant Sept. 17, 1862. Captured at Wilderness May 5, 1864. Discharged Mar. 11, 1865.

Fourth Sergeant – Joseph B. Haverstick
    Mustered out with Company June 16, 1864.

First Corporal – William R. Holmes
    Appointed Sergeant Dec. 7, 1861, 1st Sergeant July 4, 1862. Captured May 5, 1864. Died at Annapolis June 6, 1865.

Second Corporal – William W. Harper
    Promoted to 1st Sergeant Company G, Mar. 5, 1862.

Third Corporal – Charles E. Goddard
    Promoted to Sergeant Jan. 1, 1862. Discharged on Surgeon's Certificate.

Fourth Corporal – Issac B. Parker
    Transferred to Cavalry Regiment July 23, 1861.

Musician – Van Buren Eby
    Appointed 1st Sergeant July 4, 1862. Captured May 5, 1864. Died at Andersonville Aug. 12, 1864.

Musician – William A. Monyer
    Discharged on Surgeon's Certificate Oct. 4, 1862.

Lieutenant Colonel Robert Miller Henderson, c.1895. (Detail of a framed photo in the CCHS Museum Collection.)

Privates

Barton, James Jr.
Discharged May 15, 1862 by order of Gen. McDowell, on certificate of disability.

Bixler, Andrew H.
Discharged on Surgeon's Certificate Sept. 27, 1861.

Bliss, Charles
Discharged Apr. 22, 1862, on account of disability.

Bosh, Lewis
Mustered out with Company June 16, 1864.

Bratton, William
Mustered out with Company June 16, 1864

Brechbill, Charles W.
Died in hospital at Camp Tenally, Oct. 12, 1861.

Burkholder, D. Wilson
Mustered in June 10, 1861. Promoted to 2nd Lieutenant Sept. 17, 1862. Captured May 5, 1864. Discharged Mar. 12, 1865.

Burkholder, John E.
Promoted to Sergeant Mar. 18, 1862. Wounded and taken prisoner at the Battle of Gaines' Mill. Discharged on Surgeon's Certificate Mar. 5, 1863.

Cart, Jacob
Mustered in June 8, 1861. Promoted to Sergeant Mar. 5, 1863. Transferred to 190th Regiment May 31, 1864.

Cuddy, John T.
Mustered in June 5, 1861. Missing in action at Wilderness, May 5, 1864.

Curriden, David D.
Taken prisoner at hospital, near White Oak Swamp, July 1, 1862. Released on parole, July 22, 1862. Transferred to Signal Corps, Aug. 16, 1863.

Dixon, William T. B.
Discharged on Surgeon's Certificate Jan. 15, 1863.

Elliott, Isaac
Transferred to Veteran Reserve Corps.

Elliott, John W.
Promoted to Hospital Steward 40th Regiment Penna. Volunteers Aug. 18, 1861.

Ensminger, William A.
Discharged on Surgeon's Certificate Oct. 16, 1862.

Lieutenant D. Wilson Burkholder. (D. Scott Hartzell Collection, U.S. Army Military History Institute.)

Sergeant Jacob Cart. (D. Scott Hartzell Collection, U.S. Army Military History Institute.)

Faller, Leo W.
    Wounded at Second Bull Run Aug. 30, 1862. Killed at Antietam Sept. 17, 1862.

Gardner, Jacob A.
    Discharged on Surgeon's Certificate Dec. 26, 1861.

Gould, Wilson H.
    Missing in action at Wilderness, May 5, 1864.

Greason, John H.
    Mustered out with Company June 16, 1864.

Halbert, Joseph L.
    Mustered out with Company June 16, 1864.

Harkness Charles C.
    Wounded at Fredericksburg, Dec. 13, 1862. Transferred to Veteran Reserve Corps.

Harkness, William H.
    Captured May 5, 1864. Discharged Feb. 9, 1865.

Harris, John T.
    Promoted to Corporal. Captured at the Battle of Gaines' Mill. Prisoner from May 5, 1864, to Feb. 27, 1865. Discharged Apr. 1, 1865.

Haverstick, John W.
    Transferred to U.S. Marine Corps.

Hayes, Edgar W.
    Promoted to Corporal. Discharged on Surgeon's Certificate Sept. 17, 1861.

Hecker, Henry L.
    Wounded with loss of arm and taken prisoner at Gaines' Mill. Released on parole July 22 and discharged Sept. 13, 1862.

Heiser, John G.
    Transferred to Veteran Reserve Corps, Dec. 1, 1863.

Henderson, Richard P.
    Promoted to Corporal, to 2nd Lieutenant Company E. Mar. 1, 1863, and to A. D. C. staff of Brigadier General Crawford June 8, 1863, to brevet Captain and brevet Major Mar. 13, 1865.

Hendricks, John H.
    Captured at Gaines' Mill. Released on parole. Discharged on Surgeon's Certificate Dec. 12, 1862.

Humer, John S.
    Wounded in Battle of Gaines' Mill. Promoted to Corporal Aug. 1, 1862. Mustered out with Company June 16, 1864.

Humer, John W.
    Deserted Sept. 4, 1861. Returned Aug. 14, 1863. Discharged on Surgeon's Certificate Feb. 14, 1864.

Private Wilson H. Gould. (D. Scott Hartzell Collection, U.S. Army Military History Institute.)

Kempton, Sydney
> Transferred to Signal Corps. Discharged on Surgeon's Certificate Apr. 30, 1863.

Kenyon, John R.
> Promoted to Sergeant March 3, 1862. Died at Washington, D. C. May 28, 1862 of typhoid fever.

Landis, Jacob Jr.
> Promoted to Corporal May 1862. Missing in action at Wilderness, May 5, 1864.

McBeth, Samuel A.
> Promoted to Corporal March 15, 1862. Wounded at Antietam. Discharged on Surgeon's Certificate Jan. 1864.

Meloy, Jacob L.
> Prisoner from May 5 to Dec. 11, 1864. Discharged Mar. 22, 1865.

Moore, James H.
> Transferred to Cavalry Regiment, July 23, 1861.

Morrison, John F.
> Promoted to Corporal Mar. 1, 1863. Prisoner from May 5 to Dec. 11, 1864. Discharged Mar. 21, 1865.

Mullin, Charles H.
> Discharged by Order of War Dept. Aug. 10, 1861.

Natcher, John A.
> Missing in action at Wilderness, May 5, 1864.

Nevel, William P.
> Died in hospital at Annapolis May 22, 1862.

Nevin, David R. B.
> Promoted to 1st Lieutenant Company A, 109th Regiment Penna. Volunteers, Nov. 8, 1861.

Otto, John
> Prisoner from May 30, 1864 to Feb. 27, 1865. Discharged Apr. 12, 1865.

Phillips, Edward Walter
> Discharged on Surgeon's Certificate Dec. 26, 1861.

Schuchman, John C.
> Mustered out with Company June 16, 1864.

Sharpe, A. Brady
> Promoted to 2nd Lieutenant Company E, July 3, 1861, and to Adjutant July 15, 1862. Resigned July 15, 1862 to General Ord's staff.

Sharpe, Thomas
> Discharged on Surgeon's Certificate Dec. 16, 1861.

Sipe, Marion P.
> Discharged on Surgeon's Certificate Jan. 21, 1862.

Sites, William B.
>Discharged on Surgeon's Certificate Sept. 27, 1861. Died soon after.

Smith, Samuel E.
>Wounded severely at Gaines' Mill and taken prisoner. Released on parole, July 22, 1862. Died at Baltimore, Aug. 2, 1862.

Spahr, David
>Killed at Antietam, Sept. 17, 1862.

Spangenburg, John George
>Transferred to U.S. Cavalry Nov. 30, 1862.

Spicer, Charles A.
>Discharged on Surgeon's Certificate May 16, 1862.

Spottswood, Wilson L.
>Promoted to Sergeant. Discharged on Surgeon's Certificate Dec. 6, 1862.

Spottswood, Robert H.
>Died at Washington, D.C., Nov. 28, 1862.

Strohm, George
>Transferred to Veteran Reserve Corps Sept. 1, 1863.

Thompson, Joseph B.
>Discharged on Surgeon's Certificate Jan. 12, 1862.

Vantilburg, George H.
>Missing in action at Wilderness, May 5, 1864.

Waggoner, John L.
>Wounded in the Battle of White Oak Swamp, June 30, 1862. Discharged on Surgeon's Certificate Dec. 29, 1862.

Wagner, D. K.
>Discharged July 1862.

Watts, William M. Jr.
>Promoted to 2nd Lieutenant, U.S. Cavalry, March 1862.

Welsh, George H.
>Discharged on Surgeon's Certificate June 30, 1861.

Wilders, George J.
>Missing in action at Bethesda Church, May 30, 1864.

Williams, George
>Discharged on Surgeon's Certificate July 1862.

Wonderlich, Charles A.
>Wounded at Bull Run. Transferred to 190th Regiment Penna. Volunteers May 31, 1864.

Zimmerman, William
>Promoted to Sergeant June 1, 1862. Wounded in Battle of White Oak Swamp and taken prisoner. Released on parole July 22, 1862 and died in Baltimore Aug. 22, 1862.

Recruits Received After Company Was Organized And Before October 1862

Bentz, James
> Mustered in July 25, 1862. Discharged on Surgeon's Certificate.

Brannin, Patrick
> Mustered in July 8, 1861. Prisoner May 5, 1864. Died at Andersonville Aug. 23, 1864.

Callio, John
> Mustered in Aug. 28, 1862. Killed at Antietam Sept. 17, 1862.

Cockley, John R.
> Mustered in Aug. 28, 1862. Wounded at Antietam Sept. 17, 1862. Transferred to Veteran Reserve Corps.

Culp, William M.
> Mustered in July 10, 1861. Made Corporal Sept. 1, 1862. Died Sept. 20, 1862 of wounds received at Antietam.

Dubessey, Joseph
> Mustered in Aug. 23, 1861. Discharged on Surgeon's Certificate May 16, 1862.

Eby, Harry J.
> Mustered in July 12, 1861. Missing in action at Wilderness May 5, 1864.

Elliott, Samuel Jr.
> Mustered in Aug. 21, 1861. Promoted to Corporal Sept. 1, 1862. Prisoner from May 5 to Dec. 11, 1864. Discharged June 23, 1865.

Faller, John Ignatius
> Mustered in August 21, 1861. Promoted to Corporal, Mar. 3, 1862, to Sergeant Sept. 1, 1862. Prisoner from May 5, 1864 to March 5, 1865. Mustered out with Company March 5, 1865.

Fries, James O.
> Mustered in July 8, 1861. Discharged on Surgeon Certificate Oct. 27, 1862.

Fry, George
> Mustered in July 10, 1861. Taken prisoner at the Battle of Gaines' Mill. Discharged on Surgeon's Certificate Jan. 8, 1863.

Green, Henry T.
> Mustered in July 8, 1861. Killed at Fredericksburg Dec. 13, 1862.

Halbert, Charles B.
> Mustered in July 8, 1861. Discharged on Surgeon's Certificate Oct. 14, 1864.

Private Harry J. Eby. (D. Scott Hartzell Collection, U.S. Army Military History Institute.)

Haverstick, Benjamin
    Mustered in Aug. 23, 1861. Died at Camp Tenally, Sept. 19, 1861.

Haverstick, David
    Mustered in Aug. 23, 1861. Killed at Gaines' Mill, Jun. 27, 1862.

Hoffer, George W.
    Mustered in July 10, 1861. Mustered out with Company June 16, 1864.

Hubley, William B.
    Mustered in July 10, 1861. Promoted to Corporal June 1, 1862. Wounded at Gaines' Mill and taken prisoner. Exchanged Aug. 5 and returned to Company. Discharged on Surgeon's Certificate Dec. 24, 1862.

Humer, Jesse B.
    Mustered in July 12, 1861. Captured at Battle of Gaines' Mill. Discharged June 16, 1865.

Hyte, Henry E.
    Mustered in Aug. 23, 1861. Transferred to 190th Regiment Penna. Volunteers May 31, 1864.

Kistler, William
    Mustered in July 9, 1861. Appointed file-major of the regiment, Dec. 1862. Mustered out with Company June 16, 1864.

Long, Andrew K. Jr.
    Mustered in Aug. 27, 1861. Promoted to 1st Lieutenant 13th Tennessee Cavalry.

Low, Jacob N.
    Mustered in July 27, 1862. Discharged on Surgeon's Certificate.

Low, William A.
    Mustered in July 25, 1862. Died at Camp Slough, Oct. 10, 1863.

McCleaf, William
    Mustered in July 18, 1861. Captured May 5, 1864. Died at Andersonville Oct. 10, 1864.

McCune, David McClay
    Mustered in June 29, 1861. Promoted to Corporal Sept. 27, 1861, to Sergeant Sept. 1, 1862. Missing in action at Wilderness May 5, 1864.

Meloy, William M.
    Mustered in Aug. 22, 1862. Transferred to 190th Regiment Penna. Volunteers May 31, 1864.

Miller, James A.
    Mustered in August 27, 1861. Died at Washington, D.C., Dec. 24, 1862.

Sergeant David M. McCune. (Courtesy of the Shippensburg Historical Society.)

Neff, Theophilus
    Mustered in July 21, 1861. Discharged on Surgeon's Certificate Feb. 9, 1863.

Noble, Jacques W.
    Mustered in August 29, 1861. Wounded at Gaines' Mill and taken prisoner. Released July 17, 1862. Exchanged and discharged on Surgeon's Certificate Feb. 3, 1863.

Reynolds, John
    Mustered in July 16, 1861. Discharged by order of War Department Oct. 11, 1861.

Rheem, Edward B.
    Mustered in July 8, 1861. Mustered out with Company June 16, 1864.

Rhoads, John
    Mustered in July 25, 1862. Missing in action at Wilderness, May 5, 1864.

Robinson, John
    Mustered in Aug. 27, 1861. Transferred to 190th Regiment Penna. Volunteers May 31, 1864.

Shamberger, Philo H.
    Mustered in Aug. 27, 1862. Transferred as saddler to Company C. of the 5th regular Artillery, Sept. 20, 1862. Discharged on Surgeon's Certificate.

Sites, Samuel
    Mustered in Sept. 2, 1861. Promoted to Corporal Mar. 5, 1862. Prisoner from May 5, 1864 to Mar. 4, 1865. Discharged Apr. 3, 1865.

Snodgrass, William
    Mustered in Aug. 29, 1861. Discharged on Surgeon's Certificate Oct. 14, 1862.

Steel, Joseph W.
    Mustered in Aug. 21, 1861. Killed at South Mountain Sept. 14, 1862

Wise, George W.
    Mustered in July 8, 1861. Transferred as hospital steward to 1st Penna. Artillery, April 1862. Died at Richmond Dec. 21, 1862 of wounds received at Fredericksburg Dec. 13, 1862.

Wolf, Edgar J.
    Mustered in July 10, 1861. Transferred to Veteran Reserve Corps.

Wyre, William
    Mustered in July 8, 1861. Wounded at Charles City Cross Roads, and taken prisoner. Released July 22, 1862 on parole.

Private John Rhoads. (U.S. Army Military History Institute.)

Recruits Received After September 1862

Adams, John F.
> Mustered in Jan. 13, 1864. Captured May 5, 1864. Died at Annapolis Mar. 10, 1865.

Hefflefinger, Samuel
> Mustered in Mar. 22, 1864. Missing in action at Wilderness May 5, 1864.

Jarmier, Charles
> Mustered in Jan. 26, 1864. Prisoner May 5, 1864. Died at Andersonville Aug. 26, 1864.

Laird, William S.
> Mustered in Jan. 21, 1864. Transferred to 190th Regiment Penna. Volunteers May 31, 1864.

Reiff, Frederick K.
> Mustered in Jan. 15, 1864. Missing in action at Wilderness, May 5, 1864.

Schlusser, John A.
> Mustered in Feb. 29, 1864. Missing in action at Wilderness, May 5, 1864.

Stoey, William W.
> Mustered in March 23, 1864. Missing in action at Wilderness, May 5, 1864.

Walker, Edwin T.
> Mustered in Jan. 15, 1864. Captured May 5, 1864. Died at Andersonville July 19, 1864.

Walker, David S.
> Mustered in Feb. 23, 1864. Missing in action at Wilderness, May 5, 1864.

Sources Consulted

Bates, Samuel P. *History of Pennsylvania Volunteers, 1861-5*, Vol. 1. Harrisburg, Pa.: B. Singerly, 1869. 720-736.

Curriden, David, "Typo," the "Carlisle Fencibles," written at the Camp of the 7th Penna. Reserves, Sept. 29, 1862, for the *Shippensburg News*. Reprinted in the *American Democrat*, 22 Oct. 1862.

Hemminger, John D. *Cumberland County, Pennsylvania in the Civil War, 1861-1865*. Carlisle, Pa.: n. p. n. d. 14-23.

Muster Roll of the Carlisle Fencibles. *The American Democrat*, 26 June 1861.

Sauers, Richard A. *Advance the Colors*, Vol. 1. Harrisburg, Pa.: Capitol Preservation Committee, 1987. 99-101.

The 7th Pennsylvania Reserves at Antietam

by Wayne Wachsmuth

The 7th Pennsylvania Reserves formed just north of the North Woods with other units of the 3rd Division, 1st Corps, Army of the Potomac. The position shown just south of the Joseph Poffenberger Farm was the "jump off" for their advance in concert with the other units on their left and right. They were advancing toward Miller's Cornfield in the second wave of the Union assault in the early morning of the 17th of September 1862. The distance from the position of the 7th Reserves to the south boundary of The Cornfield is 950 yards.

Confederate guns located on high ground 1,000 yards west of the Miller farm were probably responsible for the shell that killed Capt. James Colwell and others in his company as they moved forward.

The 7th Reserves monument on the Antietam National Battlefield is located where the unit formed, as shown on the map. The North Woods has disappeared through the years.

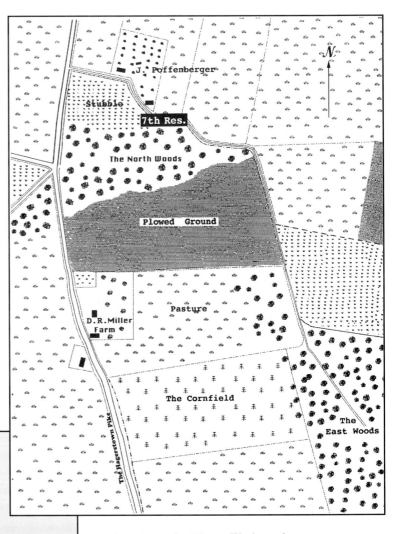

Original map by Wayne Wachsmuth.

Excerpt from the report of Maj. Gen Joseph Hooker, Commanding 1st Corps, Army of the Potomac, concerning the initial action in The Cornfield. It was subsequent to this action that the Pennsylvania Reserves advanced over this same field.

"We had not proceeded far before I discovered that a heavy force of the enemy had taken possession of a corn-field (I have since learned about a thirty-acre field) in my immediate front, and from the sun's rays falling on their bayonets projecting above the corn could see that the field was filled with the enemy, with arms in their hands, standing apparently at "support arms." Instructions were immediately given for the assemblage of all of my spare batteries, near at hand, of which I think there were five or six, to spring into battery, on the right of this field, and to open with canister at once. In the time I am writing every stalk of corn in the northern and greater part of the field was cut as closely as could have been done with a knife, and the slain lay in rows precisely as they had stood in their ranks a few moments before. It was never my fortune to witness a more bloody, dismal battle-field."

Monument to the 7th PA Reserves:

The 36th Pennsylvania Infantry started life as the 7th Pennsylvania Reserves and after the unit name change it was still referred to as the 7th Reserves by the men. The monument to the 7th Pennsylvania Reserves stands along Mansfield Avenue near the northern boundary of the Antietam National Battlefield where the unit waited near the North Woods before moving forward into D. R. Miller's cornfield. (Photo by Wayne Wachsmuth)

The Cornfield:

D. R. Miller's cornfield lies in the foreground and one half mile away to the North in the center of the photo can be seen the monument to the 7th Reserves. Captain James Colwell and four other members of Company A, 7th Reserves were killed by a shell burst as they moved to attack what has been known by Civil War historians ever since as "The Cornfield," that being the only identification needed. (Photo by Wayne Wachsmuth)

The Soldiers Monument

by Richard L. Tritt

The Soldiers Monument that stands on the square in Carlisle was erected in 1871 to honor those Cumberland County soldiers who died for the Union during the Civil War. It was the result of the efforts of many people over a four year period. The group that initiated the effort was known as the Soldiers Monument Association.

The first step in the organization of the Soldiers Monument Association of Cumberland County was the publication of a call in the Carlisle papers in January of 1867. The following notice appeared in the *Carlisle Herald* on January 4th, 1867.

"Monument Association. A county meeting of all persons favorable to the establishment of an association having for the object the erection of a suitable monument to the memory of the deceased soldiers of this county will be held in the Court House, on Monday evening the 14th instant. Our citizens from every section of our county are urged to attend."

This meeting was postponed until Monday, January 25th, and was then poorly attended due to inclement weather. At the meeting General Lemuel Todd was named to chair the Association. He stated that the purpose of the meeting was to find the means to erect a suitable monument to the memory of the sons of Cumberland County who fell in the field of battle or died of disease during the Civil War. He alluded to "the many officers and men whose bones now lie moldering on nearly every battlefield." He also alluded to what other counties were doing for the same purpose and urged this county's citizens not to be "eclipsed by any other in the magnificence of the monument."

The Soldiers Monument, engraved from a sketch by John W. Loyer. (*Atlas of Cumberland County*, F. W. Beers, 1872.)

Many Civil War veterans were involved in the Monument Association. The following are some of the veterans' names that appear in the minutes of the organization: General Robert Miller Henderson, Colonel William Penrose, Colonel Erkuries Beatty, Captain Chris Kuhn, Captain John Hays, James Hamilton, Captain S. Jacob Zug, Major John Kelso, Captain Henry Lee, Captain P. Bricker, General A. Brady Sharpe, William E. Miller and John Armstrong. In February of 1867 officers were selected, General R. M. Henderson being named President. An Executive Committee of thirteen men from all parts of the county was named to work with him. Membership was open to all county citizens for the sum of one dollar or upwards.

The association reported their efforts in the county newspapers. A plea for subscribers was printed during the spring of 1867. All the people of Cumberland County were invited to join in the effort, young and old, men as well as ladies. Subscription books were distributed throughout the county and contributors received certificates of membership for their donations.

Throughout the year of 1867 more people became involved, especially the ladies of the county. By June a sum of nearly $1000 had been raised. The "Little Helpers," a group of children, held a Strawberry Festival in June and raised $39 for the monument fund. The ladies of Carlisle held a festival on the 4th of July at the fairgrounds. A dinner was served, other refreshments were prepared, the Declaration of Independence was read and various addresses presented. The event raised $386.81 for the treasury. During the Christmas holidays, the fire companies of Carlisle held a fair and raised $1021.98 for the fund.

During the first half of 1868, the project seemed to lose momentum. An editorial in the *Carlisle Herald* on May 22, 1868 called for more expedient action and so the association decided to hold weekly meetings until their project was completed. Plans were made for renewing the labor of collecting subscriptions and a committee was formed to select a location for the monument.

Several sites were considered for the erection of the monument. Ashland Cemetery offered a free conspicuous lot, but the committee felt that the monument was not intended to be a tombstone to mark graves and should not be placed in a cemetery. The campus of Dickinson College was suggested as well as ground at the intersection of College and Louther Streets. It was felt however that the monument should be located in a central and conspicuous location. There was talk of moving the central market (now the New Courthouse) to another location so that land was considered. It was decided in August of 1868 that the shaft should be placed on the Public Square on the open ground on the north side of the Courthouse.

The monument was to be inscribed with a "Roll of Honor" containing the names of all the officers and soldiers from Cumberland County who fell in battle or who died from wounds or diseases contracted while serving in the war.

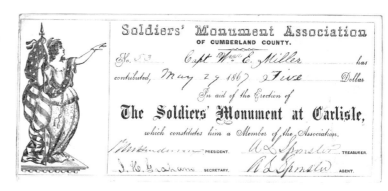

Soldiers Monument membership certificate for Capt. William E. Miller, who won the Medal of Honor for gallantry at Gettysburg. (Manuscript Collection, CCHS.)

The Soldiers Monument decorated for a patriotic occasion, c.1880. (A. A. Line, CCHS.)

A list in possession of the Secretary of the Commonwealth was obtained. In 1868 the public was also requested to forward names of soldiers who were killed in battle or who died in the service together with the name of the Company and Regiment, when and where they were killed or when and where they died. Col. Erkuries Beatty, Corresponding Secretary of the Association, was responsible for preparing the final list. In this manner the names of seventeen commissioned officers and three hundred and twenty-seven non-commissioned officers and privates were obtained for a total of three hundred and forty-four in all.

Subscriptions and fund raising continued throughout 1869 and 1870 until early 1871. Two of the fund raising events in 1869 were a Velocipede Exhibition and a picnic and dinner at Middlesex. In 1870 the Good Templar's held a festival and a number of paid lectures were held at Rheem's Hall. The total amount of money raised reached $5264.38 in 1871. The monument itself cost $5000. Additional money was needed to enclose the monument with a wall and iron fence and for the dedication ceremonies.

The monument was the work of Richard Owens, a mechanic of Carlisle "to whose taste and skill the erection of the monument was confided" in November of 1868. He was the designer and contractor, under whose supervision the work was executed.

The dimensions of the monument were, thirty feet high, the base to stand on a mound four feet high and ten and one half feet square. The base of the monument was of light gray Gettysburg granite, three feet high and ten feet square, surmounted by a pedestal of blue Montgomery County marble containing white marble tablets of the names of fallen soldiers, with a column of blue Pennsylvania marble at each corner representing cannon. This was surrounded again by a die containing the American shield, and it supported a white marble circular shaft capped by a globe surmounted by an eagle. The shaft contained a representation of folded flags, surrounded by a wreath of laurels and by a spiral band containing the names of the battles in which those whose memory the monument commemorated took part.

By July of 1869 the foundation had been laid. The monument was surrounded by a neat iron fence, and the shaft was raised to its place on February 9, 1871.

The unveiling of the Soldiers Monument took place on August 19, 1871. Newspaper accounts describe imposing ceremonies by military and civic groups. A parade was

Views of details of the Soldiers Monument, 1997. (Jim Bradley, Mother Cumberland Collection.)

followed by the formal unveiling of the monument and the delivery of an oration and other appropriate exercises.

The procession to the square was composed of military and civic groups from all over the county. The Chief Marshall was General Lemuel Todd. Participating organizations included the Keystone Band of Newville, the Shiremanstown Band, the West Fairview Band, and the Singer Cornet Band of Mechanicsburg. Many returned soldiers, military companies and secret societies joined in the procession to the square where ceremonies were conducted on a platform erected for the occasion in front of the monument. Thousands of people from all over the county were in the audience.

Ceremonies included an address of General Robert M. Henderson about the origin and organization of the Monument Association. Major General Heintzelman unveiled the statue. "The distinguished soldier was greeted with deafening cheers, and at a signal the beautiful statue of the eagle was fully disclosed to the public gaze, the bands breaking forth in stirring music."

The orator of the day was Rev. Dr. Robert Davidson, formerly a resident of Carlisle. The Governor of Pennsylvania, John W. Geary, was scheduled to speak but canceled due to unavoidable circumstances a day or two before the occasion.

"The day was one that will long be remembered by those that witnessed the demonstration. The appearance of the military, and the varied and handsome regalias of the members of the different organizations, as they dazzled the eye, preceded by the various bands, elicited the warmest commendation, not only from our own citizens, but from the thousands of visitors that thronged our borough."

View of the Soldiers Monument, 1963. (CCHS.)

Sources

History of Cumberland and Adams Counties, Pennsylvania. Chicago: Warner Beers & Co., 1886, 122-128. (Included in this book is a complete list of the soldiers named on the monument.)

Wing, Conway P., *History of Cumberland County, Pennsylvania.* Philadelphia: James D. Scott, 1879, 147.

Minutes and Treasurer's Account of the Soldiers Monument Association, Carlisle, PA, Presented to the Hamilton Library by J. Webster Henderson, 1902.

The Carlisle Herald, 4 Jan. 1867, 22 May 1868, 19 June 1868, 26 June 1868, 31 July 1868, 13 Nov. 1868, 2 July 1869, 24 Aug. 1871.

Captain Colwell Post, No. 201. G.A.R.

by Dr. Steven L. Hatleberg

The Grand Army of the Republic, or G.A.R., was a fraternal order formed by honorably discharged veterans of the Union Army, Navy, and Marine Corps to promote their social and political interests at the end of the Civil War. At the community level, men formed a post, which was often named after a local Civil War hero. The first post was organized in Decatur, Illinois, on April 6, 1866. The veterans of Carlisle, Pennsylvania, organized the Captain Colwell Post on February 24, 1881.

The first Commander of Post No. 201 was Captain William E. Miller. Capt. Miller received the Congressional Medal of Honor for attacking Jeb Stuart's calvary during the battle of Gettysburg. One of the post's first activities was a railroad excursion to the recently discovered caverns in Luray, Virginia. Other orders of business included schools for orphans, support of soldiers' convalescent homes, and pension legislation. The Post met for many years on the second floor of 34 W. Louther Street.

The national G.A.R. established May 30, 1868, as a day to remember the sacrifices of fallen comrades. This evolved into the annual Memorial Day celebration. Organizing the local and national Memorial Day celebrations became a major function for G.A.R. posts. In Carlisle, the Capt. Colwell Post involved the whole community in this event. School children dressed in their Sunday best and met in the town square, where they were given flowers. From there, they paraded to the old cemetery to place their flowers on the graves of fallen soldiers. Speeches were given and then members of the post fired a round from a small salute cannon. Ceremonies were held at the old town cemetery, the Ashland Cemetery, and the Westminster Cemetery.

Fundraising was another major activity of the post. Bean soup dinners were traditionally held on the Saturday closest to Washington's birthday. The cold weather helped to boost sales of the bean soup, ham sandwiches and homemade pies. In 1936 the Post was able to purchase a building at 32-34 South Bedford Street in Carlisle with the proceeds of their fundraisers.

Membership in Capt. Colwell Post No. 201 peaked at almost 500 veterans in the late 1880s. Thereafter, age began to take its toll. By 1936, only two veterans survived. The traditions and spirit of the Grand Army of the Republic have been preserved in Carlisle by the Capt. J. P. Brindle Camp No. 50 of the Sons of the Union Veterans, and its auxiliary.

Sources Consulted

History of Cumberland and Adams Counties, Pennsylvania.
    Chicago: Warner Beers & Co., 1886, 129.
Records of the Capt. J. P. Brindle Camp, No. 50, Sons of Union
    Veterans of the Civil War, Carlisle, Pa.

OPENING SERVICES
BY
G. A. R. Post, No. 201, of Carlisle.

QUARTETTE.	*Blest be the Ground.*	LEAVITT.

Services by the Post.

QUARTETTE.	*Sleeping only Sleeping.*	DANKS.
ORATION.		By *Rev. C. P. Wing, D. D.*
QUARTETTE.	*We Deck their Graves.*	MEES.

Presentation to the Post of a Banner from the Ladies
By *Hon. Martin C. Herman.*

NATIONAL HYMN—AMERICA.

Benediction.

USHERS:

E B. Watts, Esq., Dr. G. W. Zeigler. J. W. Henderson. Esq., R. H. Parker, Esq., D. W. F. Reily, Jas. Eckels, Dr. J. M. Bentz.

The Vocal Music under the direction of Prof. A. Newberry.

Sentinel Pt., Carlisle.

ORDER OF PARADE.

Co. G., 8th Regt., N. G. of Pa., Post 201 G. A. R., Camp 35, Sons of Veterans, Soldiers of the late war, Order U. A, M , of Boiling Springs, White Hall Soldiers Orphans' School. Indian Training School, Students of Dickinson College, Public Schools, Ex-Soldiers, not members of G. A. R., Civic Organizations.

ROUTE.

Out Hanover to Old Graveyard, down South to Bedford, to Pomfret, to Catholic Graveyard; thence down Pomfret to East, to Main, to Ashland Cemetery.

Graves of Colored Soldiers in the Cemetery on North Pitt street will be decorated at 12:30 p. m.

CAPT. JOS. G. VALE, Marshal.

Lewis Masonheimer,	*Capt. J. P. Ewing,*
Maj. S. B. King,	*R. R. Craighead.*
	Aids.

Ceremonies for Decoration Day, 30 May 1883, sponsored by the G.A.R. Post 201, taken from a printed program. (Courtesy of Bob Rowe)

Decoration Day Parade on S. Hanover Street in 1900. School children are carrying flowers to be placed on veterans graves in the Old Graveyard. (CCHS.)

Procession of G.A.R. members on Decoration Day, 30 May 1907. Left to right – Dr. J. S Bender, Jacob M. Goodyear, Prof. J. J. White (face hidden), Levi Shambaugh, John T. Ruggles, N. J. Adams. (Thomas Sharp, Sharp Collection, CCHS.)

G.A.R. Post 201 assembled on W. Louther Street in front of the First Church of God for Lindner Day, 1902. (CCHS.)

Dedication of the G.A.R. Hall on S. Bedford St., 7 Nov. 1936. James K. Snyder (3rd from left) was Commander of Post 201. He lived to be the last surviving Civil War soldier in Cumberland County. Augustus Albright (5th from left) was Adjutant of Post 201 and a Civil War veteran. (CCHS.)

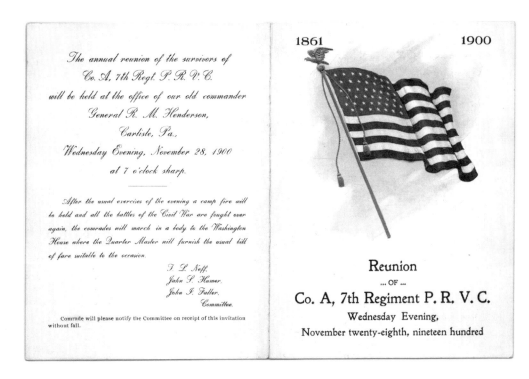

Cover and back of an invitation to the annual reunion of Company A, 7th Reserves, held 28 Nov. 1900. (Manuscript Collection, CCHS.)

Toast to "Our Dead Heroes" at a reunion of Company A, 7th Pa. Reserves, 24 Nov. 1920, held in the Henderson Law Office. At the time there were only eight surviving members of the company, three in attendance. The five other men in the photo were sons of members and one guest. (A. A. Line, CCHS.)

Left to right –
John F. Morrison, member of Co. A
John W. Henderson, son of Lt. Col. Robert M. Henderson
Marion P. Sipe, member of Co. A
William A. Monyer holding Co. A flag, member of Co A
John D. Hemminger, guest and Civil War veteran
John W. Kenyon, son of John R. Kenyon
William Haverstick, son of John W. Haverstick
Leo Faller, son of John I. Faller

Bibliography

Manuscript Materials, Unpublished Documents, and Collections

Colwell Family Papers/Collection, David G. Colwell estate, Los Angeles, California.

> Ann Hall Colwell-James Smith Colwell letters: 179 letters written 1861-1862.

> Other letters, documents, and family papers written or received by Ann Hall Colwell, James Smith Colwell, and other family members.

Lyman Copeland Draper Manuscript Collection, 1980 Microfilm Edition, Wisconsin State Historical Society. Madison, Wisconsin.

Pennsylvania Historical and Museum Commission, Harrisburg, Pennsylvania.

U.S. Army Military History Institute, Carlisle Barracks, Carlisle, Pa.

> Alexander, Bates. 1861-1864 memoirs (from the Hummelstown [Pa.] *Sun*).

> Blosser, Jonas. 1861 letter.

> Crosby, Abner L. 1861 letter.

> Haas-Jones-Curry Papers. 1861-1864 letters.

> Harrison, Hulda Papers. 1861-1864 letters.

> Heffelfinger, Jacob. 1861-1865 letters.

> Holmes, William R. 1863 letter.

> Ryan, William. 1861-1865 letters.

> Simpson, James R. 1861-1866 letters and reminiscences.

> Strock, William E. 1861-1862 memoirs and record of service.

> Wilson Family Papers.

Government Publications

Report of the Joint Committee on the Conduct of the War, Washington, Government Printing Office, 1863.

The War of the Rebellion: A Compilation of the Official Records of the Union and Confederate Armies. 128 vols. Washington: Government Printing Office, 1887.

U.S. National Archives. *7th Pennsylvania Reserves (36th Infantry) Record of Events*, Roll #169, Microcopy M 594.

Newspapers

Carlisle (Pennsylvania) *American*

American Democrat (Carlisle)

American Volunteer (Carlisle)

Herald (Carlisle)

Shippensburg News

Books

Adams, Charles Francis [JR.]. *Charles Francis Adams.* Boston: Houghton, Mifflin & Co., 1900.

Adams, John and Adams, John Quincy. *The Selected Writings of John Adams and John Quincy Adams.* Edited by Adrienne Koch and William Peden. New York: Alfred A. Knopf, 1946.

Andrews, J. Cutler. *The North Reports the Civil War.* Pittsburgh: University of Pittsburgh Press, 1955.

————. *The South Reports the Civil War.* Princeton, N.J.: Princeton University Press, 1970.

Baringer, William E. *A House Dividing.* Springfield, Ill.: The Abraham Lincoln Association, 1945.

Bates, Samuel P. *History of Pennsylvania Volunteers, 1861-5.* 3 vols. Harrisburg, Pa.: B. Singerly, 1869.

Battles and Leaders of the Civil War. 4 vols. New York: The Century Co., 1887. Reprint. Secaucus, N.J.: Castle, n.d.

Bell, Raymond Martin. *The Townships of Mother Cumberland.* Washington, Pa.: n.p., 1943.

Boritt, Gabor S. *Why the Confederacy Lost.* New York: Oxford University Press, 1992.

Bridgens, H.F. *Atlas of Cumberland County, Pennsylvania, 1858.* Philadelphia: Wagner & McGuigan, 1858. Reprint. Carlisle, Pa.: Cumberland County Historical Society & Hamilton Library Association, 1987.

Brown, George William. *Baltimore and the Nineteenth of April, 1861.* Baltimore: Johns Hopkins University Press, 1887. Reprint. Baltimore: Maclay & Associates, 1982.

Carlisle in the Civil War. Carlisle, Pa.: Cumberland County Historical Society & Hamilton Library Association, n.d.

Carlson, Oliver. *The Man Who Made the News; James Gordon Bennett.* New York: Duell, Sloan & Pearce, 1942.

Catton, Bruce. *Mr. Lincoln's Army.* Garden City, N.Y.: Doubleday & Co., 1951.

————. *This Hallowed Ground.* Garden City, N.Y.: Doubleday & Co., 1956.

————. *The Coming Fury.* Garden City, N.Y.: Doubleday & Co., 1961.

————. *Terrible Swift Sword.* Garden City, N.Y.: Doubleday & Co., 1963.

————. *Reflections on the Civil War.* Garden City, N.Y.: Doubleday & Co., 1981.

Chase, Salmon P. *Inside Lincoln's Cabinet: The Civil War Diaries of Salmon P. Chase.* Edited by David Donald. New York: Longmans Green & Co., 1954.

Chesnut, Mary Boykin. *Mary Chesnut's Civil War.* Edited by C. Vann Woodward. New Haven, Conn.: Yale University Press, 1981.

Chittenden, L.E. *Recollections of President Lincoln and His Administration.* New York: Harper & Bros., 1891.

Cleveland, Henry. *Alexander H. Stephens in Public and Private.* Philadelphia, National Publishing Co., 1866.

Commager, Henry Steele, ed. *The Blue and the Gray*. 2 vols. New York: Bobbs-Merrill Co., 1950.

Craven, Avery. *The Coming of the Civil War*. Chicago: University of Chicago Press, 1960.

Cullen, Joseph P. *The Peninsula Campaign, 1862*. Harrisburg, Pa.: Stackpole Books, 1973.

Davis, David Brion. *The Problem of Slavery in Western Culture*. Ithaca: Cornell University Press, 1966.

———. *Slavery and Human Progress*. New York: Oxford University Press, 1984.

Dowdy, Clifford. *The Seven Days: The Emergence of Lee*. Boston: Little, Brown & Co., 1964.

Dyer, Frederick H. *A Compendium of the War of the Rebellion*. 3 vols. Dayton, Ohio: Morningside Bookshop Press, 1908. Reprint. n.p., 1979.

Everson, Guy R. and Simpson, Edward W., Jr. *Far, Far from Home*. New York, Oxford University Press, 1994.

Fahner, Ralph Ray. *Horace Greeley and the Tribune in the Civil War*. Cedar Rapids, Iowa: Torch Press, 1936.

Faller, Leo W. and Faller, John I. *Dear Folks at Home: The Civil War Letters of Leo W. and John I. Faller*. Edited by Milton E. Flower. Carlisle. Pa.: Cumberland County Historical Society and Hamilton Library Association, 1963.

Fite, Emerson David. *The Presidential Campaign of 1860*. n.p., 1911. Reprint. Port Washington, N.Y.: Kennikat Press, 1967.

———. *Social and Industrial Conditions in the North During the Civil War*. New York: Peter Smith, 1930.

Foner, Eric. *Free Soil, Free Labor, Free Men: The Ideology of the Republican Party before the Civil War*. New York: Oxford University Press, 1970.

Foote, Shelby. *The Civil War: A Narrative*. 3 vols. New York: Random House, 1958.

Fox, William F. *Regimental Losses in The American Civil War*. Albany, N.Y.: Albany Publishing Co., 1889.

Franklin, John Hope. *The Emancipation Proclamation*. Garden City, N.Y.: Doubleday & Co., 1963.

Freeman, Douglas Southall. *R.E. Lee*. 4 vols. New York: Charles Scribner's Sons, 1947.

Garland, Hamlin. *Ulysses S. Grant*. New York: Macmillan Co., 1920.

Grant, Ulysses S. *General Grant's Letters to a Friend*. New York: T.Y. Crowell & Co., 1897.

———. *Letters of Ulysses S. Grant*. Edited by Jesse Grant Cramer. New York: G.P. Putnam's Sons, 1912.

Gordon, John B. *Reminiscences of the Civil War*. New York: Charles Scribner's Sons, 1903.

Harper, Robert S. *Lincoln and the Press*. New York: McGraw- Hill Book Co., 1951.

Hay, John. *Lincoln and the Civil War in the Diaries and Letters of John Hay*. Edited by Tyler Dennett. New York: Dodd, Mead, & Co., 1939.

Hemminger, John D. *Cumberland County, Pennsylvania in the Civil War, 1861-1865*. Carlisle, Pa.: n.p., n.d..

Hennessy, John J. *Return to Bull Run: The Campaign and Battle of Second Manassas*. New York: Simon & Schuster, 1993.

History of Cumberland and Adams Counties, Pennsylvania. Chicago: Warner Beers & Co., 1886

Jefferson, Thomas. *Notes on the State of Virginia*. New York: Harper & Row, 1964.

Jimmerson, Randall C. *The Private Civil War*. Baton Rouge, La.: Louisiana State University Press, 1988.

Kolchin, Peter. *American Slavery, 1619-1877*. New York: Hill and Wang, 1993.

Leech, Margaret. *Reveille in Washington: 1860-1865*. Reprint. New York: Grosset & Dunlap, n.d.

Leeds, Charles H. *Old Military Organizations*. Carlisle, Pa.: n.p., n.d.

Leib, Harry. *Harry Leib's Diary*. Edited by Richard L. Tritt. Boiling Springs, Pa.: Boiling Springs Civic Association, 1993.

Lincoln, Abraham. *The Collected Works of Abraham Lincoln*. 9 vols. Edited by Roy P. Basler. New Brunswick, N.J.: Rutgers University Press, 1953.

———. *Abraham Lincoln: Complete Works*. 2 vols. Edited by John G. Nicolay and John Hay. New York: Century Co., 1894.

Livermore, Thomas L. *Numbers and Losses in the Civil War in America, 1861-1865*. Boston: Houghton, Mifflin & Co., 1900.

Luvas, Jay and Nelson, Harold W., eds. *The U.S. Army War College Guide to the Battle of Antietam*. Carlisle, Pa: South Mountain Press, 1987.

McClellan, George Brinton. *McClellan's Own Story*. New York: Charles L. Webster & Co., 1887.

———. *The Civil War Papers of George B. McClellan: Selected Correspondence, 1860-1865*. Edited by Stephen W. Sears. New York: Ticknor & Fields, 1989.

McElwaine, Wilbur J. *Genealogical Data Abstracted from History of Middle Spring Presbyterian Church, Middle Spring, Pennsylvania, 1738-1900*. Bowie, Md.: Heritage Books, Inc., 1992.

McClure, A.K. *Abraham Lincoln and Men of War-Times*. Philadelphia: Times Publishing Company, 1892.

McPherson, James M. *The Negro's Civil War*. New York: Pantheon Books, 1965.

———. *Battle Cry of Freedom*. New York: Oxford University Press, 1988.

Martyn, Carlos. *Wendell Phillips: The Agitator*. New York: Funk & Wagnalls, 1890.

Mason, George. *The Papers of George Mason, 1725-1792*. 3 vols. Chapel Hill, N.C.: University of North Carolina Press, 1970.

Meade, George. *The Life and Letters of George Gordon Meade*. New York: Charles Scribner's Sons, 1913.

Miller, Willian Lee. *The Business of May Next*. Charlottesville: University of Virginia Press, 1992

Mitchell, Reid. *The Vacant Chair*. New York: Oxford University Press, 1993.

Morison, Samuel Eliot. *The Oxford History of the American People*. New York: Oxford University Press, 1965.

Morison, Samuel Eliot; Commanger, Henry Steele; and Leuchtenburg, William E. *The Growth of the American Republic*. New York: Oxford University Press, 1980.

Nevins, Allan. *Ordeal of the Union*. 4 vols. New York: Charles Scribner's Sons, 1947.

——. *The Emergence of Lincoln*. 4 vols. New York: Charles Scribner's Sons, 1950.

Nicolay, John G. and Hay, John. *Abraham Lincoln: A History*. 10 vols. New York: Century Co., 1886-1890.

Nye, Wilbur Sturtevant. *Here Come the Rebels*. Baton Rouge, La.: Louisiana State University Press, 1965.

Paludan, Philip S. *"A People's Contest."* New York, Harper & Row, 1988.

Pendleton, Louis. *Alexander H. Stephens*. Philadelphia: George W. Jacobs & Co., 1907.

Priest, John Michael. *Antietam: The Soldiers' Battle*. Shippensburg, Pa.: White Mane Publishing Co. 1989.

——. *Before Antietam: The Battle for South Mountain*. Shippensburg, Pa.: White Mane Publishing Co., 1992.

Quarles, Benjamin. *The Negro in the Civil War*. New York; Russell & Russell, 1953.

Raymond, Henry J. *The Life and Public Services of Abraham Lincoln*. New York: Derby & Miller, 1865.

Reunions of Ex-Soldiers of the North and South Held at Luray, Virginia, July 21, 1881 and at Carlisle, Pennsylvania, September 28, 1881. Carlisle, Pa.: Capt. Colwell Post #201, Grand Army of the Republic [1881].

Rozwenc, Edwin C., ed. *Slavery as a Cause of the Civil War*. Lexington, Mass.: D.C. Heath & Co., 1963.

Rupp, I. Daniel. *The History and Topography of Dauphin, Cumberland, Franklin, Bedford, Adams, and Perry Counties*. Lancaster City, Pa.: Gilbert Hills, 1846.

Russell, William Howard. *My Diary North and South*. London: Bradbury & Evans, 1863. Reprint. Philadelphia: Temple University Press, 1988.

——. *William Howard Russell's Civil War: Private Diary and Letters, 1861-1862*. Edited by Martin Crawford. Athens, Ga.: University of Georgia Press, 1992.

Sandburg, Carl. *Abraham Lincoln: The Prairie Years and the War Years*. One Volume Edition. New York: Harcourt, Brace & Co., 1954.

Saum, Lewis O. *The Popular Mood of Pre-Civil War America*. Westport, Conn.: Greenwood Press, 1980.

Scharf, J. Thomas. *History of Maryland*. 3 vols. n.p., 1879. Reprint. Hatboro, Pa.: Tradition Press, 1967.

Sears, Stephen W. *Landscape Turned Red: The Battle of Antietam*. New York: Ticknor & Fields, 1983.

——. *George B. McClellan: The Young Napoleon*. New York: Ticknor & Fields, 1988.

——. *To the Gates of Richmond: The Peninsula Campaign*. New York: Ticknor & Fields, 1992.

Shea, William L. and Hess, Earl J. *Pea Ridge: Civil War Campaign in the West*. Chapel Hill, N.C.: University of North Carolina Press, 1992.

Shippensburg in the Civil War. Shippensburg, Pa.: Shippensburg Historical Society, 1964.

Sifakis, Stewart. *Who Was Who in the Confederacy*. New York: Facts on File, 1988.

——. *Who Was Who in the Union*. New York: Facts on File, 1988.

Smith, George Winston & Judah, Charles. *Life in the North during the Civil War*. Albuquerque: University of New Mexico Press, 1966.

Stackpole, Edward J. *From Cedar Mountain to Antietam: August-September, 1862*. Harrisburg: Stackpole Co., 1959.

Stovall, Pleasant A. *Roger Toombs*. New York: Cassell Publishing Co., 1892.

Sypher, J.R. *History of the Pennsylvania Reserve Corps*. Lancaster, Pa.: Elias Barr, 1865.

Taylor, Frank H. *Philadelphia in the Civil War, 1861-1865*. Published by the City of Philadelphia, 1913.

Thomas, Benjamin P. and Hyman, Harold M. *Stanton: The Life and Times of Lincoln's Secretary of War*. New York: Alfred A. Knopf, 1962.

Tilberg, Frederick. *Antietam National Battlefield Site, Maryland*. Washington: National Park Service Handbook Series No. 31, 1960 (Revised, 1961).

Tousey, Thomas G. *Military History of Carlisle and Carlisle Barracks*. Richmond, Va.: Dietz Press, 1939.

Two Hundred Years in Cumberland County. Carlisle, Pa.: Cumberland County Historical Society & Hamilton Library Association, 1951.

Walker, C. Irvine. *The Life of Lieutenant General Richard Heron Anderson*. Charleston, S.C.: Art Publishing Co., 1917.

Walther, Eric H. *The Fire-Eaters*. Baton Rouge: Louisiana State University Press, 1992.

Waugh, John C. *The Class of 1846*. New York: Warner Books, 1994.

Welles, Gideon. *Diary of Gideon Welles*. Boston: Houghton Mifflin Co., 1909.

Wiley, Bell Irvin. *The Life of Billy Yank*. Indianapolis: Bobbs-Merrill Co., 1951.

——. *The Life of Johnny Reb*. Garden City, N.Y.: Doubleday & Co., 1971.

Wing, Conway P. *History of Cumberland County, Pennsylvania*. Philadelphia: James D. Scott, 1879.

Woodward, E.M. *History of the Third Pennsylvania Reserve*. Trenton, N.J.: Crellish & Quigley, 1883.

Articles

Landis, Merkel. "Civil War Times in Carlisle." Address Delivered at Hamilton Library, Carlisle, Pa., February 12th, 1931," *Carlisle in the Civil War*, pp. 1-15.

Sullivan, James W. "Boyhood Memories of the Civil War." *Carlisle in the Civil War*, pp. 1-44.

Index

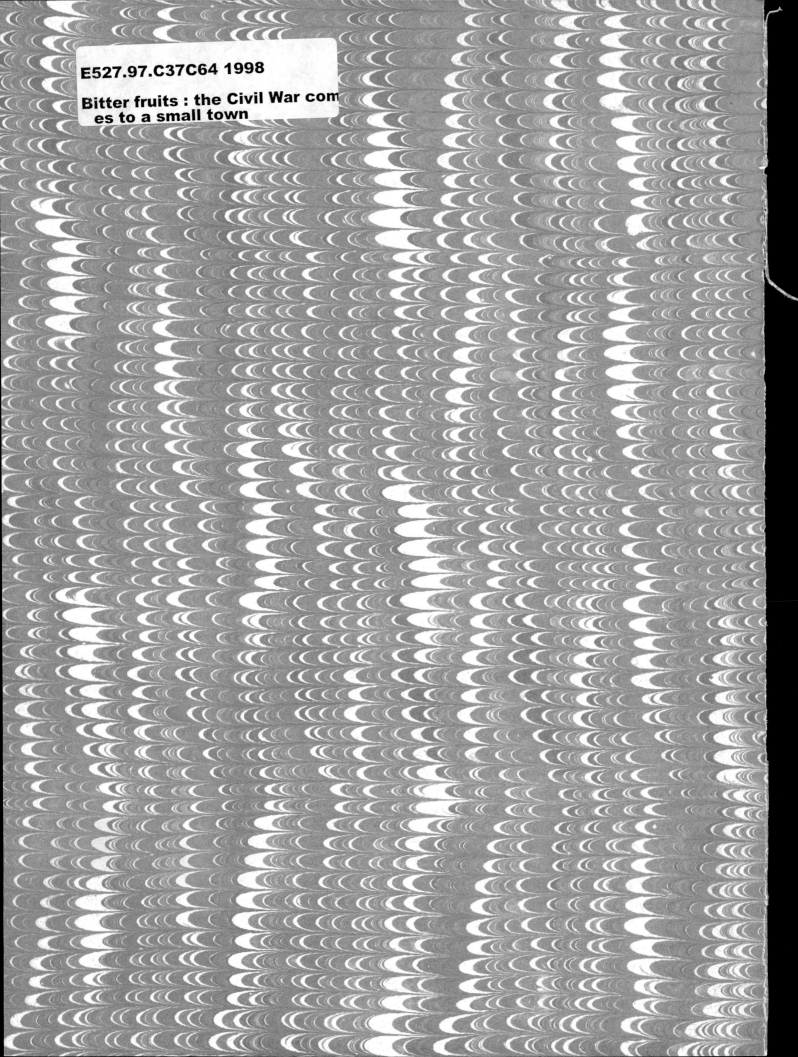